MURDER UNPUNISHED

How the Aryan Brotherhood
Murdered Waymond Small
and Got Away with It

Thornton W. Price III

The University of Arizona Press

Tucson

The University of Arizona Press
© 2005 Thornton W. Price III
All rights reserved
∞ This book is printed on acid-free, archival-quality paper.
Manufactured in the United States of America

Library of Congress Cataloging-in-Publication Data

Price, Thornton W., 1951–
Murder unpunished : how the Aryan Brotherhood murdered Waymond Small
and got away with it / Thornton W. Price III.
p. cm.
Includes index.
ISBN-13: 978-0-8165-2463-1 (hardcover : alk. paper)
ISBN-10: 0-8165-2463-7 (hardcover : alk. paper)
1. Prison homicide—Arizona—Florence—Case studies. 2. Arizona State Prison.
3. Small, Waymond. 4. Farmer, Terry Lee—Trials, litigation, etc.
5. Trials (Murder)—Arizona—Florence. 6. Prison gangs—Arizona—Florence.
7. Aryan Brotherhood. I. Title.
HV9475.A62S753 2005
365'.641—dc22
2005007581

Dedicated to my loving parents,

Thornton W. Price Jr. and Norma Adams Price

Contents

Illustrations

The administration building at Arizona State Prison at Florence.

An aerial view of the prison.

Harold Cardwell, the warden of Arizona State Prison at the time of Waymond Small's murder.

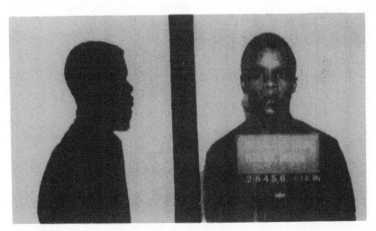

Waymond Small

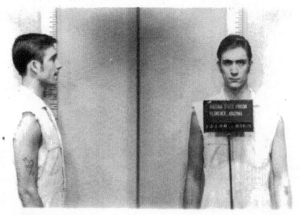

Michael Belt

Mitchell Bilke

Willard Breshears

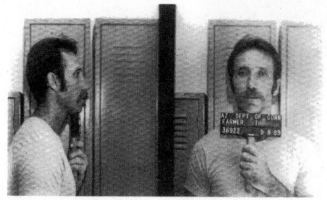

Terry Lee "Crazy" Farmer

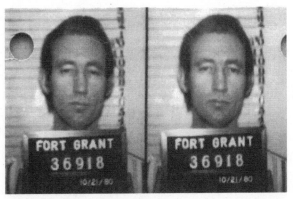

Ernest "Gooseneck" Goff

Dominic "Buffalo" Hall

Jerry "Stretch" Hillyer, aka Warren Parker

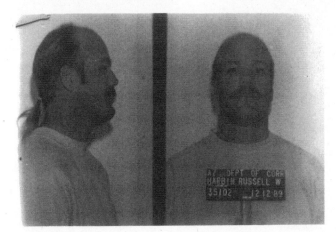

Russell "Rusty" Harbin

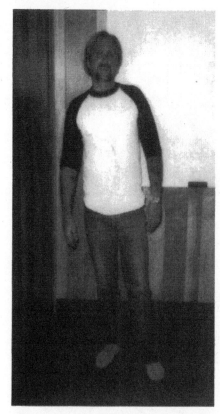

William S. "Red Dog" Howard

Troy "Baby Peck" Killinger

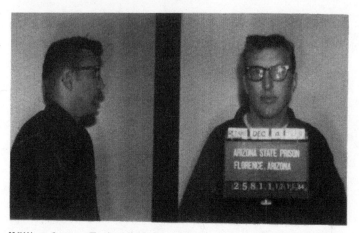

William James "Taxicab" McDonald

No photograph of Richard Compton could be located.

MURDER UNPUNISHED

Acknowledgments

I owe thanks to many who have helped me along the way. Michael Tidwell encouraged the book from inception and wrote in my behalf to his former client Terry Lee Farmer, enlisting his aid. Mr. Farmer and Mr. William Steven Howard, through their cooperation, made this book possible and asked nothing in return, simply hoping by telling their story that others would avoid their mistakes.

Deputy Pinal County Clerk Sandra Rowe found and reproduced the 16,000 pages of microfilm records from the court's file in *State of Arizona v. Terry Lee Farmer, et al.*

My relatives encouraged this endeavor in spite of the long odds against its success; for this I thank John, Sue, Carolyn, Paul, and Marian Adams.

To my former antagonists and the investigators of this crime, John DeSanti and Bart Goodwin, I extend special thanks. They contributed much to my understanding of this tale. Randy Paulsen and Ron Quaife openly and generously told me about the apprehension of Terry Farmer and Waymond Small for the crimes that sent them to Arizona State Prison. The public owes these four unsung heroes thanks for their police service and the good they have accomplished through their life work.

I imposed upon many friends to read my book, often long before it reached acceptable form. I thank Larry Sanford, Nate Ebel, Kyle Allinger, Randy Allinger, Jeff Mannix, Bud Deering, and Fred and Colette Snoy for their time, interest, and assistance.

My editors—Monica Phillips, Patti Hartmann and Alan Schroder— helped immeasurably to improve my manuscript and bring it to life.

I thank Vincent Funari of the Department of Corrections and Chris Reid of the Pinal County Historical Society for their help with photographs.

My mother, Norma Adams Price, offered me the most encouragement of all. Her ceaseless belief in my literary potential has been my life-long succor. I shall be happy if this book provides some vindication of her belief.

My wife, Kathleen Marie Price, has performed every chore imaginable to make this book possible and to encourage this enterprise. She transcribed countless hours of interviews, edited countless drafts of every paragraph and chapter, suggested solutions at every stumbling point, believed in me, aided me, counseled me — and scolded me when I needed it. She has been my secretary, proofreader, editor, and helpmate at every turn. She deserves to be called the co-author of this work, but modestly refuses to permit that form of acknowledgment, though in candor it is her due.

PART I THE CRIME

1 One Good Case

In a rural backwater sixty-five miles from the big cities of Phoenix to the north and Tucson to the south, tiny Florence in Pinal County has floundered since territorial days as the armpit of Arizona because its raison d'être has been Arizona State Prison. A steady stream of shocking news stories about Florence's prison began in 1976—front-page articles about grisly murders, stabbings, gang warfare, regular escapes, corrupt prison wardens, and the way land-fraud godfather Ned Warren orchestrated the murder of inmate Tony Serra, the snitch and former associate threatening to unravel his kingdom. The violence extended outside the prison's walls with the car bomb assassination of the *Arizona Republic*'s investigative reporter Don Bolles when he got too hot on Warren's trail.

This cacophony drew me, fresh out of law school, into its vortex, just as aspiring gunslingers in the last century were naturally drawn to the western frontier. For nine lonely months I lived in a flophouse of a trailer while working as a deputy Pinal County attorney, prosecuting every crime—mostly drunk driving, bar fights, and burglaries—originating in the three precincts to which I was assigned. By that time, I knew my youthful illusion of reaching partner in a prestigious law firm was not in the cards. Any lucky break, or one good case, and I'd gladly leave the prosecutor's office and strike out on my own as a sole practitioner. This story is about that one good case: the murder of a prison snitch. I played a bit role as the defense lawyer for the acting general of the Aryan Brotherhood, who was accused of having ordered the snitch's murder inside Arizona State Prison.

Why have I waited so long to tell this story? Time loosens tongues and unglues conspiratorial bonds. Time can soften stone-cold killers into human beings who feel compassion and become eager for the truth to be known so that others may never go down their paths. Time brings maturity, a chance to reflect, to think, to learn—and I needed this much time before I was ready. I changed, too, losing the pride I once felt for my part in earning my client's acquittal. I now realize that prejudice, manipulation, and ignorance—not lawyerly skill—accounted for the series of acquittals handed down by the good jurors of Pinal County to the bewildered prosecutors who began the case thinking of themselves as latter-day Marshall Dillons, expecting to serve death warrants upon all the Florence Eleven conspirators.

I considered writing about this case after the fifth and final trial ended in 1981 and my client, Richard Compton, was acquitted with my help. Eight years passed. Still I'd done nothing. So I threw away all forty volumes of trial transcripts and nearly all of my case files. Another decade passed. I married, raised a child, and grew prosperous as a lawyer. Yet the story remained fresh in my mind. So in 1997 I began to write.

I drove five hundred miles to the Pinal County Courthouse in Florence, where Sandra Rowe, a helpful deputy clerk of court, found and duplicated at minimal expense the sixteen thousand pages of microfilmed court records from the *State of Arizona v. Terry Lee Farmer, et al*. From their prison cells, Terry Lee "Crazy" Farmer and William Steven "Red Dog" Howard agreed to help me reveal the truth about the crime, the trials, and prison life. And my old nemeses John DeSanti and Bart Goodwin, Arizona Department of Public Safety investigators of the murder, agreed to help as well. They told me how they had calculated to pit black witnesses against white killers until one black would break the prisoners' code of silence and provoke feuding within the Aryan Brotherhood.

As a young lawyer, I aspired to a role akin to a hired gunslinger. I wanted a duel, leaving a clear winner and loser determined by the jury's verdict after fair combat under the rules of the lawyers' game. As a middle-aged man bearing emotional scars from legal battles inflicted in both victory and defeat, however, I have learned that the courtroom's verdict and natural justice usually coincide. The Florence Eleven eventually got justice and punishment—just not in the way the system intended.

Arizona's taxpayers got something out of this era in the history of its penal system. The crescendo of prison crimes and violence between 1975 and 1978 created the political consensus for Arizona's massive investment in new prisons. After Waymond Small's murder, Arizona built a prison system that would never again be controlled by gang violence. At an incredible price, Arizona largely succeeded. To give credit where it is due, the next unit in Arizona's penal archipelago should be named after Waymond Small, the obscure inmate whose death galvanized public opinion and made its construction a top priority.

2 The Murderer

On November 30, 1977, twenty-year-old white Terry Lee Farmer walked up to Waymond Small, a snitch, in front of sixty witnesses working in the prison's tag plant. He looked square into the eyes of this notorious and vicious black inmate and impaled his heart with a shank. Small died as he attempted to take his next breath. Throughout the five trials of the Small murder, Farmer steadfastly stood by the gang's story: he had killed Small in self-defense over a bulldogging incident. He claimed Small had tried to turn him into his boy toy, but he had refused.

Before writing this story, I had only seen Farmer in person once — when I called him as a witness at the fifth trial of his co-conspirators. At that time, all I or any other defense attorney needed to know was the content of a convict-witness's proposed testimony; nothing else mattered.

But to unravel how the Florence Eleven evaded justice, I now needed to know why this callow youngster, all the while facing the death penalty himself, first volunteered for the murder rap, then steadfastly insisted his co-conspirators were uninvolved, "taking the case" himself — especially since he could easily have turned state's witness and spent the rest of his life term on easy street.

I learned about Farmer's pitiful infancy from a letter in the court file. His foster mother had written to the sentencing judge after Farmer's conviction for murdering Small (a conviction later overturned and then superceded by a plea bargain). She wrote to Judge Platt "in hopes that perhaps it will help to have better understanding of the behavior pattern of Terry Farmer." Mrs. Rita Grace Scott explained that as an eighteen-month-old, Farmer was found abandoned, along with his nine-month-old sister. Farmer's father was in jail and the mother had left the children unattended for several days in a locked upstairs apartment in Jacksonville, Florida, in September 1957. Hearing their cries, a neighbor climbed a porch to reach the second story and left diluted milk for the two children. When retrieved by juvenile authorities, Farmer was malnourished and underdeveloped. One eye was damaged. His feces-covered buttocks had bleeding sores. For weeks afterward, his skin peeled with each diaper change and he screamed in pain. The Scotts cared for the boy as his foster parents until he was adopted by the Farmers. He didn't walk until age three.

I learned about the crimes that sent Terry Lee Farmer to Arizona State Prison for life from Farmer himself and the detective who put him behind bars, Randy Paulsen. Paulsen's persistent pursuit of a missing person report sent Farmer to prison before his twentieth birthday. Detective Paulsen and I met over coffee and dinner late one night in downtown Phoenix in 1997 at an all-night Denny's off Interstate 17 at 23rd Avenue and Thomas. Paulsen was working narcotics for the Department of Public Safety and would have to leave on a moment's notice if one of his snitches paged him during dinner.

In early September 1976, during his third year of police work and filled with youthful vigor, Paulsen sat at his desk in the Coconino County Sheriff's Department in Flagstaff, Arizona, mulling over a commonplace missing-persons report concerning Kathleen Herman and Tilfred Oso. Paulsen had rapidly advanced from uniformed patrol deputy to detective in the sheriff's office. Though younger and more handsome, Paulsen bears a striking resemblance to a prominent Arizona politician who would play a part in this tale: Bruce Babbitt, Arizona's attorney general at the time of Waymond Small's murder and shortly thereafter its governor and then President Clinton's secretary of the interior. Both Paulsen and Babbitt grew up in rural northern Arizona. Intellectual, intuitive, and articulate, Paulsen developed a clear, well-defined sense that the world is divided into good and evil, right and wrong.

Over the Labor Day weekend of 1976, Herman and Oso had been reported missing by their coworkers at Paul Harvey Concessions inside Grand Canyon National Park, eighty vacant miles north of Flagstaff, the county seat of vast Coconino County, the second largest county in the lower forty-eight states. Paulsen learned that nineteen-year-old Kathleen Herman, an average-sized brunette from Erie, Pennsylvania, had been hired by the park concessionaire just two weeks earlier. Tilfred Oso, a Navajo Indian, was a twenty-four-year-old native of Winslow, Arizona, with a large extended family. He also worked for Paul Harvey. Herman had hooked up with Oso at a park employee hangout the night before, and they decided to hitchhike to Flagstaff. Herman planned to purchase a small refrigerator for her apartment. Oso was headed to nearby Winslow for a few belongings to finish his apartment. Both had uncollected paychecks and left behind their clothing and belongings. Their friends did not believe they had just run off together, abandoning new jobs and all their possessions.

With no leads of any kind, Paulsen turned to publicity, calling radio, television, and newspaper reporters in Flagstaff and the distant metropolis of Phoenix, asking for information about the pair's disappearance. Numerous potential sightings were reported before a truly promising lead materialized two weeks later.

"Paulsen," Randy answered tersely as he picked up the phone in his small cubbyhole at the sheriff's office.

"I think I saw those kids get picked up," the caller began, explaining that he worked in Phoenix and had noticed a short news account about the missing hitchhikers. "I took my wife and kids to the Grand Canyon over the Labor Day weekend. It was raining when we left, and we saw two kids, a white girl and an Indian guy, hitchhiking at the entrance to the park. We thought about picking them up, but our car was crowded. After I drove by, I saw a car stop to pick them up. I told my wife, 'Good, someone got those kids out of the rain,' so we kept driving. About ten miles later, the same car passed me, going real fast. I remembered it because the driver and passenger were wearing the same hats. Perfectly round, flat brimmed, brown leather. Goofy looking. The kind you see at carnivals and fairs. Not a cowboy style at all. The car was a green-and-white Monte Carlo with Texas plates."

Paulsen asked the man his name and job. "I work as a truck driver. I don't read the paper much and don't get to work early very often. I did today and was reading an old copy of the *Arizona Republic* with a story about missing hitchhikers near the Grand Canyon. I just knew I'd seen them as soon as I read the story, so I had to call you. Maybe it's nothing."

"Thanks a lot. Let me know if you think of anything else," said Paulsen.

Something about the story gave Paulsen a sense of foreboding, a premonition he'd been right—something sinister had happened to the hitchhiking pair.

Texas plates, green-and-white Monte Carlo. Not much of a lead, but better than nothing.

On the off chance the driver of the Monte Carlo had brushed up against the law, Paulsen meticulously combed through every police report in the past four months within 150 miles of Flagstaff that he could get his hands on—Highway Patrol accident reports along Interstate 40, routine patrol and arrest reports from the cities of Flagstaff and Williams, sheriff's office and FBI reports. He was looking for one thing: a Monte Carlo with Texas plates. The search yielded a surprisingly long list, so Paulsen hit the Teletype wires and phones to narrow the field, calling the Texas county sheriff where each Monte Carlo was registered, asking for the vehicle's color.

Two more weeks passed. Answers came in, but none reported a green-and-white Monte Carlo in their jurisdiction. Following up on a nonresponding department, Paulsen called the Leon County sheriff's office to speak to the detective bureau.

"Detective Randy Paulsen, Coconino County sheriff's office, Flagstaff, Arizona, here. I'm working a missing persons case and need help identifying a Chevrolet Monte Carlo that might be registered to someone who lives in your county. Did you get my Teletype?"

"Funny you should call," the Texas detective answered. "A guy and gal just came into my office today and dumped a plastic bag of junk on my desk. They wanted me to tell them what to do with the items. They found the stuff inside a car they'd retrieved from Nevada that belonged to their brother, Kelly Paul Bryan, a twenty-four-year-old insurance salesman. The car is a green-and-white Monte Carlo. They got a call from the Boulder City, Nevada, police department telling them the car was there. It had been abandoned after a high-speed chase but the occupants got away. Until they got the call about the Monte Carlo in Nevada, they thought their brother was on a business trip. They don't know how the car got to Nevada. None of the stuff belongs to their brother. They're quite mystified."

"What's in the bag?" Paulsen asked.

"Not much. Some papers with names and phone numbers, clothes, and a hat. Brown leather, flat, round brim. The people say the Boulder City PD found another hat just like this one at the scene where the car was abandoned."

"That's the car!" Paulsen screamed out, no longer restraining his excitement at the miraculous find.

"There's more," the investigator continued. "Turns out Bryan never showed up for work. To top it off, a body was found out in the weeds at a roadside rest alongside I-35 in Texas, and the family identified it as Bryan. Murdered. Shot in the head and his skull smashed with rocks."

His pulse racing, Paulsen asked, "Could you send me a license photo of the victim? I need it in my own investigation."

The driver and passenger of the green-and-white Monte Carlo may have killed Herman and Oso between Flagstaff and Boulder City, Paulsen surmised. That didn't narrow it down much. Hundreds of miles of lonely highways, barren deserts, obscure washes and canyons, windswept mesas, and sagebrush prairies festooned the remote emptiness of northwest Arizona along the route to Hoover Dam, where Arizona ends and Nevada begins at Lake Mead.

Paulsen looked back through his lists. What had brought this Monte Carlo to the attention of local law enforcement? The report mentioning its license plate was inconsequential and yielded no new leads on the identity of the driver or passenger. Late one August night while checking for stolen vehicles, a Flagstaff patrol officer had written down a list of license plates on cars parked outside one of the long string of motels along old Highway 66 through town. The Monte Carlo hadn't shown up stolen that night, but the patrolman's notes proved its presence in Flagstaff.

The missing person's case took a backseat in Paulsen's pile of assignments. He had no other leads to follow, no clear plan.

Cops are a social bunch, and in spite of what their work reveals, they generally like people. The image of lazy cops, their patrol cars parked for long hours outside Denny's and the local Winchell's Donut Shop fits into a stereotype, a popular mythology, an accepted prejudice about the men in blue. The cops see it another way: during coffee breaks over donuts, stories are shared, odd incidents are mulled over, connections are made. The bad guys get identified; crimes get solved.

It was just so for Paulsen.

"I've got this odd missing-persons case. It bothers me," Paulsen told his cop buddies one day at Denny's. He related the tale of the hitchhikers picked up by two men driving a fast Monte Carlo with Texas plates.

"Randy, I got something you might want to check out," offered an FBI agent stationed in Flagstaff. "A pair of guys burglarizing national monuments along Interstate 40 sounds like the class of characters you're looking for. They got caught, but only after a high-speed chase and a running shootout with New Mexico Highway Patrol."

Geography told Paulsen this hunch was illogical. To get from Boulder City to Petrified Forest National Monument, site of one of the burglaries, the pair would have had to return through Flagstaff. Would they really be so brazen?

Nonetheless, an undeniable impulse told Paulsen to check it out. "I'd like to read the report," Paulsen found himself saying. At the FBI office, the agent showed the incident report to Paulsen. During an interview, one of the pair from the Petrified Forest incident, a man named Larry Hartley, admitted being arrested in Lawton, Oklahoma, along with a man he called Ray on charges of possession of a stolen vehicle. Paulsen wanted to talk with Hartley, but first he contacted the FBI in Oklahoma to request the mug shots of Hartley and Ray, his cohort from the Oklahoma arrest.

Armed with three photographs—of Hartley, Ray, and the murdered owner of the Texas Monte Carlo—Paulsen decided to follow up on the names and phone numbers found in the abandoned Monte Carlo. One number had Flagstaff's prefix of 774 and the name Cookie. Paulsen called the number, then drove to a motel where Interstate 17 from Phoenix merged into Milton Street in south Flagstaff. Twenty-year-old Cookie Orosco had agreed to meet him at her parents' motel to discuss her relationship with the suspects. "I met 'em in the bar," she told Paulsen, pointing to the photographs of Hartley and Ray. "We shot some pool and drank some beers, they called each other Will and Ray. They wanted me to take a drive with them to the Grand Canyon, but I didn't want to go." She had nothing more to add.

Paulsen waved to Cookie as he left the lobby and headed on to his next stop, Roswell, New Mexico, an eleven-hour drive east across sagebrush deserts, red-rock canyons, the Navajo reservation, and vast empty spaces dotted with gaudy sights: Chief Yellowhair's Trading Post, a tourist trap filled with cheap Indian trinkets and Mexican saddle blankets; and highway signs tantalizing passersby with the slogan "Winslow: For Men." He drove Interstate 40 for 380 miles to Albuquerque, then headed south on U.S. Highway 285 for another 140 miles. Paulsen drove fast, hoping Hartley hadn't posted bond yet on the charges from the Petrified Forest incident.

The Coconino County Sheriff's Department could never afford to assign two detectives to an investigation and certainly wouldn't do so for a missing person investigation requiring so much time and promising so little prospect of success. Paulsen began to devise a plan. How would he confront Hartley? How would he build up from the burglaries, the car chases, and the shootout before springing the questions he really wanted to ask about the disappearance of Herman and Oso?

When Paulsen finally arrived in Roswell, he wasted no time. "I'm Detective Paulsen, Coconino County sheriff's office, Flagstaff, Arizona. I'd like to talk to you," Randy told Hartley. The cocky youth slouched into his chair in the interview room, twitching his nose and cocking his head back as he sized up his inquisitor. He had a handsome face, shoulder-length hair, and a Fu Manchu mustache. At first he did not appear sinister or threatening, just arrogant and cocky. As quickly as his first impression sank in, Paulsen sensed a second, ghastly undercurrent that drew him up short as he felt his muscles tighten. The numbing drive had not prepared Paulsen for what now struck him most—Hartley's eyes.

"Sure, what about?" the twenty-four-year-old Hartley answered. His outward appearance was friendly, but his eyes flashed, revealing a fire burning inside a diseased mind, a fire hot enough to sear flesh. His eyes laughed back at Paulsen, but they failed to hide the hateful, cunning mind driving his actions. Behind those eyes dwelt a demonic persona that resided in a world utterly detached from the placid and deceitful words that flowed mechanically and unconvincingly from his mouth.

Hartley admitted being in Flagstaff, meeting Cookie, and traveling with Ray. He admitted the theft of the Monte Carlo, but he didn't mention what had become of its owner. He denied going to the Grand Canyon and picking up two hitchhikers. The lies were unimportant. Paulsen only wanted Hartley's story. He'd pick it apart later. After he caught up with Ray and got his story, it wouldn't match Hartley's. This he knew for certain.

An hour and a half of Hartley's fabrications gave Paulsen enough material to punch full of holes. In spite of himself, Hartley had done Paulsen one huge favor. Hartley had said he first met Ray when they worked in Oklahoma as carnival roustabouts. He talked about road dogging with Ray and admitted to many less-serious crimes they had committed. During those travels, Hartley said that Ray had used a half-dozen aliases—Ralph Mark Bell, James Starling, James Farmer—but that the actual person behind each alias was Terry Lee Farmer.

"I know you're lying to me," Paulsen growled, cutting off Hartley as he stood up. "You killed Kathleen and Tilfred. I'll prove it and I'll see you in the gas chamber."

"Yeah, sure you will," were the last words Paulsen heard from Hartley, who acted amused by the threat.

Now Paulsen needed to find Terry Lee Farmer and have a little talk. With luck, Farmer would be arrested and Paulsen would learn about it. He didn't have to wait long. Three months after the disappearance of Herman and Oso, Paulsen's nationwide detainer request hit pay dirt. A Teletype message arrived from the FBI's Fargo, North Dakota, office informing him of Farmer's arrest. Farmer was being held on a charge of reckless endangerment. He had been the driver of a vehicle when one of the occupants shot at the windows of the FBI office.

Expecting a short first interview with Farmer, Paulsen flew to Fargo with only one change of clothing and a return ticket booked for the next day. Paulsen expected little, but he went for broke. He was emboldened by the nineteen-year-old's appearance — not as possessed and demented as Hartley but scary nonetheless. The vacancy of Farmer's lifeless left eye drew in Paulsen until he snapped back to attention in the cramped interview room at the Grand Forks county jail.

"My name's Randy Paulsen, Coconino County Sheriff's Office, Flagstaff, Arizona." Paulsen let the words "Coconino County" and "Flagstaff" roll slowly off his tongue, intently gazing at Farmer, hoping the shock of a deputy from the scene of his atrocious crimes would cause him to recoil or flinch.

"I've been talking to your partner, Larry Hartley," Paulsen continued, intending to hit Farmer hard and fast with blunt details he could have known only if Hartley had talked, then winging it from there. "He told me a lot about what you two have been up to."

Paulsen sat across the table from Farmer, rubbing his chin and staring at the young man. He then pulled a stapled stack of papers from his satchel and read them aloud, beginning in known territory where Paulsen could trip up Farmer on a lie and blow his confidence in his web of aliases. Paulsen began reading from the FBI reports on the Oklahoma car theft. Once Farmer knew his aliases were blown, he would realize Hartley had talked too much. He would quickly figure out that Paulsen had done his homework, since he had connected Farmer and Hartley to criminal activities in both Flagstaff and Oklahoma.

Paulsen proceeded to the Boulder City, Nevada, chase and the recovery of the green-and-white Monte Carlo. Now Farmer became even more worried as Paulsen read from police reports about the murders in both

Texas and Arizona. An odd hat and Flagstaff phone numbers had been found in the Monte Carlo.

Paulsen took his time, reading each report of the crime spree in full to Farmer, leaving in all the stilted police-speak of officers "exiting vehicles" and times being denoted in twenty-four-hour military style.

Paulsen read that Cookie had identified Hartley and Farmer as the "Will" and "Ray" she met in Flagstaff driving a green-and-white Monte Carlo with Texas plates and that Will and Ray had asked her to go to the Grand Canyon but she declined. Farmer now knew that Paulsen had placed Hartley and himself uncomfortably close to the Herman-Oso disappearance.

As Paulsen read the reports, he watched Farmer for the slightest sign of discomfort. Slowly he shifted into more fragile territory, inserting details based on hunches.

"This officer interviewed Larry Hartley in Roswell, New Mexico. Hartley was in custody on federal burglary and theft charges for offenses committed at Petrified Forest National Park and El Morro National Monument. Hartley was arrested following a high-speed chase and shoot-out with the New Mexico Highway Patrol. This officer determined to interview Hartley in connection with the possible double homicide of Kathleen Herman and Tilfred Oso."

As if entranced, words unconsciously flowing, Paulsen brilliantly fabricated a plausible confession of murder from Hartley.

"Hartley admitted to this officer that the victims had been picked up while hitchhiking on September 4, 1976. The victims were picked up on Highway 180 at the entrance to the Grand Canyon National Park during a rainstorm. Kathleen and Tilfred were the same ages as Hartley and Farmer and seemed hip. Hartley offered marijuana to the two hitchhikers during the drive toward Flagstaff and they accepted. After an hour, while Hartley was driving, Farmer pulled a gun and told Kathleen and Tilfred to keep quiet. He told Hartley to take a dirt road off the main highway and ordered Kathleen and Tilfred at gunpoint into the woods. Hartley waited in the car for thirty minutes. Farmer returned to the car alone. When Hartley asked about the two passengers, Farmer said, 'I offed the Injun and fucked the girl. She's tied up if you want to go get some for yourself.' Hartley said no, then Farmer walked back into the woods. Hartley heard gun shots. When Farmer returned this time, he just said, 'Let's get out of here.'"

Falling silent, Paulsen shuffled the reports and put them back into his satchel. A long pause passed and Farmer seemed ready to break the silence, fidgeting and squirming in his seat. Paulsen looked into Farmer's eyes and let sigh a sympathetic sounding "Huum." Farmer was wavering; Paulsen kept up the pressure.

"He's putting the jacket on you, Terry. He probably did it. Why in the hell should you protect him?"

Farmer decided Paulsen already knew too much about the murder, so time to play dumb was over. "I'll talk, but I've got to have a deal. I don't want the death penalty," Farmer blurted out.

"Give me all you got and I'll see what I can do," Paulsen prodded.

Once the dam broke, Farmer gushed an admission to the murders. Still, Paulsen cautiously took his time.

"We'll need to get a lawyer appointed for you. I'll have to get approval for the deal from the Coconino County Attorney."

Paulsen couldn't contain himself as he left the room, eager to call Arizona.

"I've got him ready to lay down," Paulsen told Coconino County Attorney J. Michael Flournoy over the phone, trying to project a detachment and calm that he did not feel. "I just need your approval of a plea bargain. Farmer will cop to the murders, give up the bodies, and testify against Hartley. We only have to agree to no death penalty. I don't have the bodies, I want the deal. What do you say?"

It was a no-brainer. Flournoy gave Paulsen the green light. What else could he do for a cop who had solved a murder before the police had a body? "You've got it. Be sure to get a confession he can't worm out of. And make Farmer give up the bodies."

Five days later, after daily trips to the Laundromat in Dakota's freezing November to wash his only change of clothes, Paulsen flew back to Flagstaff with extradited prisoner in hand and Farmer's confession to the murder of Herman and Oso tucked safely in his briefcase. Farmer had agreed to testify against Hartley for the Texas and Arizona murders and promised to show detectives the location of Herman's and Oso's bodies. For his cooperation, Farmer would get life in prison and escape the death penalty.

"Hartley was driving when we saw them," Farmer had told Paulsen back in Grand Forks, North Dakota. "We'd spent two or three days at the Grand Canyon. Picked up two hitchhikers on the way back to Flagstaff.

We blew some grass in the car. I needed to take a leak. When I came back to the car, Hartley had the gun pointed at 'em."

Paulsen believed Farmer had tilted the story to minimize his involvement. Farmer claimed Hartley had taken the lead in the crime, with himself always a passive observer. Paulsen doubted Hartley had pulled the gun on the hitchhikers without Farmer expecting it. He doubted that Hartley had chastised Farmer when he didn't tie their hands tight enough and retied them himself, that Farmer had no idea Hartley planned to kill, that Hartley had strangled Tilfred and then raped and strangled Kathleen, that Farmer had touched neither until both victims were dead, when he finally went into a frenzy and smashed their skulls in with a rock. But it didn't make sense to press Farmer too hard before he led Paulsen to the bodies.

Early the morning of December 17, 1976, Detective Paulsen drove north from Flagstaff on Highway 180, the same route millions of Americans take every year to see the Grand Canyon on their summer vacations. Terry Lee Farmer sat shackled and slouched in the backseat of the detective's cruiser, and his mind drifted as he remembered his past two and a half years of aimless travels from one end of America to the other. He knew it had to end. He couldn't keep it up. And now he realized that this was possibly the last time he would be on the free and open roads of the Southwest. He had liked this area best, for amidst its open blue skies, stark landscape, eerie silence, and pastel sandstones, he had found a place with enough rawness to momentarily quiet his inward tempests.

The many dirt roads off Highway 180 into the uninhabited vastness of Coconino National Forest confused Farmer. Paulsen followed his prisoner's uncertain directions to two bodies somewhere amidst the high desert sagebrush and Ponderosa forest. Hours dragged by as Farmer told Paulsen to drive down the same back roads more than once, but time after time he found something not right with each dirt track.

As the hours passed, Farmer thought back for the thousandth time over the events that most plagued his mind: his estrangement from his family.

"Dad, am I adopted?" ten-year-old Farmer asked his father, a Southern Baptist who sold insurance.

"No, son, you're ours, just like Vicky," Dalton assured the little boy.

It didn't ring true. In his heart Farmer felt certain it was a lie. How else could he feel and be so different from his father and mother and Vicky, too? The lie made him angry, so angry he burned inside.

He remembered catching himself the next week, in shock, when he killed his black cat after it scratched him. He had flung his pet against the wall and killed it. He didn't know why, but it made him feel better. Soon his adolescent violence spread to people. When he struck his mother in rage, he left home for good, realizing that if he didn't leave, someone in his family would be seriously hurt, or die, by his hand.

At seventeen he became an aimless drifter, and two years later he took the same drive that would end Paulsen's investigation and recover the two bodies decomposing with the help of coyotes, crows, and magpies. What would the bodies look like? he wondered. As Farmer stared out the window at the snow-covered sagebrush prairies, he relived the day in Texas when the deadly duo first got their hands on the Monte Carlo, with its 440-cubic-inch engine.

"You'll never get away with it. We'll catch you and run you down!" declared Kelly Paul Bryan, the Monte Carlo's owner. Those words seared Farmer's mind and spelled doom for the owner.

"Why'd he say that to me?" Farmer wondered for the thousandth time. "Dumb little shit. If he'd kept his mouth shut, he'd be alive today."

Farmer knew now what had happened. Even with a loaded gun to his head, the idiot wouldn't shut up. He'd dared him to shoot, so he did.

Farmer thought he understood what had happened when the Monte Carlo's owner died. It was a macho thing. Man to man. It didn't bother him nearly as much as Kathleen's murder. With his confession Farmer believed he had traded his freedom forever to avert killing another woman—a taboo in his warrior's mentality.

"Girls were always my downfall," Farmer thought to himself. It was a girl that led Farmer to commit the first crimes he considered serious—animalistic acts of revenge for the assault and rape of Diana, his girlfriend and early partner in crime.

While riding around in Paulsen's squad car, feigning uncertainty about where to find Oso's and Herman's bodies, memories flooded his mind. At age sixteen, Terry and Diana had run away from home to live on the streets of Atlanta. Alone, broke, and on the run, he supported the pair using Diana as bait. Playing the part of prostitute in a southern big city's ghetto, a seedy, rundown fleshpot of cheap bars and low-rent rooms, Diana's delectable young figure lured unsuspecting johns out for quick fun in the dark alleys between bars, where Terry jumped from the shadows and rolled the marks for their wallets.

This game had worked well for them until one night two men, posing as friends, duped Terry into leaving Diana unprotected on the streets. They quickly took from Diana what she had pretended to offer so many times. Soon thereafter, Diana got sick and returned home. Her parents filed a peace bond to keep Terry away, and the pair drifted apart. A few months later Terry left home for good. It was time for him to take care of unfinished business in the big city's ghetto.

Three knife-point robberies of 7–11 convenience stores put four hundred dollars in his pocket, and Farmer began prowling the ghetto's night clubs in search of Diana's attackers. He bought a .25-caliber automatic handgun for a hundred dollars off a street dealer and patiently waited for his prey at a club where he knew he would find them. He smiled for the first time in weeks when one of his targets entered the club, duded up and acting like he was a cock of the walk. "That asshole's attitude's gonna change real soon," Terry thought.

The mark made the job easy. He left the bar with a young girl in tow. She presented a problem, but he'd deal with it on the fly. The pair walked through a dimly lit parking lot, then out of sight around the corner of a building. Terry picked up his pace to stay within striking distance. As he turned the corner, he almost ran into the pair next to a garbage dumpster, where the girl was already giving the mark a blow job. Terry snuck up behind her and tapped her on the shoulder. The girl jumped back in fright and accosted Terry with "Hey, fucker," while the john looked up to see what had interrupted his date. Terry drew the pistol from his back pocket and instinctively thrust the muzzle into his quarry's very surprised face.

"Hey, I don't want no part of this," the startled girl gasped.

"Get the fuck out of here, whore," Farmer growled, and the girl bolted away.

"Move, asshole," he ordered the mark, dragging him down the alley by his arm, gun in face.

"Hey man, what's up? I ain't done nuthin' to you," the mark protested, frantically tucking his shrinking, wet penis inside his pants.

Terry remained quiet, moving his man along until he slammed him into a warehouse wall.

"Where's your little shithead road dog? You know, the maggot fuck with the zit face!" Terry held the gun to the mark's head. He could smell his fear. He was intoxicated by the sights, sounds, and odors, and his rage boiled. He didn't wait for a reply. Instead, he pistol-whipped his face, splitting his cheek. The mark gasped and pleaded, "Who are you, man? I ain't done you no wrong."

"Look at me shithead. Remember me now?"

By the look on his face, Terry knew he did. He recoiled just like all the others. His one dead eye gave him the evil, half-crazed look of the devil's own.

Terry knew gunfire would attract attention, so he beat and kicked his victim into unconsciousness. He considered finishing the job by cutting the slumped man's throat, but his anger had subsided and he still had another score to settle. He stomped and kicked the mark's head as hard as he could and left the unconscious man near death's door.

Two hours later, the second mark recognized Terry first and fled in panic to a public restroom in a dark city park, directly across the street from where he and the other man had taken Diana. He ran to the last toilet stall, where he stood trembling and waiting. Terry quickly found him and kicked the stall door until it opened. The mark sprang out, screaming, "You're dead, man," and impaled himself on Terry's upraised knife. Both men crashed against the wall opposite the stall, and Terry saw a look of astonishment and heard a grunt of surprise. Then a gush of air rushed from his victim's gut as he drove the knife to the hilt. His body slumped onto Terry's, and he twisted free from his victim and let him collapse to the floor, blood flowing from his wound. Clutching his innards, he screamed and rolled. But Terry was excited by the smell of blood. He kicked the mark's head so violently he slipped on the muck and fell to the floor. Jumping up, he began kicking the man again, first in the head, then in the guts. Blood shot onto the wall, stalls, and floor, spraying Terry with a stream of gore. He stomped until the man laid still. Finally satisfied, he wiped the knife on the wet grass and fled to his hotel room, his clothing drenched in blood and sweat.

Luckily he got to his room unseen. He tore off his clothes and stood in the shower for an hour to let the warm water erase all traces of the attack. He watched the trails of blood flow down the drain and with it the anger. He placed all his bloody clothing into a bag, redressed, and walked several city blocks before disposing of the evidence. Sleep eluded him that night as he relived the fights, saw the marks' faces, heard their cries, and smelled their fear. Still, he did not feel he had done wrong. The next morning Terry left the city and began a two-year road exodus and crime spree.

Now he had reached his road's dead end.

During the first long day of driving down the narrow dirt tracks off Highway 180, Farmer did not give up the location of the bodies. But on one side road Paulsen sensed Farmer had acted differently. On the way back to town, Paulsen let Farmer know he was suspicious.

"It's that road we just left, where we went back twice, isn't it?" Paulsen confronted Farmer.

"You're right," Farmer admitted, realizing Paulsen was on to him again.

The next day, Farmer took Paulsen directly to the bodies, hidden amongst a clump of trees, their skulls crushed with rocks.

Paulsen had called the families during every step of the investigation—when Paulsen found Hartley, when he found Farmer, when Farmer confessed. Now he called to tell them that the fate of their children was finally known. He didn't want a strange policeman to walk to their doors with the grim news.

In Farmer's confession, the impetus to rape Kathleen and murder them both had been Hartley's alone. Paulsen believed that, to a point. When Hartley was arrested, he had worn around his neck a talisman of his crime: an unusual piece of Navajo jewelry made of silver, turquoise, and bear claws. Tilfred's father recognized it immediately from Hartley's mug shot. Tilfred Oso's distinctive bear-claw necklace hung beneath his murderer's mocking face. It sickened his father's heart to see evil incarnate wearing Tilfred's talisman. Tilfred's family name means "bear" in Spanish. The bear symbolizes power and wisdom to the Navajos. His wise and powerful son had been maliciously slain as if he were a wild animal, and his necklace had been kept as a trophy. Such feelings never would be shared out loud by Tilfred's family. The Navajos do not speak of the dead.

Tilfred's extended family showed up, though Paulsen had asked only the father to come to the sheriff's office to identify the necklace Hartley wore. The Oso family sat in silence, showing no emotion, as only Paulsen and the old man quietly spoke. Navajos remember their jewelry, a symbol of their wealth. They design, fashion, and wear it every day. The distinctive piece around Hartley's neck was no exception. The old man had made the bear-claw necklace himself and given it to Tilfred. That Hartley had worn it was proof to the Oso family that Paulsen had found the beast who murdered their Tilfred.

As the family filed out the door, Tilfred's mother asked Paulsen, "Do you want to know why I came here?" Paulsen nodded yes.

"I wanted to see the one who caught the bad man," she quietly replied.

After Farmer's sentencing, Paulsen again talked with Tilfred's family in his office. The Navajo family broke down crying. He knew any display of emotion to someone outside the family was highly unusual for any Navajo, and he felt accepted as someone special to the Oso family.

Kathleen's mother sent Paulsen a thank-you card several months after Farmer's sentencing. Twenty-three years later, Paulsen and Mrs. Herman still exchange Christmas greetings.

To this day, Paulsen remembers his appreciation and acceptance by the Oso and Herman families as the finest compliments paid him during his law-enforcement career. No jury's verdict of guilty could ever mean as much or so reward his efforts. Nor could an execution of Hartley have more satisfied Paulsen, but he got that as well in a form perhaps more just than a painless and quick execution by the state.

On the day of his extradition to Arizona to face first-degree murder charges for the death of Kathleen and Tilfred, Hartley committed suicide by swallowing a prison-made poisonous concoction of ground glass, metal shards, and ink that produced a death more hideous, protracted, and painful than any legal execution. Reading a news account of the suicide, Farmer felt Hartley had acted out of weakness, taking a coward's way out. He kept the newspaper clipping for years among his few personal mementos.

Farmer arrived May 4, 1977, at Arizona State Prison in Florence to serve concurrent life sentences for the Arizona and Texas murders. Not yet twenty years old and facing life in prison. How much worse could his life get?

3 The Victim

Investigating the life of the Florence Eleven's victim, Waymond Small, I began with a blank slate. To defend Richard Compton against a charge of murdering Small, I had only needed to know how to portray Small as a violent predator. Now I wanted to know about the person whose death became the cause for war between the State of Arizona and the Aryan Brotherhood.

I learned of Small's life and crimes through reading old court records — in cold storage at the Maricopa County Clerk of Court's Annex — from the 1977 first-degree murder case that sent him back to Arizona State Prison for the last time. That file revealed the details of Small's life. It also told me I would learn a lot more by talking with Phoenix police detective Ron Quaife, who along with his partner, Detective Harry Jennings, had apprehended Small.

Quaife and Jennings were the lead investigators on another first-degree murder case in which I had defended James Fisher, a sociopathic alcoholic. Fisher's and Small's crimes had eerie similarities. Both Fisher and Small had bludgeoned elderly women with hammers, killing them behind closed doors of small, downtown Phoenix apartments and stealing trivial sums of money — $500 and $600 — money they could easily have taken from their victims with one ounce of force. Both cases were easy to solve and prosecute. Both merited the death penalty.

Small had been in and out of mental and penal institutions his entire life, so much so that if the State of Alabama in 1977 had extradited him from Arizona to serve an overdue term of imprisonment for his escape eleven years earlier, Quaife and Jennings never would have been called late at night on April 13, 1977, to investigate Grace Ascher's murder.

Like Farmer's captor, Ron Quaife exemplifies the highest ideals and achievements of law enforcement. I learned his life story in 1997 during a leisurely three-hour visit to his north Phoenix home, where he lived in retirement with his wife. In 1963, Quaife, his wife, and five children moved to the Southwest after selling their inheritance of Illinois land for barely enough money to make a down payment on a home in Phoenix. Police work became Quaife's career by default when the Phoenix Police Department became the first prospective employer to call him back for an interview. The work suited his personality and talent.

By 1977 Quaife had moved up the ranks from beat cop to detective in the Phoenix Police Department's Homicide Bureau. Quaife and his longtime partner, Harry Jennings, put a quick end to Waymond Small's first and only legal interlude of adult life on the streets. From the age of eight to thirty-two, Small spent only three weeks as a free man. Every other day, this average-sized, ebony-colored son of grinding Alabama rural poverty was either in state custody or an escaped fugitive.

Detectives Quaife and Jennings were called to the scene of Grace Ascher's murder, an apartment in the heart of the city near the campus of Phoenix College. Flipping through Ascher's checkbook, Quaife and Jennings learned that the nearly blind woman had written a check to have her carpets cleaned the day of her death. This clue led Quaife and Jennings straight to Waymond Small, an ex-convict and newly employed carpet cleaner randomly assigned to the Ascher job. Small's employer described the cleaner's vehicle: a blue 1968 Chevrolet Impala. Quaife and Jennings posted a lookout for the vehicle, which turned out to be stolen, to stop and detain Small upon suspicion of murder and car theft.

Small fled when a patrol car spotted the Chevrolet. Quaife and Jennings followed the course of the chase and capture on their radio. They reached the Canterbury Apartments as Small was being handcuffed. He was taken to Phoenix Police Headquarters at Seventh Avenue and Washington, where he made an odd confession: Yes, he had killed the elderly lady, but Black Hands made him do it.

Quaife's doleful, bloodhound-like expression and calm, unassuming midwestern demeanor hid his feelings of revulsion as Small spun his fanciful tale. "Okay, tell me more about this Mr. Black Hands," became Quaife's broken-record refrain during the suspect's long-winded confession. The Black Hands cult, Small said, had initiated him in a desert mountain mine shaft outside Globe, Arizona. Eventually, according to Small, the cult threatened to kill his eight-year-old son unless Small killed Ascher. With Small's admission of murder, Quaife had heard all he needed and charged Small with the murder of Grace Ascher. Small's best defense, Quaife told the Maricopa County prosecutor, would be insanity.

Maricopa County paid for Waymond Small's criminal defense. Small was fortunate to have his defense assigned to Brice Beuhler, a wheel-chair-bound, well-known, and well-regarded former prosecutor with the Maricopa County attorney's office. He had just started a private practice and kept his office open by taking on indigent defense work.

Beuhler's first motion filed in Small's behalf sought an examination of his mental competency to stand trial. Prosecutor Jim Braden requested that Judge Sandra Day O'Connor appoint Dr. Michael Cleary, longtime head psychiatrist at Arizona State Hospital, as one of the psychiatrists to undertake Small's evaluation.

Dr. Cleary knew Small well. He was a repeat customer at the Maximum Security Division, where he had been examined many times between 1970 and 1977. Small's dog-eared, massive file told a sorry tale. Born June 9, 1945, in Cedar Bluff, Alabama, Small thought he had four or five living brothers and sisters. His father deserted the family when they lived in Columbus, Ohio. Small was sent to a children's home when at age nine his mother gave up on him. His schooling ended at the seventh grade. He logged four separate juvenile detentions between the ages of twelve and fifteen. His adult FBI rap sheet began in 1961, at age fifteen, with his conviction for armed robbery and sentencing to the Georgia Industrial Institution.

It is doubtful whether Small ever knew—from the day of his birth to his death in Arizona State Prison—a single day of normal life. Small spent very few days outside institutional control after age nine. He certainly spent every day from April 1968 to March 1977 either in the Maricopa or Gila County jails, the Arizona State Prison, or the Arizona State Hospital—except for his brief escape from the Gila County Jail.

Small's first period of institutionalization lasted six months at the juvenile diagnostic center in Columbus, Ohio. While there, he threatened to hang himself. Between the ages of nine and fourteen, Small bounced back and forth between the streets, foster care, and Ohio's School for Boys at least three times, often running away from psychiatric wards.

Georgia convicted Small of armed robbery and sent him to prison for twelve to fifteen years, but again he escaped. Small spent some of this time aimlessly wandering with his dad from Houston to Phoenix, where he was suspected of burglary and rape, and where he definitely fathered a child. This spree ended in 1963 in Columbus, Ohio, with his arrest for stealing shirts. He didn't give himself up easily. Small struck out violently at the policeman attempting to arrest him and jumped off a high bridge into a river. The psychiatrist pegged this as "not a suicidal gesture but an attempt to escape arrest."

Stealing shirts, however, wasn't the reason for his next four years of confinement in Ohio's mental hospitals. He had cut a girl with a knife, sodomized a young boy, and placed a shotgun at the throat of another victim and pulled the trigger, but the gun did not fire.

After Small won a transfer from prison back to the Columbus hospital, he escaped, staged an armed robbery, and shot at an Ohio highway patrolman to avoid arrest. This earned Small three more years at Lima. The authorities blew it again and released Small to the less secure confines of Columbus State Hospital. Within three weeks he escaped again, on August 27, 1967.

Small was always cagey in giving his history, so educated conjecture leads to the conclusion that a documented 1967 shotgun armed robbery in Indiana and confinement to a state mental hospital in Indianapolis fit into the short but otherwise unaccounted-for time frame after the escape in Ohio.

Small followed his mother's path to Arizona, where yet again he committed an armed robbery, got arrested, escaped from Gila County jail, and was recaptured after taking a shot at the Gila County sheriff. Small may have come to Arizona to see his son, Raymond, the issue of his procreative union with Laura Street in February 1963.

Small might well have repeated his Ohio, Georgia, and Indiana scenarios of confinement-escape-confinement if Arizona had had an adequate hospital for the criminally insane. After his escapades in Globe, Arizona, Gila County Superior Court Judge Robert McKee requested that psychiatrist Maeir Tuchler assess Small's mental condition. Tuchler's report spelled out the system's deficiencies in order to assure that Small went to prison this time.

> Lima State Hospital is a maximum security institution for the criminally insane. The various state hospitals in Ohio transfer their unmanageable and violent patients to this institution for the criminally insane. Arizona has no such institution, the maximum security ward at Arizona State Hospital is quite inadequate to control behavior of such potential violence of which this subject is capable.
>
> He is quite devoid of any inner controls and most ingenious in

maneuvering escapes. The only safe security for Waymond Small is in a penal institution rather than in a mental hospital.

Small returned to Arizona State Prison and was there until July 13, 1976, when the old Georgia escape charges caught up with him. He was extradited to Georgia, where he acted as his own lawyer and prepared a successful writ of habeas corpus challenging the legality of the guilty plea that sent him to prison at age fifteen. Relieved to be rid of him, Georgia released him with a bus ticket to Arizona on January 29, 1977. For the first time in his adult life, at age thirty-one, Small had no holds, paroles, or warrants over his head. Thus began his last foray outside institutional walls, destined to last only three months.

After reviewing Small's files, Dr. Cleary dictated his last report on him:

Describing events [on the evening of Grace Ascher's murder], when he returned to the victim's house, he relates an experience in which the victim reportedly came up behind him, called him a bad name and attacked him with a claw hammer and knife, one weapon in each hand. He then moves from an apparently factual account to the realm of fantasy, fiction or fabrication. The victim changed into a man who had tried to kill him when he was 5 years old, a one-legged man who tried to throw him into a cesspool; he saw a series of clear pictures, then disarmed and fought the attacker, backhanding the hammer and slapping at the knife. He heard a weird chanting in the background and the man "a brown skinned brother, with medium Afro and burns on his face," spoke to Small telling him he moved fast. In addition, the small dog of the victim assumed the proportions of a huge German Shepherd. On leaving the house, he could not recall how he got out but then realized that Mrs. Ascher was dead.

Compared with the tale Small later told at his trial for Ascher's murder, the jurors who convicted him could easily have said to psychiatrist Cleary, "Doc, that was nothing." And though they would hear an even wilder tale, the jury's verdict would agree with Dr. Cleary's diagnosis: "no mental disorder."

Armed with Dr. Cleary's report, Judge O'Connor found Small competent and sane on July 6, 1977. Disappointed but not dissuaded, Small tried again. Brazenly, he wrote a letter in his careful, effeminate, nearly perfect handwriting, beseeching Judge O'Connor to spend some quality time alone with him.

Trial judges routinely receive handwritten entreaties from defendants, victims, and their families and friends, seeking special favors or the opportunity to tell the judge the whole story so that justice can really be done. Judges ignore the pleas and instruct their clerks to dutifully file the letters in the court's official case file in order to preserve a complete record.

Small's letter deserves recognition as a classic of the genre: sickly sweet, transparently manipulative, with oddities of English usage, syntax, and word choice that betray the con man's warped mind-set in spite of his charade of rationality.

> Re: Waymond Gene Small, CR 97388
> Dear Judge O'Connor:
> Will you please permit me an off the record, informal and irregular confidential conference with you. I am hoping that what I have to communicate to you will influence you in your dealing and understanding me and my case, cause number supra. I promise not unnecessarily waste your time and my behavior will be that of a gentleman and above reproach. However, if you feel for any reason that I may constitute a security exposure to loss or harm in anyway, then by all means take whatever steps you deem necessary so that we may have a few hours alone, so that you and I can sit down and talk about what I would like to talk to you about.
> Thank you in advance for your time and to any consideration you may give my request as stated above. I am
> Sincerely yours,
> Waymond Gene Small

Prosecutors and public defenders have a special name for murder trials like Small's in which the evidence of guilt is so great, the crime so horrible, and the defendant so unsavory that the outcome is never in doubt: the slow-form guilty plea. The only matter in doubt: would Small receive the death penalty?

Prosecutor James Braden wasted no time convincing the jury of the horror of Small's crime. He began with Dr. Jarvis's autopsy. Before the second witness took the stand, the jury knew that a defenseless, nearly blind, seventy-year-old lady had been viciously attacked with a hammer and knife and strangled with an electric cord. Dr. Jarvis's autopsy report described atrocious stab wounds and hammer blows to the chest, neck, and head, with a cord ligature double wrapped and tied around the neck in a square knot. Even Jarvis's sober, technical descriptions conveyed Small's brutality: "*Cause of Death:* Head injury. Stab wounds, neck and chest. Strangulation by ligature. *Manner of Death:* Homicide. *Narrative Summary of Circumstances Surrounding Death:* Found Beaten and stabbed; house ransacked, dog killed. Found dead April 13, 1977, 9:15 p.m."

Ascher's body was found by Wayne Buechler, her nephew, who divided his time between staying with his aunt at her apartment in Phoenix and working on his parents' land in the outlying farm community of Buckeye. On the evening of April 13, Wayne headed to the city, on foot since he didn't own a car. Just as Small completed his bloody work, Buechler turned the busy corner of Fifteenth Avenue and Thomas Road. Using his own key, he entered the unusually quiet apartment. Ascher's lap dog didn't even greet him with its high-pitched, yippish bark. Then he saw his aunt, slumped on the floor in a pool of still-fresh blood.

The slow-form guilty plea hit its high point with the introduction of Small's two confessions—one to Laura Street, the mother of his son, Raymond; the other to Leslie Haboush, his most recent female interest.

After murdering Ascher, Small had gone on a midnight drive around Phoenix, stopping first at the apartment he shared with his roommate, Alan Gannt. There, he took all his belongings and packed them into the stolen 1968 Chevrolet Bel Air. He drove to the projects where Laura Street lived with his son and her four other children. Knocking on her door at 1:30 a.m., he offered all his possessions to Laura and Raymond. Why? He had told Laura he was "leaving town because he thought he'd killed a woman." He confessed that he had hit her on the head with a hammer and stabbed her in the belly and throat and killed her tiny dog. He had done this "because he had beat her out of some money or something." Street asked Small if he was sure the woman was dead. He answered that "she should be." Defense attorney Beuhler asked Street if Small told her that morning that he had to accept the blame for this act because otherwise his son would be in danger or even killed. "No, he didn't say that," she deadpanned.

Small gave his second confession to the newest woman in his life, Leslie Haboush. Pulling the sting himself, before the defense counsel could, Prosecutor Braden asked Haboush to admit her unseemly past before unfolding her tale. Only twenty years old, she admitted to her conviction for prostitution and a pending charge for possession of dangerous drugs. She then told the jury she met Waymond Small on April 10, 1977, at an apartment complex off Seventh Avenue as she stood outside waiting for a ride. Small was driving a 1968 Chevrolet Bel Air. He stopped and asked her if she needed a lift. Small told Haboush he was "doing really well" and "putting up money in investments and getting his self situated." Small asked her to move into an apartment with him; she told him she would think about it.

The next afternoon Haboush saw Small at her friend's apartment and told him she would be shooting pool in a tournament that evening. Small told her he was going to see "some woman about getting some money and see if the carpet had dried." She saw Small the next morning at 5:45 a.m., and he said he had to leave Phoenix because he had murdered a woman and ripped her off for $600. Small said he had taken samples of the carpet to the woman's apartment, but she came after him with a hammer and a knife, so he grabbed her by the legs, beat her on the head with the hammer, cut her throat, and killed her dog, cutting his thumb during the scuffle. Small told Haboush he wanted her to go to Ohio with him. At that point, she asked him if he had any regrets, and he said he had no feelings about it whatsoever. He seemed perfectly normal, said Haboush. The killing didn't bother him in the least.

Haboush didn't know whether to believe Small's murder confession until she heard "a radio broadcast that a woman had been found in her northwest home, beaten to death." When Haboush told him what she'd heard, Small "just looked at me and said he thought I was bullshitting." She asked him what time he went to the victim's apartment. He said 8 p.m., that he had stayed twenty minutes, left, then came back "to torch and fire the apartment," but "the ambulance and the police were already there."

Haboush and Small were captured when they returned to the Canterbury Apartments. True to form, Small made wild efforts to escape capture. Realizing policemen were inside the complex, Small fled to the car. In the nick of time, another police vehicle sped into the parking lot and blocked the Chevrolet's exit. Small jumped out and ran toward the apartments. The officer yelled, "Stop or I'll shoot." Small never broke stride, and the officer ran after him. Surrounded by officers, Small was finally restrained and shoved, still struggling, into the back of a police car. After a short, handcuffed drive in a separate car to police headquarters at

Seventh Avenue and Washington Street, Haboush immediately dropped the dime on Small.

On August 4, 1977, Small got his wish: twelve jurors heard his story; the same story he would have told Judge Sandra Day O'Connor if she had granted his request for a personal conference; the same story his attorney rejected; the same story Detective Quaife ignored when Small offered to solve ten unsolved murders.

To common sense, Small's story proved him insane; in the legal sense, it did not. Defense Attorney Brice Beuhler, now relegated to an advisory role since Small was acting as his own lawyer, set the day's ground rules for Waymond Small's delusional monologue by saying: "Your Honor, if I might interject at this point, I have advised Mr. Small in light of representing himself I feel a proper way for him to proceed would be in a narrative form to simply recall the facts surrounding this case and directing it to the jury since he cannot very well pose questions of himself and answer them himself."

Judge O'Connor agreed: "I know of no other way to do it."

With this open-ended entrée, Small began an uninterrupted spiel lasting all day. His phantasm started in 1968, when he met his father's seventy-five-year-old friend Mr. Jackson, who ran a dude ranch. Jackson propositioned Small to transport cars from California to Phoenix for one hundred dollars a run.

"It would be a full-time job. I would have no say-so over what I did. I would have to obey the orders regardless of what the orders were, and at any time I showed any reluctance to obey such orders they would not hesitate to kill me. I was 22 years old and didn't care a damn if the sun didn't come up the next day. I thought I was one of the toughest sons of a bitches that walked the face of this earth. I took the proposal." For $100,000 a year, "no questions asked," Small became "part of Black Hands's personal organization."

Small's initiation into Black Hands's group sounded like a medieval rite of passage, complete with modern touches like truth serum, psychological profiles, and delectable female assistants serving as Satan's handmaidens, just like Goldfinger's vamps in the James Bond flick.

Irene was the name of Black Hands's female consort. After Black Hands's men picked up Small in a 1966 Lincoln Continental like Odd Job's in Goldfinger, they blindfolded him, drove around for hours, and took him to a tunnel with an elevator shaft. Irene showed Small to the dormitory where other men were being evaluated by doctors and Irene using "psychological profiles" and "hypnosis, drugs, basically sodium pentothal and lie detector tests. They would know at all times what you were thinking and what you were doing."

As part of his indoctrination, Small claimed he listened to tapes describing "murder, kidnap, arson, extortion, and bribery of high officials" committed by Black Hands's organization. From these tapes he learned about people "marked for death and people that were marked to be set up." Small told the jury he'd offered to help Detective Quaife "clear up" unsolved murder cases by telling him what he had learned during his indoctrination. According to Small, Quaife "investigated and found out it was absolutely true, that in fact these murders had been committed and were unsolved. I offered to do what I could if necessary, to clear up as many of these past homicides as I could recall, and if necessary—which I didn't mention this part to Detective Quaife—I would submit to hypnosis and I have 100 percent recall under such conditions."

Small said Detective Quaife turned on him and "convinced the County Attorney that I may have committed these crimes." Small asked to talk with the county attorney, but "Mr. Braden would have nothing to do with me." This rejection led Small to his last resort. He wrote Judge O'Connor and requested a personal interview, but, "because of the rules of procedure that she is bound, she couldn't grant me that interview." Unable to convince Detective Quaife or to get the county attorney or Judge O'Connor to hear him out, Small couldn't even get his own lawyer to believe him, and he had insisted upon portraying Small as insane and deluded.

In spite of rejection from all corners, Small told the jury he valiantly persisted in his quest to tell his story. Small enjoyed the spotlight, and he scanned the courtroom looking for any sign that the judge, the jurors, the bailiff, or the lawyers were taken in by his story. Behind a facade of outward calm, his cunning mind calculated the scene, looking out for the slightest opening for an escape route, for a fleeting moment when he could throttle his captors, seize a gun, take a hostage, and break out of his bondage.

Small told the jury about the job's excellent perks: "Girls were available for the needs of the men anytime they wanted. If the girls didn't consent to total submission there was always girls to take their place." Black Hands confronted one of these sexual objects, snatched her heart from her chest, literally pulled it out, and told another girl to eat it. "Black Hands hit her and knocked her silly. He had a pit in one of the back rooms about as long as that table sitting there and twice as wide. It was made of glass. At the bottom of that pit there was sand and nothing but ants. And he put her in there screaming and suffering. He liked that. While this girl was in the pit screaming, he was having sex with a third woman. He had two of the guys to hold her legs and he kept telling them to pull on her legs and spread them, make her holler, make her scream, make her suffer until he took a knife and he went to cutting on her. Finally he killed her.

"Irene noticed the way that I was looking at Black Hands, and she said, 'I guess you think he's pretty sick, don't you Waymond?'"

"I just told Black Hands, 'You're a sick mother fucker.'"

"He hit me with his open hand."

"Normal people out there in society can't even believe what goes on down there in the penitentiary, so it's hard for them to open their minds to believe what I'm telling them. Anyway, I felt that I had made a bad mistake when I said that, and I thought he was going to kill me. Irene said, 'I don't think Waymond will ever make that mistake again.'"

"He took me out. He just said, 'I want to have a talk with you so that you don't ever make that mistake again. As long as you live, don't you ever so much as think that, because if you do, it will be your last thought.' We were in the mountains and he put a blindfold on me and we drove about ten minutes."

But clever Small escaped from Black Hands, leading to the armed robbery and jail escape in 1968 from the Gila County Jail in Globe, Arizona—the convictions that sent him to Arizona State Prison in the first place. Small explained away the criminality of his conduct by recourse to Black Hands's evil genius.

Small enjoyed a fanciful escapade in the mountains before returning to talk with a deputy sheriff in Globe. "I went through several miles of the mountains that night around Globe until I came to an old man's ranch. His name was Joe Schue. I recall his name. I asked Mr. Schue for some water. He gave it to me. I knew there was no way I could explain my predicament to him. If there was any way I could get away from Black Hands, I wanted to do that. So I hot wired Mr. Schue's Jeep, drove it further up in the mountains. I left the Jeep up in them mountains and went back to Globe. Mr. Schue had a rifle in his Jeep. I took that with me. I went back to the county jail. The Deputy was standing out on the corner. The minute he saw me he started shooting. I was in the middle of the highway. I fired a shot back at him, ran across the alley and up around the courthouse."

Small fled back to the mountains, hiding under bushes and evading roadblocks. Before he was finally captured at another roadblock outside Apache Junction, he had managed to accost another victim in a campground before getting a lift to Phoenix in the back of a camper's pickup.

At this point in the story, Judge O'Connor called for lunch recess. Undaunted, Small continued the Black Hands story all afternoon.

"Well, let me give you a description of Black Hands. He stands about 5' 9½", maybe 5'10". He's an average person physically. He has very big wrists. He's white. He has blue eyes. You can't tell what kind of hair he has because he dyes it, colors it so much. It's usually black or blonde, very muscular person. Doesn't look like a weight lifter or anything like that but he has good muscle tone. He has a distinguished voice. If you heard his voice, you'll never forget it.

"Nails, he's a black dude. He stands about 5'9", average weight, average height. When I said black I mean black. He's black. He doesn't have any scars or anything on his face. He has a very wide African type nose. Fingers, Palms, Thumbs, Hands, Knuckles, they're all white, as average as anybody you'd ever want to meet. They are mercenaries. I don't think any of them is from the United States."

Adding spice to his slow-brewing fantasy, Small changed the subject and offhandedly threw in some personal history.

"The Judge accepted my plea of guilty and gave me 12 to 15 years in the Arizona State Prison" on the robbery and escape charges arising from the just-related adventures in Gila County.

"I was aware of the potential dangers in prison. I had described the first attempt on my life to you. I think it would be important to describe the other two, although I could never get anyone to testify to it, short of holding a gun on them. The second attempt was supposed to be a sure thing. And if it wasn't for the fact that I had heard these tapes, they would have killed me.

"I was released from the Arizona State Prison August 13, 1976. I was placed in the Pinal County Jail, pending extradition to Georgia. When I was 15 years old, I was put in prison in Georgia for a crime I didn't commit. I went back to Georgia. I wrote a Writ of Habeas Corpus. The judge heard my arguments, checked the evidence and facts and ruled in my favor that there was no way I could have committed the crime. So I was released from the Jackson State Prison in Jackson, Georgia, January 29 of this year.

"I was going to stay in Georgia and work on some legal actions, but my foster parents were short of funds so I returned to Arizona. After a three-day bus ride I arrived in Mesa, Arizona. I saw an ad to become a carpet technician for Miller's Carpet Care, caught the bus and went there and I talked to the manager. I told him I was an ex-con. He gave me a job. I trained for 3 days. I learned the job fast."

Small rambled on about how he'd found his roommate, Allen Gannt. Of course, Gannt turned out to be one of Black Hands's confederates and so testified against him.

Well into Smith's fifth hour of monologue, he reached the day of Ascher's murder. He explained how he dutifully drove to Ascher's apartment and began to take carpet samples to test for germs, bacteria, and stains and examined the spot that was supposedly still wet from cleaning earlier in the day. While doing these tasks, Black Hands magically appeared.

"I was about to take a sample of carpet from this area right there when an individual entered into the home. [Ascher] recognized this individual immediately. There was no alarm about it, nothing to be upset about.

"The person came out of this area and walked out to the front door.

"Four men came through that front door. These four men—one of them I did recognize, and that was Palms. He's the only one at that time that I recognized from having stopped me in Phoenix previously. Then I recognized Black Hands from his voice. He had on some theatrical makeup as well as the rest of the four people that had entered the home.

"There was three other guys attacked Miss Ascher immediately, and one of them held a gun on me. It was my effort to try to intervene that caused me to get cut on my thumb. I told Leslie Haboush otherwise. I told Leslie Haboush that Miss Ascher had attacked me, but she didn't.

"These three guys, each one of them had a weapon. These guys killed Miss Ascher. I'm standing there and watching. This is not the first time that I witnessed Black Hands at work.

"Mr. Black Hands explicitly told me, 'The only fingerprints that are in this house are yours, and the only way.'

"Let me come back to that; okay," Small interrupted himself, realizing he hadn't yet explained away the cut on his finger, though in his own mind, he had satisfactorily explained away his mere fingerprints on the murder weapon by recourse to Black Hand's wizardry.

"Anyway, as incredible as it is, Little Dog, this little pooch, started barking. Black Hands reached down and grabbed the little dog around the throat and he was choking the dog, he was hitting Miss Ascher in the head with a hammer. Palms was trying to keep her from hollering. He shoved a knife in her throat and held it there. He was standing behind the chair. The other one, I believe would be identified as Fingers. He had stabbed her in the chest. This is when the chair was turned over. Palms turned the chair over and stepped on Miss Ascher's glasses.

"Palms pulled a knife down through her midsection there. Black Hands took the hammer and he was holding the little dog, still choking it. He cracked it on the head with the hammer, swung it on the floor there. The little dog hobbled into the bedroom. Black Hands went in there and hit the dog in the head with the hammer again."

The details, so vividly and calmly recited, probably convinced the jury that Small had enjoyed himself as he tortured the defenseless elderly woman and her little dog. Small thought otherwise, believing the details convinced the jury that the evil genius of Black Hands accounted for the mayhem.

"It was at this point that Fingers told me to go into the bedroom. Black Hands had throwed the hammer on the bed. He told me to empty boxes of things on the bed. I told him no, I wasn't going to do it. I leaned my hand up against the door there and just told him flat I wasn't going to do it, that I knew he was going to kill me, and just wasn't going to do it.

"So he emptied them on the bed and that's the reason there was no fingerprints there and that's also the reason why that it would have been so impossible to see that hammer. It was almost completely covered up with letters, jewelry boxes and items of things like that.

"He told me that if I valued—if I valued the life of my son, whom I personally knew that not I or anyone else could protect from him, that I had better keep my mouth shut and accept the blame for Miss Ascher's death. I told him that I couldn't do that. He said, 'Think about it. Give the boy a chance to grow up.'

"Since I hadn't seen nobody around there, it occurred to me if I burnt Miss Ascher's house down, it would be about the best way of getting out of the problem I was in, the situation that I was in."

Small had already heard the testimony of Laura Street and Leslie Haboush. However insane his story might be, every testifying criminal defendant seeks to align his story with as much of the rest of the trial evidence as possible. Small fell into this pattern by agreeing with Street's and Haboush's descriptions of his actions after Ascher was murdered. Apparently, Small did not comprehend that in so doing he gave the jury yet another backhanded confession that he was the murderer.

"I put everything in the car and then I went over to my son's house. I knocked on the door. His mother answered the door. I told her not to wake him up. I told her that I had my personal items in the car, and I wished to leave them there for her and my son, that I wouldn't need them anymore.

"She asked me what was wrong. I told her, 'I think they killed a person.'

"I referenced to that which I did not explain to her, I was actually thinking about myself.

"She said, 'What did you say?' I said, 'I think I killed a woman.' I wasn't referencing to myself then. She said, 'Waymond, what happened?' I said, 'I can't tell you.' She said, 'Why not?' I said, 'Because the police will be after me.' She said, 'For what?' I said, 'They're going to charge me with murder.' She said, 'Murder?' I said, 'Yeah.' She said, 'Murdering who?' I told her, 'A woman.'

"She didn't believe me and I told her, 'You may think I'm joking, but the police will be here. They'll send detectives around to ask you questions.'

"She said, 'What kind of questions will they ask me?' 'They'll try to find out where I'm at.'

"She said, 'Where you going to be at?' I said, 'I don't know.' She said, 'Well, what happened?'

"I said, 'I went to a woman's house on business and when I left there her throat was cut and her dog was dead.' She said, 'I don't believe that.' She said, 'You may have done something but I don't believe that.' I said, 'Believe it.' She said, 'You ain't no killer and I don't believe you killed nobody.'

"I said, 'The woman's head was beaten with a hammer.' She said, 'Maybe she's not dead.'

"I left my personal items at my son's house for him and his mother.

"I drove over to a parking lot behind the Glenrosa apartments. I went to sleep on the front seat for a short while and when I woke up I went to Miss Haboush's apartment.

"I was let in. I had a conversation with Miss Haboush where I related that I had ripped an old lady off for $600 and that she came at me with a knife and a hammer.

"I informed Miss Haboush that the police would be looking for me for murder. Miss Haboush didn't believe me. She asked me or indicated to me that she would like to know why the police was going to be looking for me.

"I hadn't told her at that point that it was going to be for murder."

Small's canard having run its course, prosecutor Braden didn't bother with a single objection or question. Judge O'Connor called a recess. The jury had heard more than enough for one day.

Waymond Small's trial, which began on July 21, should have wrapped up quickly once he testified on August 4. But seven more days passed before the jury got the case. Those days tested the patience of the prosecutor, defense lawyer, and jury as Judge O'Connor patiently and competently wove her way around Small's maze of manipulations to assure any higher court would sustain his conviction if he were to appeal. Painstaking recital of the day-to-day machinations can be quickly characterized by describing the pages Small used from the con man's playbook.

Small's maze played off the inherent tensions between the concept of "legal" and de facto insanity. Small threw in an added complication: he vacillated between exercising a criminal defendant's constitutional right to act as his own lawyer and exercising his constitutional right to be represented by a competent lawyer. The law gives the defendant the right to proceed as he prefers, though the man who represents himself has a fool for a client. In Small's case, these principles, and their inherent conflict, danced alongside each other throughout the trial. Judge O'Connor deftly tackled Small after every snap of the judicial football; he tried to bob and weave for a first down, but O'Connor played a better linebacker to Small's halfback, holding him scoreless.

Small repeatedly expressed dissatisfaction with his court-appointed lawyer and asked to represent himself. As long as Small possessed mental competence to make an informed decision and Judge O'Connor assured herself that Small indeed wanted to represent himself, he could—and he could flip-flop back to representation by counsel, unless Judge O'Connor concluded that each change unduly disrupted the trial. Judge O'Connor could not refuse Small's request to represent himself just because it was a "bad idea" or showed "poor judgment." Knowing he could change his mind, Small did so almost daily or expressed his dissatisfaction with the status quo, whatever it was. Each change dictated a new hearing, outside of the jury's presence, to decide the rules of the game. Was Small competent today to make this decision? Did he understand what he was doing?

Immediately after telling his fantastic tale about Black Hands, Small had a change of heart; once again he wanted Brice Beuhler to be his lawyer. Small's tactics showed remarkable presence of mind and manipulative skill. He had been able to present his Black Hands defense while acting as his own lawyer, but Brice Beuhler resumed the reins and conducted the trial while psychiatrists offered opinions that Small's highly delusional defense showed he was legally insane. Once Beuhler took charge of the defense case, their irreconcilable conflicts would again come to the fore. Beuhler defended Small using the legal insanity defense even though Small insisted that his Black Hands story was literal truth and that he was not insane.

Small's deranged behavior looks, feels, sounds, smells, and tastes like insanity to any layman, as indeed would the actions of many murderers. However, the law distinguishes behavioral insanity—sociopathic, psychotic, and other all-too-common behaviors that might appear to be insanity—from the exceedingly rare cognitive insanity that shields a true madman from criminal liability. The law defines legal insanity as a mental disease or defect so severe that the defendant is unable to appreciate the nature and quality or the wrongfulness of his acts. A mental disease or defect of any other kind does not constitute a defense. As long as Beuhler was responsible for Small's defense, he called psychiatrists to the witness stand, hoping to show that Small was legally insane when he killed Ascher.

By his ploys, Small got to have his cake and eat it, too, first asserting he was sane, then that he wasn't, as he alternated between self-representation and representation through counsel. The charade took time, and a week passed from Small's telling of the Black Hands fantasy until the jury began deliberations the morning of August 11, 1977. Small tried to have it both ways to the very end. He asked Judge O'Connor to permit both Brice Beuhler and himself to give closing arguments to the jury;

O'Connor gave Small his choice. Betraying his rationality, Small opted for Beuhler.

Though Small's trial stretched over twenty-two days, it nonetheless played out as a slow-form guilty plea. The jury members easily recognized Small's overt lunacy and outright perjury and found him guilty after six hours of deliberation. Their verdict delivered, the jurors went home, since in Arizona juries at that time decided guilt but not punishment for first-degree murder. At a sentencing hearing before the judge, the prosecutor attempted to prove that "aggravating circumstances" warranted the death penalty, and the defense argued that "mitigating circumstances" warranted life imprisonment.

Judge Day O'Connor, destined in four years to become the first woman appointed to the U.S. Supreme Court, decided Small's fate on September 7, less than five months after Ascher's horrid murder. If ever the good Justice O'Connor shall be thought cold-hearted, let it be recalled that she spared Waymond Small's life.

The prosecutor easily proved, and Judge O'Connor found, that Small qualified for the death penalty because two "aggravating circumstances" existed. Small's prior Arizona convictions for robbery in 1968, for assault with a deadly weapon in 1973, and for aggravated battery in 1974 created one aggravating circumstance. Judge O'Connor found that the murder of Grace Ascher had been committed "in an especially heinous, cruel or depraved manner," creating a second aggravating circumstance. Judge O'Connor also found that Small's mental illness was a "mitigating circumstance" because his "capacity to appreciate the wrongfulness of his conduct or to conform his conduct to the requirements of law was significantly impaired, but not so impaired as to constitute a defense to prosecution." Balancing the two aggravating circumstances against this one mitigating factor, Judge O'Connor decided that the mitigating factor outweighed the aggravating factors and spared his life from execution by the state. Whether mitigating factors outweigh aggravating factors in a first-degree murder case will forever remain highly subjective. Would one judge in ten have been so lenient?

Within four months of each other, Farmer and Small arrived at Arizona State Prison as convicted murderers who had narrowly escaped the death penalty. In prison parlance, Terry Lee Farmer and Waymond Small were doing "all day" or, in the legal jargon of Arizona's criminal code and each judge's sentencing order, "imprisonment in Arizona State Prison for

life without the possibility of parole until service of 25 calendar years."
However expressed, both men believed they faced the same reality: they'd
never live to see the day of their release from Arizona State Prison. One
did not; the other may not.

Once sentenced, Terry Lee Farmer, the volunteer, and Waymond
Small, his victim, were launched via parallel paths on a collision course
and became cannon fodder in a politically motivated war to reclaim
Arizona's prisons.

4 A Gang Is Born

Borrowing the name and idea from California convicts, Stretch Hillyer and Red Dog Howard founded the Aryan Brotherhood within Arizona State Prison. Though others might claim the honor of being the group's originators, no one doubts the role these two played as prime catalysts in the toxic brew that loosed the gang's scourge in the prison's walls.

I first met Red Dog when venturing inside the prison to interview potential witnesses during defense of the Waymond Small case. Red Dog was charged, along with my client Richard Compton, with being one of the Aryan Brotherhood officers who had ordered Small's murder. Why I interviewed Red Dog, or what he said, I don't recall. That I still vividly recall his persona from that day testifies to his uniqueness. Though at the time he was shackled hand and foot, escorted by three guards, indicted for murder and facing the death penalty, being held along with his Aryan Brotherhood confederates in Cell Block 4's lockdown, Red Dog acted as if he had the world by the balls. More significant, even the prison guards acted as if maybe Red Dog was powerful; they acted deferential and oddly respectful toward him. They laughed at his jokes, enjoyed his high jinks, and played along with his horseplay antics. Guards and prisoners alike used Red Dog's nickname and knew how he had acquired it. Over time, Howard's moniker and its genesis, and his outlandishly low prison number, which signified exactly how very long ago he first went to prison, indelibly defined his status as an institutional legend.

In 1997, after his conversion to Christianity, Red Dog and I began an extensive correspondence, and I learned how he earned his nickname in 1969. His story, now four decades old, remains a classic amongst Arizona State Prison institutional lore.

"Pass the hooch to me," Howard hollered to his drinking buddies, Butch and Ray, as the threesome—ostensibly at work at their jobs in the maintenance department—became increasingly more intoxicated on a "home brew" prison concoction. Any position with the maintenance department was an institutional plum, a sweet job, affording as it did access to a shop full of tools, widgets, tubes, pumps, tape, electrical out-lets, grinders, screw drivers, hammers, and ever-precious garbage that could be sifted through for special tidbits and odds and ends, all under the minimal supervision granted to prisoners who performed the work of running day-to-day operations.

With their basic needs of food and shelter supplied by the state, idle convicts naturally and inevitably turn to smuggling contraband intoxicants inside the prison walls to ease the passage of time. They hoard fruit from lunch sacks and garbage bins, squeezing the juice into pilfered plastic bags until fifteen cups — sufficient for a batch — are secreted. Flavor and fermentation are enhanced with sugar, lemon drops, and Kool-Aid. Bread dough provides the yeast. So much creative enterprise to blot out feeling, to dull consciousness, to self-medicate, to feed the serpent of addiction.

When Red Dog earned his nickname, he was well stewed on prison brew, as were Butch and Ray. The drunken trio engaged in idle conversa-tion about petty items pilfered and set aside:

"Hey, Red, how much do you want for the TV antenna?" Butch asked Howard, whose nickname derived at that point only from the color of his hair.

"I already sold it to Abe for two cartons of smokes," Howard re-plied.

"I'll give you twenty-five for it," Butch slurred, offering five more packs than Abe.

"Butch, what did I just say?" Howard sneered back, a sarcastic edge to his voice. "It's sold, bro!"

Butch wouldn't let it go. "Why would you prefer to sell a greaser some-thing for less than what a peckerwood like me wants to give you?"

"Butch, I gave my word to Abe when I made the deal, so that's it! I won't sell to you no matter what you offer!" Howard snapped at the stronger, larger weightlifter.

Hoping the heated exchange would escalate into an entertaining fight, Ray kicked back and clasped his hands behind his head.

"Look here, Red, I need this antenna bad, so here's what I'm going to do," Butch finally declared. "I'm going to take it and pay you, store day, what I said I'd pay you. You can tell that greaser anything you want, but he's not getting this antenna."

As Butch reached for the antenna, Howard grabbed his arm.

"Okay, Red, if that's the way you want it!" Butch screamed, as he came around the bench between them and pushed Howard into the wall, seizing him in a bear hug and pinning Howard's arms to his side, squeezing the breath out of his chest with all his might. Nose to nose, the two men turned red, Howard from lack of breath, Butch from the exertion of squeezing the wind out of Howard.

Howard, unable to break Butch's hold, was about to pass out. He twisted his neck forward and viciously bit Butch's left ear, tearing half the cartilage away. Blood gushed and Butch let go of Howard to grab his tattered ear. The top half was missing, and it took eight stitches to close, but Butch didn't snitch. Howard received no prison discipline for the incident. When the two saw each other the next day, Butch admitted he was wrong. They shook hands and remained friends, and Howard earned the moniker "Red Dog." Such a nickname bestowed honor within the prison walls. Howard's rabid, wild dog tendencies made him a man to be feared, admired, and respected.

Howard was released in 1969 but returned to prison, with serious time to do, in 1975, again for one too many armed robberies. Howard's extracurricular activities in prison stacked more time onto his original sentence, so this stint stretched out to eighteen years, with each escapade adding to his institutional legend. A man's reputation isn't built in a day, nor upon one incident. Red Dog's was earned over twenty-three years, including receiving multiple convictions for armed robbery; stabbing Flash in 1965; fighting "four niggers" alone rather than pay protection in his Gladiator School days; biting Butch's ear in 1969; attempting to escape in 1971; running lucrative protection rackets and hustles; turning corruptible guards into prison mules; forming and leading the Aryan Brotherhood; ordering Small's execution as lieutenant in the brotherhood; and surviving a reprisal shotgun attack in 1980 between feuding factions within the brotherhood. No prisoner would deny that Red Dog had earned a reputation as one of the hardest and toughest convicts at Arizona State Prison.

With a thin, six-foot-seven-inch frame, Jerry Joe "Stretch" Hillyer looked like he'd survived the rack. His most-valuable asset was his reputation for violence, earned by deeds, not words. In June 1977, Stretch parlayed this reputation into the generalship of the Aryan Brotherhood.

Stretch cemented his institutional reputation on June 7, 1975, by shooting Larry Fassler. The very day of his release from isolation, Stretch walked to the milk dispenser during the evening meal. In full view of all the inmates and guards inside the chow hall, he pulled a pistol supplied by the Padilla brothers and shot Fassler six times.

Fassler, in prison for drug smuggling, was reputedly running his own operation from inside the walls. He owed Hillyer $10,000 from a drug debt and an IRS fraud—at least that was one yarn, but not a very believable one. Another highly believable story amounted to simple jealousy over Fassler's sweet scam. Any convict receiving regular government checks—veterans' benefits being the prime example—could arrange "check cashing" services and credit with Mr. Fassler, the prisoner's banker. The vet would have his government check sent to Fassler's street connections. Funds would be forwarded to Fassler, who could smuggle into prison "green money"—the most highly desirable contraband of all—carried into prison by a guard acting as his mule. For his services, Fassler charged 20 percent. Convicts accepted this extortionate rate of exchange because drugs, supplied primarily by the guards earning 100 percent for their services, sold for twice their street value inside the walls. So, by prison logic, green money was worth twice its face value.

Besides his 20 percent skim, Fassler made fast money on loans. Knowing his clients were good for the money, Fassler would extend loans against funds to be received at rates that would make street bankers green with envy. A ten-dollar loan had to be repaid in seven days for fifteen dollars—with a one dollar per day late charge for every extra day.

The main yard gangsters—Stretch, Big Head Red, Taxicab, the Padillas, Jim Black, and Big Dave—got frustrated with Fassler's entrepreneurial activities because they could never figure out how to burn or rob him, and he would never loan them large sums of money, just the usual ten dollars now, fifteen dollars in seven days. So Stretch volunteered to shoot Fassler to get his annoying presence permanently "out of sight, out of mind."

Stretch botched the job, in a sense. Fassler survived six bullet wounds, losing one eye, but Stretch did as much damage to Fassler as he could and still escape punishment. If he had killed Fassler, he would have risked a death sentence, but to maim him he risked nothing. When charges were filed against Stretch for shooting Fassler, the Pinal County attorney gave Hillyer a plea bargain that did nothing more than close a file and clear paper. There was no more to be done; Stretch's sentences already exceeded his life expectancy by several decades.

Particularly memorable lore, passed along from the old-timers to the "fish" (prison slang for newly arrived inmates) survives for decades to create the enduring reputation of the institution and its hardcore convicts. To this day, the institutional status of Stretch and Red Dog is preserved in Arizona State Prison's culture and oral history.

Red Dog was released from Arizona State Prison after his second stint in April 1975. During his six months on the street, he shot heroin daily, drank heavily, and robbed to pay for his habits. His suppliers extended credit, so when he went back to prison on two armed robbery convictions with a sentence of fifteen to thirty years, he still owed the Sanchez brothers a hundred dollars. The Sanchez brothers on the streets, Eddie and Johnny, told their brothers in prison, Robert and Mike, to collect the debt.

Freshly back on the yard and having no money on the books yet, Red Dog was approached with a favor to straighten out the debt. "Just let me know what you need," Red Dog told the messenger, wanting the debt cleared as quickly as possible, given the violent reputation of the Sanchez brothers. A certain person was making business difficult. Would Red Dog hit him? "Okay," he agreed, "but I need a weapon."

"I'll be back later," the messenger agreed.

He returned shortly with a large surgical scalpel. "We don't have a shank so this will have to do."

"Who's the snitch?" Red Dog asked.

"Shawn Jones."

"Okay, but tell Mike and Robert to send me two papers of stuff to get my mind right before I do it. Okay?"

When the messenger returned with the dope, Red Dog asked, "Whose snitch is he?"

"Captain Jimenez."

Days passed. Red Dog shot the dope. He never caught Shawn in the right circumstances, so, throwing all caution to the winds, he approached Jones in the chow hall in front of guards and inmates galore.

Red Dog sat beside Jones, striking up an amiable conversation.

"How's it going, Shawn?"

"Okay, Dog," Shawn answered, suspecting nothing.

Without warning, Red Dog grabbed him by the shirt collar, drove him into the wall, pulled the scalpel from his back pocket, and slashed Shawn's neck repeatedly. Dropping his victim, considering the job done,

Red Dog turned to see inmates flee out the doors of the chow hall. A guard yelled, "Dog, drop that knife," and he slid it across the floor, offering no resistance. Quickly and easily handcuffing a now-passive Red Dog, the guard hustled him to the yard office as other guards swarmed to the scene with a stretcher for the wounded man.

In less than thirty minutes, Warden Harold Cardwell arrived to question Red Dog, who wondered none too seriously about the fate of his victim.

"Well, you really did it this time, Red Dog," the warden began.

Red Dog sat in complete silence, forcing the warden to continue his haranguing monologue.

"We knew Shawn had a contract out on him from the streets, Dog, for killing that young couple out in the desert. There are people wanting him dead. They say he should have gotten the gas chamber and not two life sentences."

"Warden, I don't know nothing about that, except he's a rat," Red Dog allowed. "He ratted on me while I was out on the streets. He set a trap for me by sending me to buy dope from cops."

Red Dog offered a plausible lie to cover up the reason for the hit in order to avoid snitching on the Sanchez brothers.

"Dog, that don't add up," Cardwell reasoned. "You don't have any dope charges on your record, and you weren't back in prison two weeks and you tried to kill Jones in the chow hall. So I'm going to treat this like a contract hit from the streets."

"Lock the asshole up," Cardwell barked, sending Red Dog to lockup in the basement of CB-4 to await trial on an attempted murder charge.

The Warden might as well have thrown a birthday party for Red Dog. He knew everyone else locked down in the basement—Stretch, Frank, Troy Killinger, Marvin, Boots, Shitty Leg Red, Big Head Red, Freight Train Red.

"It looks like old home week," Red Dog told Stretch as he walked by his cell on the way to his own, escorted by a guard, shackled hands and feet.

"Yeah, and it gets better all the time," Stretch agreed as he stuck his long arm out of his cell and extended a lit Camel for Red Dog. The guard slapped it out of Stretch's hand, provoking a string of profanity, but the guard didn't flinch. The tirade was so familiar, so predictable, so ineffectual.

Red Dog's "house" became the last cell on the back of CB-4. The hollering back and forth lasted all night as the convicts caught up on the news and gossip from the yard.

"How much time you get for shooting that fat Jew?" Red Dog asked Stretch.

"Fifteen to twenty-five. Imagine that," Stretch laughed along with the others. What difference did another sentence make to Stretch? He was already serving life without the possibility of parole.

Red Dog got called out for interviews with street police, who believed Red Dog had been paid by someone on the street to hit Jones. Red Dog stuck to his story. With a thirty-year sentence hanging over him already, he never expected to see the streets again, so why sweat the small shit?

Robert Sanchez got word to Red Dog he wanted to be Red Dog's jailhouse lawyer for his prison disciplinary case, a clever ruse to allow the two to talk together confidentially, which worked in a matter of days.

From Sanchez, Red Dog learned that everyone in prison, including Shawn Jones, thought the hit was a contract job from the outside. The Sanchez brothers were satisfied. "Dog, you did a good job. My bosses on the street are satisfied," Robert told Dog during their meeting. "You are all paid up and your credit is still good."

"If I don't hurry up and get out of here, I won't need no credit," Red Dog laughed.

Sanchez accurately told Red Dog what to expect from the "courts," both the prison and "outside" versions.

"You'll get solitary for thirty days, and six months in the adjustment center, down in CB-4 basement, from the disciplinary court," Sanchez predicted.

"What about downtown? Not that it matters a whole lot. But I'd like to know," Red Dog asked.

"Most of the dudes with a lot of time, like you, they will usually give 'concurrent time,' in other words, another sentence, but it runs at the same time as your other sentence, just to clean up the paperwork," Sanchez told Red Dog.

"Well, that's not bad," Red Dog conceded.

Sanchez got it right. Red Dog copped to assault with intent to commit murder and received a sentence of fifteen to twenty-five years concurrent with his two armed-robbery convictions.

During their lockup, the boys in the basement laid the plans and sealed the pact to run the prison themselves once their disciplinary confinements ended and they returned to the yard. CB-4's basement lockdown became the incubator for the Aryan Brotherhood, which would be a stumbling block to the rug heads and greasers. White prisoners would now take care of their race instead of getting bulldogged and pushed around. If there was any jacking up to do, they'd do that too. The Mau Maus, Mexican Mafia, Native Brotherhood, and now the Aryan Brotherhood had jelled into large groups, ostensibly for self-protection along racial lines. Only the old-timers with notorious reputations wouldn't need to join groups for self-protection.

Out of detention, Stretch, Red Dog, Troy, Frank, and Marvin agreed to recruit good white dudes with a lot of time to do. No child molesters, no Jews. Only upstanding convicts—murderers and armed robbers. When twenty-five or thirty recruits agreed, everyone would swear allegiance and wear the Aryan Brotherhood AB tattoo verifying their allegiance.

Koolaid Smith became the first victim of a racial reprisal carried out by the Aryan Brotherhood. As prison gossip described the news, "A nigger got shitty with a couple of our brothers on the truck, so the next day Little Red and Little Ritchie stuck Koolaid." A brother had access through the yard office to prison records, so the Aryan Brotherhood quickly learned that another toad intended to testify against Little Red and Little Ritchie over the Koolaid Smith attack. His name was Waymond Small.

From his CB-4 lockdown isolation in November 1977, "General" Stretch Hillyer would order the killing of Waymond Small. After Small's death, a new chapter began in the history of Arizona prisons and politics.

5 The Hit

The frigid and violent currents of San Francisco Bay confirmed to the prisoners of Alcatraz the impossibility of escape. Isolation amidst the desert vastness of Florence equally cowed Arizona's outlaws—a virtual relic of territorial days. Inmates make no attempt at escape before first assuring themselves vehicular transit across the flat and hostile desert expanse that separates Florence from Arizona's population centers—seventy miles north to Phoenix or sixty miles south to Tucson. To the east and west, nothing beckons fleeing inmates but packrats, scorpions, and rattlesnakes.

Upon becoming a subject of the Arizona Department of Corrections' jurisdiction, inmates are assigned a number to be theirs alone for their term and for as many times as recidivism brings them back. Assigned in numerical order, these numbers are badges of honor acknowledged by inmates and guards alike. Inmates with high numbers are "fish"—the fresh meat in the prison pond until they are more than one hundred from the highest number assigned. As new game, they are prey—soon to be sorted through, tested, pigeonholed, stereotyped, tagged, and cataloged by administration and convicts. Administration does its sorting and assigns the inmate to the suitable institution; inmates sort to decide between the victim and the prey, the protector and the punk, the abuser and the extorted. A modus vivendi prevailed inside the Arizona State Prison in Florence: the administration ran the prison; the prisoners ran the prisoners. In the sixty-five-year history of the prison, November 3, 1977, proved to be one of its most violent and chaotic days. It was the day the administration lost charge of the prison and the prisoners.

Florence's desert isolation makes escape dubious from the gun gang and farm labor details outside the walls. Newcomers, snowbirds, and passersby along Highway 79 were astonished at the large numbers of inmates working outside the walls in the prison's extensive vegetable fields and animal farms or in largely unsupervised litter patrols along the highways. But an inmate afoot stood no chance of escape. Few were ever enticed by the futility of trying to outrun dogs and mounted posses over the barren landscape.

Inmates counted among the greatest of privileges the opportunity to work outside the prison walls. The most privileged were outside trustees, who were given jobs in which they were allowed to drive trucks on the farm roads connected — without barrier or guard station — to Highway 79. This unguarded junction is the same junction those trustees' wives, mothers, and friends drove from Phoenix and Tucson on weekends to visit.

Though convicted of first-degree murder and sentenced to life imprisonment only two months before, Waymond Small had been assigned to outside work on the gun gang the day of November 3, 1977. Small, like every other inmate, was "shook down" in a quick search of his person for weapons upon passing through the main gate and climbing aboard the truck carrying the gun gang to its work destination somewhere on the prison's farms outside the main walls. A single guard rode inside the cab of the gun gang truck, and an inmate drove. The tightly loaded pickup carried twenty inmates, perpetually on guard against attack from their cohorts and preferably armed with a prison-made shank, slim and stealthy enough to escape detection during the cursory daily shakedowns by lethargic guards. Either John Ward's shank escaped detection that morning or it was passed to him on the truck by another Aryan Brother.

Until the aftermath of November 3, Warden Cardwell never admitted knowledge of the brotherhood to anyone outside his trusted staff, but if he was truly unaware of its existence, the man had to be blind. How could he have learned so much in only one day? For by day's end, twenty-eight members of this brotherhood — who were "behind" the stabbing of Koolaid Smith and Malone, as Dominic "Buffalo" Hall would later explain it — were moved to investigative lockup, a high-security lockdown within CB-3. Cardwell didn't get a fast education on November 3; he just decided the Aryan Brotherhood had gone too far.

When the lockdown was finished, the administration knew Koolaid had been stabbed in the presence of nineteen inmates in the bed of the gun gang truck in the early morning. Malone had been stabbed the same evening in an escalation of the prison's race and gang warfare.

Who stabbed Koolaid? Who stabbed Malone? The administration did not know the identity of the assailants in either episode on November 3, yet that day it began a systematic lockdown of every inmate with an AB tattoo. It knew who stabbed Koolaid one week later — once Waymond Small chose to talk.

Prison officials—collectively and pejoratively called the man, hacks, cops, or pigs by the prisoners—use a thousand petty devices to control and manipulate the inmates. No technique was less subtle than calling out a prisoner to come talk to the man at the yard office. When the call-out goes down in plain view of an entire population of gossiping prisoners, no good can come to the inmate who's been talking with the man. He's been "put out on front street" and custom fit for all time with a "snitch jacket."

As with most of his behavior during his last short stay at Arizona State Prison, Waymond Small defied the convict's code. Small's trip to see Captain Davis and Captain Pierce, seven days after Koolaid Smith's stabbing, was made without anyone trying to conceal his destination or purpose. Consequences be damned; Small wanted to talk and consented to a taped interview.

"Waymond Small. Number 28456. You're here today because you want to tell us about an incident you saw. Is that correct?" Captain Davis began. "This concerns the assault with intent to commit murder on Albert L. Smith, prison number 32368, that occurred on the gang truck going to work the morning of November 3, 1977, about 7:30 a.m. At that time, you were housed in CB-4, Ida run 11, and had been working on this particular gang truck for a month. That right? Why don't you tell us about it?"

Small needed no more prompting.

"Okay. On that morning when we was going out on the gang, between Gate 3, after we were shuck down, Ward accosted me, told me that something was coming down and he didn't want me to get paranoid because it had nothing to do with me and it had nothing to do with any type of racial issue. And I told him, I said 'Well, why you telling me?' He said, 'It's a one-on-one thing and we don't want you to be involved in it.' I said, 'Well, okay, if that's the way you feel. It's one on one.'

"So we went to get on the truck and we all got on the truck and I was thinking, you know, who could be, you know, gonna get in a fight or something. There was no knives mentioned or anything and we had been shook down so I had no idea there would be a knife involved. So the only person I could figure he would tell me about was Koolaid Smith and so I said, 'In a one-on-one, I looked around the truck and I don't believe there's a guy on the truck that could whip Koolaid.'

"It was something to put out of my mind. Nothing to worry about 'cause he could fight for his self, you know, fight individual in a fight such as that. Koolaid is young and powerful.

"We got out of the prison and started driving down the paved highway. Ward was standing on left beside me, leaning against the back of the truck as I was. And he grabbed the side of the truck — the boards — and pinned my arms down with my hands in my pocket and pulled his knife on me and put it under my throat. And he said 'one-on-one, stay out of it.'

"And a white inmate stabbed Koolaid twice that I saw, you know, but I don't know how far the knife penetrated in Koolaid. At the time that I saw this, Ward had his knife on me and I was more interested in what Ward was doing and I saw this inmate stab Koolaid twice. Koolaid turned and started fighting him to keep him from sticking him anymore and Koolaid was handling it so well that you could obviously see that if the fight continued Koolaid was going to overpower the guy and take that knife away from him. And Ward was observing the same thing that I was. He swung from the left of me, grabbed the knife in his right hand and brought it down on Koolaid's back with his right hand and the damage had been done then, there was nothing I could do. Koolaid groaned and made a semi gesture to try to reach the knife in his back. And then, you know, he didn't go any further. He left it alone and continued to fight the guy in front of him. The guy in front made several more attempts, you know, to stick Koolaid again.

"We had turned off the highway and headed toward Ranch #1, the hog farm, and the guy threwed the knife out of the truck and Koolaid groaned and leaned on the side of the truck and went down to one knee. Well most of the guys had moved from the front of the truck where the fight was at and had me pinned to the back of the truck.

"The officer in the truck had opened his door and had the rifle or shotgun, whichever one he had, and was hollering telling him to get back, he knew something was wrong.

"The guy that was fighting Koolaid took off his sweatshirt and put on somebody's coat, or his coat — maybe somebody was holding his coat — I saw him take off the sweatshirt and put on the coat and then Koolaid looked at me and said, 'Somebody stop the truck. I'm hurt.' Then nobody moved.

"I pretended to Ward that it was, you know, alright with me, what they had done, but it wasn't. I didn't want to put myself in jeopardy at that particular time 'cause, you know, I knew how they do. They stab you in the back, they don't give you no chance to fight.

"Anyway, when he got out, Koolaid told him, 'Man I'm stuck.' And he said, 'Are you hurt bad?' And Koolaid said, 'Yeah, real bad, man.' And he walked up to the back of the truck and Koolaid was sort of leaning to the side with his right hand on his knee and the officer saw the knife handle sticking out of his back and said, 'Alright. You guys get back.' He said, 'Come on out Koolaid.' And Koolaid went and was getting out. He was — the officer had took his gun and give it to the other officer and was going to help Koolaid down. Koolaid said, 'I can get down by myself.' And jumped down off the truck and closed the gate back up. And he was on his radio all the time asking for an ambulance to come out there and told they had a man hurt pretty bad. He'd been stabbed and that's when I think the ambulance and you guys came out there. I believe you know the rest from there."

Captain Davis did. The twenty-four-minute interview ended with Davis clearing up a few nitpicking specifics that cops, judges, juries, and lawyers love to know but that don't really matter. The shank Ward held to Small's throat and later stuck in Koolaid's back was about "7 inches long, wrapped in white tape." It was "a round ice pick type shank except much bigger than an ice pick — the size of a ballpoint pen." The shank the first inmate had used to attack Koolaid "was a blade about 3 inches long that looked like the blade off of a hunting knife. Light colored, stainless steel stick, had white tape on it. This was used to cut and stab Koolaid."

Small explained, "When Ward came back there with me in the truck, I felt that his promise was good, 'one-on-one, you know, that this guy's going to fight somebody, you know.' I didn't have anything that I felt would threaten me or me was in danger of anyway." Small now had his "own personal reasons" for going against the prisoner's code of silence and being willing to testify in court. "I'm doing it because I feel that if I don't, it's going to continue to happen and I feel that it's for my own personal safety as well as the rest of the inmates that something has to be done."

"Why was Koolaid hit?" Davis asked. "Have you heard of an organization called Aryan Brotherhood? Was the Koolaid incident an organizational move, or do you think that it was strictly an individual move?"

"It was an organizational move," Small told Davis, "because of the way that they were united in the way that they isolated me and Koolaid out of that truck. Later that evening there was another incident that Ward was involved with on another organizational move and another inmate that I thwarted myself."

Small had seen Ward twice that day try to stab a black in the back. Ward was armed with a knife, and "he had it drawed back to stab Gomes in the back." Later that same day in CB-4 there was another incident. Small was not present, but he knew about it. "Not the exact incident per se with regard to Malone but I overheard some conversation on my way back in from chow," Small said. Davis then made a note: "Small can identify the man who started the attack on Koolaid. Will set up a lineup. Small is positive he will be able to pick out the man."

"Why did the Aryan Brotherhood attack Smith?" Davis asked.

"I don't think that Koolaid did anything to provoke that attack," Small told him. "He was my cell partner prior to that incident and I have knowledge that Smith is the type of individual that he very rarely even talks to other inmates and he causes no trouble whatsoever. It appeared at the time when they were [on strike] he said he felt there might be some aggression toward him because of that." Small was not in the institution at that time, but Koolaid told him that he had worked and not gone on strike.

"Do you want us to put you in protective custody?" Davis asked Small, knowing Small's life was now in peril because he had talked so freely. He could have sent Small to protective custody against his will, but Small could prevent that with a simple threat, which he used. If Davis sent him to protective custody, he would refuse to testify against the Aryan Brotherhood. "Those AB honkies are not pushing me around. It's time for the blacks to stand up against them. I want to do it the right way," Small said.

There are no secrets in prison. Through the grapevine, just as Captain Davis and Small knew would happen, the entire prison learned that Small had snitched off the AB before the six o'clock news that evening. In twenty days, Small would be dead for his transgression.

"This kite's from the brothers in the basement lockup," cell block porter James "Watermelon" Waltman whispered to Buffalo Hall before he shuffled off on his rounds, delivering to each cell clean sheets and fresh "blues"—blue jeans and blue work shirts with each prisoner's number stenciled in large block numerals.

"What's da' kite say?" Danny "Cowboy" Farrell asked his cell mate as Hall read the message hidden inside their stack of laundry.

"Just more shit," Hall said, feeling uneasy about the last part of the missive: "You're in charge now till I get out." The crumpled paper was signed "Red Dog."

Red Dog was one of the twenty-eight suspected Aryan Brothers locked down by Warden Cardwell after Koolaid got stabbed on the gun gang truck. The convicts made it easy since they all sported a small fresh "AB" tattoo somewhere on their bodies. The AB oath was a mixture of bravado and half-witted nonsense: "I swear to uphold all obligations and decisions, and to honor, respect and be loyal to my Brothers of the Aryan Brotherhood. Knowing that if I do not, it will mean my death. I take and accept this oath, and swear to abide by it, body and mind. This is the way I shall remain." Prisoners pledged their lives to the cause of white supremacy, with unquestioned loyalty to fellow "brothers," obedience to the group's rules, and a promise never to talk about the secret brotherhood to any outsider. Any violation of rules was made punishable by death; one could only leave the brotherhood "beyond earthly life."

When Hall initiated Cowboy into the brotherhood, the cell mates had something new to break up the monotony of prison existence. They'd shoot the breeze about how this new hustle would play out.

"What's this shit I hear about the AB's wanting to run a store?" Cowboy asked Buffalo. "Just sounds like cover for a protection racket to me. Kites say Big Richard's gonna run the store now that Red Dog's locked up. How much shit's gonna end up in his veins now?"

"With him, for sure that's where it all goes," Buffalo agreed.

"What do we do with Puff locked down?" Cowboy asked.

"Like it says, run the brothers till he gets out. Hope they don't get too many crazy ideas while they're locked up."

"We'll pass it on to the other brothers in the cell block. Gotta let 'em know who's boss now."

With that, the pair lapsed into their own thoughts. The next day, Watermelon brought another kite signed by Red Dog.

"What this one say?" Cowboy asked.

"Lotta jive about look out after his boys and getting them to pay so Red Dog can get his store," Buffalo answered.

"This brotherhood shit," Buffalo mused, "started with all the shakedowns and hits from the blacks on the fish and punks. Now we're turning the fish into our own punks. How did Red Dog do it? In the joint for the last ten years but never broke. Always got credit at the store."

The kites came regularly from the locked-down brothers, who kept in touch with prison doings by kites from outside the basement of CB-4, even though they were supposed to be isolated from the general prison population. Like any village, prisons are full of gossips. In this case, Watermelon and Cal the Barber, the porters between CB-3 and CB-4, kept the brothers in CB-4's basement informed and passed their orders back to AB captains and lieutenants.

Too lazy or too understaffed to do the work themselves, prison guards used trusted inmates to bring clean jeans and T-shirts to each cell in the lockup. James "Watermelon" Waltman, an old southern sexual pervert, as tough and institutionalized as Red Dog and in his fifteenth year at Florence for rape and kidnap, carried the brother's kites back and forth so they could manage business as usual. Waltman earned his prison nickname when he was discovered in the kitchen using a watermelon specifically sculptured for sexual satisfaction.

"Nick, more kites for you from the brothers," Watermelon whispered most every November day as he passed Hall's cell. Being an AB captain when the brothers got locked down now meant Buffalo Hall bore the brunt of their frustrations and demands.

"Hit Small and Gomes. Troy."

"Don't like the way you've been taking care of business. Small and Gomes are still walking the yard. Get the niggers or we get you when we're out. Rusty."

Troy and Rusty couldn't be ignored; they were AB captains and tight with Stretch. Their say-so was as good as an order from the general. Buffalo stalled for time while telling the other brothers about the escalating demands for a hit on Small. Maybe the kites would quit; maybe someone else would get the heat; maybe someone would step on Stretch's heroin too bad; maybe Big Richard would piss off the brothers and take too much store money for himself and his habit. The brothers can't do much else in CB-4 lockup but send nasty kites, so why get uptight and think they mean anything?

Ten days passed. Watermelon's daily kite delivery service was becoming more and more an irritant to Hall. "Read this one, Nick," Watermelon whispered, casting a furtive downward glance with his eyes to the stack of clean blues he passed into Nick and Cowboy's cell. "Brothers are hot as hell you're not taking care of business. Say you're in for it once they get outta the hole unless the nigger dies, and soon." Buffalo's temper flared inside, but he showed no sign of emotion and just grunted.

The kites were getting hotter all right.

"Why's Small still walking the yard? Red Dog."

"Take care of the nigger Small. He talked about Ward hitting Koolaid. Troy."

The tone of the kites became more ominous with each passing day, and Buffalo and Cowboy talked about them with more alarm. The brothers were locked down for two weeks, and there were no signs of the administration loosening up soon.

Even after the lockdown of the suspected ABs, daily routine for the other inmates didn't change much, giving them plenty of opportunities to gossip, swap lies, pass kites, shoot the breeze, and jack up punks for protection. With three meals a day, eight hours at work in the industrial yard, trustee work outside the wall, gun gang, weights exercise, basketball hoops, and jogging the perimeter of the wall under the watchful eyes of armed guards, freedom abounded for inmates in the general population to talk, scheme, and jive.

Church on Sunday was a free-mixing social hour as long as the conversations were held in hushed tones. A tight knot of Aryan Brothers who'd avoided Warden Cardwell's lockdown—the Greek, Compton, Hall, Farrell—sat together at Mass, the better to plan and scheme. For Hall and Farrell, Sunday services became their weekly bull session with "Big Richard" Compton, Stretch's acting general and the second oldest AB member.

"That nigger Waymond Small choked Little Ritchie in the chow line last week with a wire," Compton whispered to the bunch. "He was on the truck when Ward and them hit Koolaid. He's talking to the man. He's gonna talk before the legislative committee looking into all the shit going down. You gotta hit him, man, the motherfucker's on your side of the yard," Compton whispered to Hall, Farrell, and the Greek as they knelt during Mass.

Watermelon brought more kites: "Till I get out, you watch my kids and be sure the niggers don't hit on them. You gotta be sure my kids keep paying my store and you collect the goods. We need more coffee and Camels down here. You heard how Small hit Ritchie with a wire. He's in your building, you gotta hit him now. Red Dog."

Hall and Cowboy agreed they had to make a plan and talk to Willard Breshears and the brothers in the plant. The heat from the brothers wasn't going to stop. Hall had a plan to take the heat off himself, but he didn't dare tell even Cowboy, his most trusted friend in prison. Small and Gomes were Hall's problem because Hall was the highest-ranking AB who had avoided the warden's dragnet and who still lived in a medium-security cell block and worked in the yard, as did Small. Why not tell Captain Davis to put Small and Gomes into protective custody because their lives were in danger?

Captain Davis's office received official, legal prison kites collected from the administration's kite boxes on every cell run. This system ensured a continuous flow to his office of anonymous tips and prison gossip from snitches and putative victims. Now several came from Hall himself, telling Davis to put Gomes and Small into protective custody.

Hall had hoped to snitch off the plan so he wouldn't have to do it, but Small wouldn't take the easy way out.

The regular jobs in the tag plant, the industrial yard, and the farm—for which the prisoners were paid ten cents an hour—were closed for business on Saturdays, so Hall and Farrell had other preoccupations when the stream of kites to get Small showed no sign of letting up.

Bubbles, Stan, Bilke, Farrell, Breshears, Belt, the Greek—the brothers on the field—heard the word from Hall: "Brothers in the unit say we got to hit Small. Big Richard tells me the same. Small works over in the tag plant. Got any ideas?"

"There's this young fish celled with me, wants to make a name for himself. He's been asking me 'bout the AB. Wants to know how he can get in," Cowboy offered. "Maybe we can get him to do it and make him a member."

"What's his name?" Hall wanted to know.

"Goff. Goofy-looking kid with a big Adam's apple. He's tagged Gooseneck," Farrell answered.

"He works in the print shop. Where's Small work?" Mitchell Bilke asked.

"Nigger's over in the tag plant. I can point him out when the time comes," Breshears offered.

"How do we get Goff over to the tag plant from the print shop?" the Greek asked.

"Destiny gave me her keys. One fits the lock to get out the gate," Bilke suggested.

A plan emerged.

The interior walls of the prison house the chow hall, the tag plant, the industrial yard, and the cell blocks where prisoners sleep. Each man has his assignment, and being out of place without a pass is a violation with an automatic write-up and detention if a prisoner was caught by the guards. Security was lax during the day, but armed guards from the tower walls could bring any disturbance to a quick and brutal end. Major transgressions, attempts to escape, fights in plain view of the guard stations—the security is good enough to thwart any overt disturbance of prison order. Below this smooth surface, a gulf stream of covert, devious, and illegal activity can boil, hidden below the ebb and flow of the tide.

Does that prisoner, ambling slowly along, have a shank hidden in his coat? a dime bag in his pocket? or is he just walking to the yard to pick up a roll of wire, a tool, a piece of tape to finish his work? Nothing about his demeanor betrays his goal; not everyone can be stopped and checked. Guards and inmates fall into routines, trusted patterns, rhythms of the simple day-to-day comings and goings of the small city of men living, working, and daydreaming inside the prison walls. Little things slip by; this much the prisoners can count on, whatever the goal.

Weapons? Not hard to come by, and it's not hard to see why. Even death-row inmates have their own shanks, made from any sharpened object that can stab, poke, and gouge an enemy. Toothbrushes; toilet bowl brushes; spoons, knives or forks from the chow hall; a single blade from a garden rake; any scrap of metal retrieved from the tag plant's manufacture of license plates for a million Arizona vehicles—the sources of supply are boundless. The resourcefulness to fashion even the most innocuous fragment into a lethal weapon springs from the paranoia and fear of each inmate, bidding to do his own time unmolested.

Finding a weapon for the Small job proved easy.

"I'll talk to Mac. He's got access to the grinder in the print shop. He'll make something up," Hall thought to himself.

By next weekend's athletic field meeting on November 27, the pieces had fallen into place, much to the consternation of Hall's attempts to avoid the onus.

"The kid's got a friend who wants to help him do it," Farrell told the gathered conspirators. "Another fish. Heard about the rumor on the yard 'bout the hit on Small. Wants to do it if we'll make him AB."

Lying in his cell at two in the morning, wide awake, Hall realized his chances to avoid the hit were disappearing. "Crazy kid really wants to do it," he thought to himself, remembering how Farmer approached him in the darkroom at the print shop that day.

"Want to talk to you," Farmer had muttered, motioning Hall behind the curtain in the darkroom. Hall guessed what was coming. The kid was Ernest Goff's friend. He'd seen them together often enough in the chow line and eating together. Hall realized they must have come to the joint around the same time. Their numbers were mighty close. He figured they had probably met in the diagnostic unit on intake and partnered up.

Once inside the darkroom, Farmer came to the point. "You want someone to off the nigger. I'll do it. Make me AB."

"Can't do it yourself," Hall answered. "You'll need help. If you can get someone, you can. Go talk to whoever will help you and decide amongst yourselves if you really ought to do it. I'm not going to hold anything against you for not wanting to do it."

Half an hour later, Farmer returned to Hall's work area with Gooseneck. The trio adjourned to the darkroom. Mike Belt was there working.

"I'll help Farmer do it," Goff told Hall. "I'll hit him on the head with a hammer, and Crazy'll stick him."

"Get me a good shank about seven inches long, sharpened on both edges," Farmer requested.

"They'll need a change of clothes when they come back. Might have blood on 'em. I got some spare duds they can change into to do the job, then get back into their own when they come back," Belt offered. "They can change here in the darkroom; I'll be here and watch out for them."

"I got someone with a key to the gate. That way you won't have to walk the long way around the yard," Hall suggested, thinking of Bilke's hiding place under the sink by the darkroom for Destiny's treasure trove of master keys to the gates inside the walls.

"Willard can show you where the nigger works over by the packing room in the tag plant. He says he's got a hammer hid over there, too," Hall told the eager fish. "Want a rep? Pull this off and you got it."

"There's Small," Willard Breshears whispered to Farmer and Goff. Mixing in with the other whites at the front of the tag plant, where Breshears worked, Farmer and Goff came over from the print shop on November 28 to identify their target. Farmer and Goff had no business in the tag plant, but no one forced the stalking pair to move on or noticed they were out of place, so they leisurely surveyed their prey.

Small was average in height, about five foot nine or ten, and weighed around 175 to 180 pounds. He was stocky, with a callous, cold aura, the intimidating persona of a bulldogger, the mannerism of the ghetto black—or so he appeared to Farmer. Farmer thought he could read Small's mind by reading his body language: "Thinks the whole world is wrong if they don't give him a handout, oppressed by a system that won't give him a chance. Always acting loud and obnoxious; brazen and boisterous. Thinks his Boulevard Stroll gives him an aura of cool, saying, 'I'm not to be messed with.'"

"The man's a warrior," Farmer acknowledged to himself. "He'd throw in if one of his kind is jumped."

Having volunteered for the hit, Farmer was treated differently by the prisoners on November 29. The day took on a surreal quality. Time was suspended, his mind absorbed. At breakfast he sat with others but paid no heed to their presence. Silence enveloped him wherever he wandered that day, as if the other prisoners, knowing what was about to occur, kept their distance and held their tongues, sensing another hot fuse in an overloaded circuit of racial warfare was ready to blow.

The basic plan was in place. Farmer checked out everyone else's readiness. The hit was scheduled for today, whenever Farmer was ready. The bit players, relieved and emboldened by the paucity of their individual responsibility, fell to their tasks.

"You know your part?" Farmer whispered to Michael Belt first thing in the morning as Farmer loaded and primed the print shop's small press in the main yard.

"Yeah, I got the blackout clothes. You can change in the restroom. I'll keep Benjamin occupied in the darkroom fiddling around all day on nonsense. He won't see you two coming and going."

MacDonald couldn't talk much—too many ears around—but his nod told Farmer the shank was finished, ready to be placed in his hand when he asked.

Goff was Farmer's most serious concern. "You won't have to pay protection if you do this. It will make your time easier. But I got to know if you're up to this," Farmer asked Gooseneck over lunch, sensing his partner's uneasiness and precarious state of mind and instinctively doubting Goff's ability to cover his backside from interference by other blacks at the tag plant when the time came for action.

Shortly before lunch time, the first hitch came: Small had changed work areas. Word had it he had moved from the tag plant to the metal fabrication area, which was cut off from the tag plant by a chain-link fence. The plan was still in place for an afternoon hit in the tag plant. As the one with his ass on the line if things went wrong, Farmer decided on a solo dry run to metal fab to check out the new information. One glance around told him someone had run out some BS. Small wasn't there. Farmer wandered to the tag plant and found that Small had changed job sites from the small-press area to the roller coater area. Small was now situated deeper within the recesses of the tag plant and surrounded by a segregated cocoon of other blacks. "Good move," Farmer thought to himself, assessing Small's changed job site as the conscious act of a man aware of his jeopardy, "but it only delays the inevitable."

Small was too alert, as were those around him, and the roller coater crew seemed too edgy for a strike on this day. They were courting disaster. Farmer returned to the print shop and passed word to the conspirators, "Tomorrow."

After bunking down in his cell, Farmer slept fitfully. Voices rang up and down the tier as always, but oddly it was quiet enough for conversations to be overheard amidst the low rumbling. Alone with his thoughts, Farmer remembered the pocket of silence that followed him all day as he'd walked the yard, to and from work and chow, and back to evening lockup in his cell. At midnight, thoughts repeated themselves like a record stuck in a groove: "Tomorrow, kill or be killed," followed in endless succession by, "Will I be a hero or play the fool?" At 4 a.m. the two thoughts still ran after each other, like a dog chasing its own tail. The realization of the finality of his decision and the haunting question — hero or fool? — would not leave his mind.

He reasoned only within a twenty-year-old's simple logic circumscribed by the laws of prisons and prisoners, not free men. Waymond Small was a bulldogger jacking up whites for protection, hitting those who wouldn't pay and forcing sex upon white fish. He was snitching on the brothers over the Koolaid and Gomes hits, and he knew too much. He would tell all to the legislative committee. For these transgressions it was right to kill him. Farmer would be a prisoner's hero, the beginning of a legend, someone to be feared—or at the very least, he would be left alone for the rest of his life in prison. Farmer saw himself as the tool to work the collective and institutional will of the inmates, and even the administration, making him—within the prisoners' code—no different from a sheriff carrying out a sentence imposed by a court of law.

Farmer's reasoning that night overlooked a change no one had foreseen. Every prior prison stabbing and murder had been lightly brushed off by the system with a perfunctory investigation. If prosecuted in the courts at all, past offenders had received sweet plea bargains with concurrent sentences. Viewed in context, Farmer and his co-conspirators risked little by killing Waymond Small.

How could any convict have known this killing would awaken an apathetic public and unleash the full power of the state to prosecute *this crime*, which was so like the many others that had been largely ignored?

"He's over there," Breshears whispered to Farmer and Goff, though there was no need for stealth and silence amidst the cacophony of yelling, banging, slinging, and pounding made by the seventy prisoners at work in the tag plant, now in full swing at 10:30 a.m. On November 30, two massive presses clattered as they imprinted aluminum sheet metal; the belt drive conveyed sheets to knives that separated the newly minted licenses from the roll stock fed into the press from stacked sheets. Small worked in the shipping room, where stacks of freshly imprinted plates were sorted, boxed, and labeled.

No one noticed Farmer and Goff missing from their stations. With only one guard and one civilian supervisor at the print shop where Farmer and Goff were assigned to work the presses along with sixty other inmates, the pair's fifteen-minute sojourn to scope out Small's workplace went undetected.

"Come back after chow, before the press fires up work for the shipping crew," said Breshears. "They'll just be jiving, playing cards outside. You can get Small alone. I'll have a hammer." The pair departed the tag plant for a casual stroll back through the gate to the print shop, where Bilke fiddled with his silkscreen, acting busy as he waited to catch sight of the two's return and quickly relock the gate.

With Farmer and Goff back in their places, the first of the chow whistles blew. Time was running out. Small was scheduled to testify the next day at the state capitol in Phoenix before a legislative committee investigating gang violence inside Arizona State Prison. No inmate was supposed to know this, but everyone with an ear to the ground did. The hit had to go down after lunch.

The pace of inmate work within Arizona State Prison's industrial yard is never taxing. Returning from lunch, segregated groups of inmates idle away time. The blacks play cards on the backs of overturned crates, shucking and jiving as they would in any ghetto street scene; the whites sullenly hang around in tight-lipped groups, speaking in low grumbles like the guys in a street scene outside a burger joint across the street from any urban high school.

After lunch, Belt kept the print shop supervisor distracted inside the darkroom while Hall kept the guard busy with idle chitchat and make-work. Meanwhile, Farmer and Goff slipped into the restroom and donned garb with their prison numbers blacked out. Farmer recovered MacDonald's custom-made shank from its hiding place, slipped it into his waistband, and slowly ambled out of the print shop with Goff.

By 1:15 p.m., the crews had begun to reassemble at their stations within the tag plant. From the previous day's reconnaissance, Farmer and Goff knew that the island around the roller coater, where Small was assigned to work, was a racial island where twelve blacks were separated from the twelve whites at the presses.

"Are you one hundred percent sure you want to do this?" Farmer asked Goff, still uncertain of his stature for the work of murder.

"Yeah," Goff nodded.

Sliding open the side door to the tag plant, the pair walked quickly to the roller coater area before the blacks became aware of their presence. Farmer walked alone into the sea of black faces surrounding Small's station; Goff approached from the opposite direction. Waymond Small fed newly stamped plates into the roller coater for painting, a huge maul hammer within easy reach of his left hand. Farmer took a license plate wet with paint and showed it to Small. "You missed this one," he coldly growled, thrusting the painted plate into Small's hands. Farmer's personal code prevented him from attacking from behind. He believed in giving his victims a fair chance.

Small looked Farmer square in the eye and took the plate from his hands, nonchalantly brushing aside his threatening tone, no doubt bolstered by the surrounding presence of blacks who would fall upon the lone white if he struck Small while his back was turned.

As Small turned around to face him a second time, Farmer nodded — the signal to Goff, standing behind, to strike Small on the head with his claw hammer. Farmer quickly spotted the maul hammer to Small's left, and as Goff swung, Farmer slashed Small's left armpit. The shank severed his pectoral muscle and punctured his lung. He slumped to his left, his arm dropping uselessly to his side. Farmer struck his second blow, driving the shank into the center of his chest. He twisted the blade until he felt the heart muscle tear. Small struck out at his attacker, but Farmer escaped to the rear of the plant.

Small sprinted in pursuit, the hammer in his right hand, but his oxygen-starved body collapsed, having run as far as his last breath could take him. Small's body crumpled at the restroom door. Only three months after his being sentenced to Arizona State Prison and one day before he planned to escape yet again, Waymond Small was dead.

Farmer tugged on the partition door, Small's body near his feet. The door wouldn't open, and Farmer realized his point of greatest peril lay ahead. His only route of escape from the building was back the way he had come, past the twelve stunned blacks. Slowly, he walked back to the group, holding the bloody shank upraised, and coolly staring straight into the yellowed eyes of Paris Toney, who, now that Small was struck down, became the most aggressive and dangerous of the blacks left in the tag plant. "You're next," Farmer warned Toney as he walked by, throwing the shank at his feet.

Farmer calmly walked past the whites and out the door of his entry. Under the eyes of the guards manning the walls and towers, Farmer crossed the open spaces of the industrial yard in blood-spattered clothing. He was out of place; the alarm should have sounded from a guard's discovery of the murdered man's body or an inmate tipping him off with a furtive glance or head bob in the direction of the corpse lying in a pool of blood. But no one stopped him. He nonchalantly walked back to his press in the print shop, his concern now focused on the small nick on the finger of his left hand. Belt had sliced up his blood-spattered clothes and flushed them down the toilet. Knowing he had to disguise the origin of the nick, Farmer deliberately mashed his finger into the press. With blood streaming down his hand, he pointed out his wound to supervisor Richard Benjamin. "Shit, I busted my finger," Farmer explained, before the alarm was raised and all hell broke loose. For good measure, Farmer rubbed black ink from his press into the small wound.

When the shakedown and strip search came, the print shop supervisor accounted for Farmer's wound. "He got it on his press." Did he forget the odd coincidence of the proximity of Farmer's press wound to the crime? Did he fail to make the obvious connection? Was he so easily fooled? Or did his sympathy for white inmates, victimized by racial predation, provide a thin veneer behind which he willingly hid any doubts about Belt's oddly oversolicitous attitude and work ethic and Farmer's finger injury on this fateful day? Regardless, when the evening sun set upon the locked-up and shook-down prison—with every prisoner minutely inspected for signs of injury or struggle—the administration remained none the wiser that Goff and Farmer had struck the fatal blows that murdered Waymond Small.

From his post atop Tower 3, Capt. John Vargas, under whose eyes nothing truly out of the ordinary could escape detection, lifted his phone set at 1:20 p.m. and dialed directly to the shift commander's office. "We've got something going down at the tag plant. Inmates are running out the doors. Send help."

Captains Houlihan and Rushing ran to the plant and found Waymond Small lying in a pool of his own blood, with a hammer in his right hand. The body lay next to the restroom, against screen partitions separating the tag plant from the print shop. His chest bubbled, and pools of red collected on the ground at his left side. Small heaved and sighed a few times before becoming still; he failed to respond to Houlihan yelling his name.

As more guards swarmed into the tag plant, Houlihan barked out commands to the inmates: "Everyone! Back out the doors!" Then he yelled to the guards: "Get these men stripped down and searched for blood and weapons, now!"

News of the eruption at the tag plant spread like fire. Supervisor Richard Benjamin came out of the print shop darkroom, his eyes taking a few moments to adjust to the light, and watched the commotion fifty yards away.

"What's up, Mike?" Benjamin asked Belt, who was also standing in the print shop doorway.

"Sounds like a shanking went down in the tag plant, sir."

Behind Benjamin's back, Belt caught sight of Farmer and Goff. With a flick of his head, he let them know he'd flushed their clothes down the john.

Captain Davis, chief of prison security, examined Small's body at the prison hospital. Dr. Demosthenes pronounced him dead. A one-inch-wide stab wound in the middle of his chest was still bleeding heavily but had stopped pulsing. "Must have got him right in the heart," Davis thought to himself. Another stab wound in the left shoulder and two sets of gouge marks on his head like the impression from the claw end of a hammer told of a brief yet violent struggle. Davis called the guards at the tag plant. "You're looking for a long, thin shank and a claw hammer," he told the men.

Captain Davis was a laconic, gray-haired bear of a man in mood and size. He was on the stretch run to retirement, and his eyes were permanently bagged and puffy from the irritation of chronic chain smoking and sleepless nights amidst the crises of numerous shankings and shakedowns. He allowed himself fleeting feelings of regret that he hadn't tried harder to get Small to accept protective custody. But, he thought, what good could he do with a con like that, a know-it-all bulldogger, a murdering thug?

"Waymond Small's dead. Stabbed in the heart. Must have been some ABs that took him down," Davis told Warden Cardwell over the prison phone.

Davis knew Warden Cardwell's commands before he bellowed them: "Search everyone in the yard. Then we'll lock down the sonsabitches for good. Fuckin' Judge Muecke can go freeze in hell before I'll let 'em out this time! A dead witness about to talk. The governor and the legislature'll be on my ass." Cardwell ordered a complete prison lockdown—all prisoners would remain locked behind cell doors or in dormitories, and all visitors would be barred.

Cardwell told *Arizona Republic* reporters that Waymond Small's death was "a gang hit by either the Aryan Brotherhood or the Mexican Mafia. I've got an idea which it was, but I'm not going to say right now." The *Republic*'s story of Small's death made clear that the warden's true suspect was the Aryan Brotherhood. Cardwell told reporters two stabbings on November 3 led to his locking up twenty-eight Aryan Brotherhood members "for investigative purposes." "We feel there is a conspiracy. This thing's getting out of hand. Over three-quarters of the stabbings, we feel, involve this group."

PART II ARIZONA DECLARES WAR

6 The Politics

The state's needs and motives for a vigorous prosecution of the murder of Waymond Small sprang from threads and tentacles spreading in all directions into the corrupt culture of Arizona State Prison, with the criminals and crimes intertwined. One crime cannot be understood without understanding another; one feud cannot be understood without understanding another. One gang's action causes another's reaction. One hit leads to the next until each act of violence seems to propagate its successor in a cycle without end. Before long, the sheer number of interconnected crimes, feuds, and frauds leads in all directions, like the flash of light radiating outward in all directions from a bomb's explosion. So it seemed with Tony Serra and Waymond Small, the first and last murder victims of 1977 at Arizona State Prison—Tony Serra on January 4 and Waymond Small on November 30.

Inmate Tony Serra was murdered in plain view of seventy-four convicts, yet when questioned, no one had seen anything. The shakedown in the immediate aftermath discovered a zip gun and three shanks. Before he died, everyone in Arizona had known for months that Tony Serra was willing to talk, for indeed he already had. "Tony Serra, a con man and former associate of land fraud kingpin Ned Warren, Sr., was beaten and stabbed to death at his prison work site Monday four months after he revealed his version of certain Warren activities," reported the January 4, 1977, edition of the *Arizona Republic*. The *Republic*'s headlines tied Serra's murder to Arizona's and Warren's legacy of land fraud: "Serra's death is the 13th linked to mob or land fraud in the state." The paper reported that "before the Serra killing, the most recent was the bombing death of *The Arizona Republic* reporter Don Bolles. . . . Bolles was fatally injured June 2, 1976, when a bomb exploded beneath his car in the parking lot of a Phoenix hotel."

The longest-running, most violent, and most reported land frauds in Arizona history were masterminded by Ned Warren, the godfather of Arizona's fraudulent land sales industry, whose exploits single-handedly made synonymous the words "Arizona" and "land fraud" in the national press during the 1960s and 1970s. By 1977, Warren was dying of cancer and was unlikely to serve any of his twelve-year sentence for fraud, still under appeal. Everyone convicted in his swindles sat behind bars, but his name and legacy lived on. The public knew Serra's name well, too, from extensive news reports of Warren's demise.

Warren's companies owned land and sold it—*many* times. They repeatedly resold the same land to different customers, and then sold each successive new mortgage to a different bank. The companies carried off the fraud for years by never recording any deeds of sale showing the purchaser to be the new owner. Each bank believed it owned good commercial paper with a paying customer, who would receive a deed for the land only once all payments were made on their long-term purchase contracts. The buyers were unsophisticated out-of-state purchasers, most never seeing the land they had "bought," and never understanding their victimization until they had made years of payments. In the end, no one knew who owned what.

Tony Serra "was sentenced to 8 to 10 years in prison in August 1974, for 11 counts of fraud stemming from the operations of Great Southwest Land and Cattle Co., a crooked land firm . . . controlled by Warren." Serra had been the company's "sales manager." Two years into his prison term, Serra had a peculiar change of heart. On August 13, 1976, the *Republic* reported that prison inmate Tony Serra had given a sworn statement asserting that in 1968 the Maricopa County attorney, Serra, and Warren had removed a three-foot pile of records of Arizona Land's swindles from the county attorney's office after they had been surrendered to the prosecutor's office by Richard Frost, Warren's successor as president of the firm. Serra's revelation offered the tantalizing hint that "the records are hidden not far from here [Florence]." Serra was "willing to disclose the hiding place of land-fraud evidence allegedly smuggled out of the County Attorney's office six years ago," though he never did so before being murdered.

Prison Warden Cardwell was "very irate" at the prospect of Serra talking and said this "could get a couple of finks killed." John Moran, director of the Arizona Department of Corrections, paid a "highly unusual" visit to Serra in his cell after his revelation. Then, three days after Serra's death, the *Republic* reported prison director John Moran's denial "as an absolute lie," as the content of Serra's posthumously reported letter to his lawyer described visits and threats from Moran and Warden Cardwell. An unrelated story on the same page told of "four escapees and hostages spotted east of Yuma." Cardwell denied that these escapees could be considered suspects in Serra's murder—which, though true, nonetheless damned him again, since having to answer so potent a charge was proof of his weakened stature.

Serra's death rang in the 1977 New Year, the opening round in the wildest, most violent year in the history of Arizona State Prison. As with most murders before his, Serra's murder merited virtually no investigation, and no one was ever successfully prosecuted for his death. But eleven months later Small's murder started a war against the Aryan Brotherhood. Why the metamorphosis from ennui to war? Too much publicity. After fourteen murders and twenty-five stabbings at Arizona State Prison during 1976–77, politicians were finally forced to act by the *Republic*'s sensational coverage of the carnage that government officials appeared unable to stop.

Amidst Arizona's prison crisis, three men occupied the governor's chair from October 1977 to March 1978. The first, Raul Castro, vacated the office one month before Small's murder to serve under President Jimmy Carter as the U.S. ambassador to Argentina. Then came Wesley Bolin, Arizona's secretary of state and Castro's constitutional successor. The lovable, ineffectual, over-the-hill Bolin, a bolo-tie western-style Arizona institution, crowned his thirty-year career of public service as secretary of state by serving as governor the last four months of his life. As secretary of state—essentially an elected head-clerk's job—Bolin couldn't botch a thing so long as he stayed out of the way of his hired clerks, who carried on the office's utterly humdrum business of recording financial statements and counting election ballots. Unexpectedly elevated to the governorship, Bolin did not have time to annoy any constituency during his four months in office.

Governor Bolin displayed his stripe as a "give the public what it wants" politician in a speech delivered shortly after his ascension to the governorship, reported November 24, 1977, in the *Republic*. Speaking to a joint meeting of the Prescott Rotary and Kiwanis Clubs, Bolin announced his order to the director of the Department of Corrections to put state prison inmates to work in an effort to control stabbings and other violence: "We are going to see that those prisoners go to work down there. All they do is sit around and think up mean things to do to each other."

Not to be outdone, Majority Leader Burton Barr introduced a bill requiring inmates to be engaged in productive measures. Six days later, on November 30, Governor Bolin fired John Moran as the Department of Corrections' director "for failing to solve Arizona's prison crisis and for taking political potshots at the state legislature."

Perhaps at the very moment Governor Bolin's pen signed Moran's dismissal order in Phoenix, Terry Farmer and William Goff walked from the print shop to the tag plant with Willard Breshears to identify Waymond Small as their intended victim. Or perhaps Farmer and Goff engaged their victim in small talk moments before thrusting a shank into his heart and smashing his skull with a claw hammer. Or perhaps John DeSanti and Bart Goodwin received their orders to Florence for the most challenging investigation of their lives. Or perhaps Waymond Small was murdered at the same time the politicians at the Capitol were crafting their quotes to attack Bolin's firing of Moran, for as the *Republic* reported; "In the Legislature, leaders in both the House and Senate accused the governor of using Moran as a 'scapegoat for a 50-year-old problem' and 'a carcass to hang his hat on.' Several legislators called the governor's decision 'premature and precipitous.'" In any case, Governor Bolin acted decisively and forcefully when news of Small's murder reached his office. With Governor Bolin's firing of Moran on the same day that the Aryan Brotherhood murdered Small, the defining moment arrived in a long-simmering crisis of public and institutional confidence.

For Moran's immediate replacement, Governor Bolin tapped imported experts from the Texas prison system—calling the Lone Star State's system "the finest in the world." Ron Taylor, administrative assistant to Texas's prison director, was "loaned" to Bolin for ninety days to make his recommendations. On January 12, 1978, Taylor announced his immediate recommendations to the House Government Operations Committee—the same committee before which Small had been scheduled to testify:

Arizona's Attorney General should prosecute all crimes committed by persons in the custody of the Arizona Department of Corrections. . . .

Investigators and attorneys should be assigned to the Department of Corrections to ensure vigorous prosecutions. . . .

In addition, I support legislation being drafted to specifically provide for the capital punishment of inmates who kill or conspire to kill another inmate, either in jail or prison. . . .

The current level of violence at the state prison is a despicable situation and I pledge every effort to correct it.

On the same day as Taylor's appearance, the legislators got the dog-and-pony show they'd sought and that Small had volunteered to provide on December 1, 1977. Prison inmate George Warnock, wearing a black hood, though incongruously his name was given, told the legislative committee that Ned Warren, the Aryan Brotherhood, and the Mexican Mafia had all placed contracts on Tony Serra's head before his slaying in prison—Warren for fear of Serra's knowledge of land-fraud schemes; the gangs because Serra "ripped them off in a heroin deal."

When Wes Bolin died in the saddle on March 5, 1978, with the prison crisis still escalating, Attorney General Bruce Babbitt became his constitutional successor. A politician of enormous ambition—Babbitt later made a serious run for the Democratic nomination for the presidency in 1992 and served as President Clinton's secretary of the interior from 1993 to 2001—Babbitt could not afford to let a few prison gangsters sully his law-and-order image—not on his watch, not if his ambitions were to be fulfilled. Throughout Arizona's entire prison crisis, Bruce Babbitt had been the one constant in the highest echelons of the executive branch, having served either as attorney general or governor. Babbitt had been the one politician able to expand or curtail Arizona's commitment to prosecute the Florence Eleven for the murder of Waymond Small.

But Babbitt's career aspirations alone do not explain Arizona's all-out declaration of war on the Aryan Brotherhood on November 30, 1977, though certainly Babbitt either lobbied for or didn't resist Governor Bolin's direction that the attorney general's office take over the prosecution of the Waymond Small homicide. So, although pressure to do something about violence at Arizona State Prison didn't begin with the murder of Waymond Small, Arizona's institutional reaction to the murder—from the governor's office to the head of the Department of Corrections; the warden and the captains, lieutenants, and sergeants at Florence; the Department of Public Safety investigators; and finally to the prosecutors at the attorney general's office—was to declare all-out war on the Aryan Brotherhood and to throw every available institutional asset of the state into the investigation, prosecution, and conviction of its members.

The declaration of war coincided with an event that made it impossible to ignore the prison crisis any longer, just like a homeowner finally calling the plumber after the home's pipes had burst, spilling sewage and fouling the air. Yet those bursting pipes first began with a single drip from a small crack, hard to detect at first and easily ignored for a while. The all-out response to the murder of Waymond Small began after a trickle of prison violence had grown to a flood. The year of Small's murder began with the murder of Tony Serra. Many had speculated that Warden Cardwell and his favorite among the inmates, murderer Gary Tison, had been complicitous in Serra's murder. By failing to send Waymond Small into protective custody when he knew Small was a marked man, Warden Cardwell again faced conjecture of the same vein.

The Tony Serra and Waymond Small attacks had much in common: both murders occurred during the workday in front of hundreds of prisoners, with the perpetrators aided in both committing the crime and evading detection. As if suddenly struck deaf, dumb, and blind, prison guards found only dead bodies, bloody shanks, and witnesses. Serra and Small were both snitches who told authorities about gang and organized crimes. Warden Cardwell could have prevented both murders by removing either snitch from harm's way, but he may have deliberately chosen not to, for complex political, personal, and institutional reasons.

With Small dead and Governor Bolin taking jurisdiction out of Warden Cardwell's hands, the struggle to retrieve the asylum from the inmates began. It's one thing if the prisoners are running the institution and only the warden, the guards, and the Department of Corrections know it. That equilibrium may persist—and may always remain the natural state of affairs so long as institutions confine the human spirit. But this equilibrium is disturbed and no longer acceptable if the public ever comes to believe that the prisoners are running the asylum. When Arizona newspaper stories created the public perception of a system run amok, with prison gangsters freely ordering the unprosecutable cold-blooded shankings of their rivals week after week, politicians had no choice; now they demanded that names be named, that heads roll, that law and order be restored to the prison—lest they not be reelected.

With Waymond Small's murder, the rumble of prison violence had reached a crescendo heard around the state. Black ink had splashed across hundreds of pages of Arizona newsprint. The collective public and political minds demanded that the offensive wail from Florence be silenced.

7 The Investigation

While the Waymond Small case worked its way through the legal system, the relationship between the state's lead investigators—Department of Public Safety Detectives John DeSanti and Bart Goodwin—and the defense lawyers became ice cold. When I began investigating this story, I hoped twenty-two years were enough for a thaw.

In my first phone call to Goodwin, I asked for a chance to talk in person and explain my request. Goodwin, now retired from public service and working in Tucson as director of corporate security for a gaming company, only agreed to hear me out. I drove the five hundred miles to Tucson, hoping for the best yet unsure we would even recognize each other. Our paths had barely crossed during the prosecution; Goodwin had not sat in the courtroom through a single day of any trial in which I had defended Richard Compton.

We met after work in the small employees' kitchen area at his place of employment inside a large industrial park. Our nervous conversation began with an easy topic: how good we still looked after twenty years. Bart proudly told me he worked out regularly and could bench press over three hundred pounds. His huge barrel chest, massive shoulders, bulging biceps, and enlarged forearms, wrists, and hands offered undeniable proof of his disciplined training regimen.

Like a good cop, Bart quickly fell into an expressionless, neutral silence, leaving me the burden to speak and prove myself deserving of his cooperation. Getting quickly to the point, I said: "I want to write a book about the Waymond Small murder that's completely true. I'm not doing this to make the defense lawyers look good and you guys look bad. I don't think the convicts got a raw deal when you guys prosecuted them. They're telling me you had it right all along. The Small hit went down exactly the way your snitches said it did. Even Farmer's telling the truth now. I know they were guilty, and no one's saying they weren't. It was an AB hit. All the defendants were guilty as hell. They did exactly what Hall and Farrell said they did. Now I want to figure out why the jurors let them off. That's the story I want to tell, and I want to tell it from everyone's point of view — the prisoners', the prosecutors', the investigators', the defense lawyers'. When I'm done, I hope everyone will say, 'Price got it right.'"

Goodwin had heard a lot of lies in his time; his BS detector is finely honed, and he had no reason to cut me any slack. My project depended upon this man's cooperation; the fate of my hopes rode on his decision. Would he believe me? Emulating Goodwin's technique once I'd said my piece, I fell silent, putting the ball in his court. He sat silently — waiting, thinking, deciding.

"I didn't know what you had in mind," he began. "Since this won't be some bullshit fairy tale about how the system fucked over some poor convicts, I guess we should call DeSanti and see what he thinks." Goodwin rose from his chair, walked to an adjoining office, and picked up the phone. I sat across the desk in silence, nervously awaiting his next move.

After a few calls, Goodwin located DeSanti's cell phone number and left a message asking John to return his call right away. We sat, wondering if DeSanti's call would come anytime soon, but in less than three minutes the phone rang.

Goodwin hadn't talked to DeSanti for several years. Ten minutes passed as two old partners and longtime friends chewed the fat, called each other bad names in jest and affection, and caught up on the basics of jobs, kids, and wives before getting down to what had precipitated this unexpected call.

"Terry Price, remember him?" Goodwin explained. "He was one of the defense lawyers in the Waymond Small case. He wants to write how it really went down. It won't be some dumb liberal's fairy tale how the system fucked over the convicts. I think we should work with him. What do you think?" Goodwin's endorsement was as good as a decision for them both. The chance DeSanti would contradict his friend's recommendation was nil. They knew it; I knew it; a deal had been struck.

Several months later, Goodwin booked a room in the Embassy Suites Hotel on Grand Avenue in west Phoenix. DeSanti lived nearby, still working in law enforcement for the State of Arizona, and he drove each day to our meetings. Over the weekend, during ten hours of tape-recorded interviews, Goodwin and DeSanti answered questions. Men I had known only as opponents in a legal game came alive. For the first time I learned the intimate details of the investigation. Rapport grew quickly between former antagonists as we traded stories, such as the time DeSanti single-handedly captured escaped convict Richard L. Davis in 1968. DeSanti had a reputation for toughness, and it was apparently well earned.

While Waymond Small's still warm but thoroughly dead body lay on a gurney at the Arizona State Prison hospital, DeSanti and Goodwin were in the midst of a weeklong homicide seminar at the Department of Public Safety Training Academy. Nothing they could have learned the rest of the week in the classroom—indeed, nothing anyone in officialdom could have taught them in a month, a year, or a decade—could have prepared them any better than they already were for the investigation of Small's murder. They were Arizona's finest, handpicked for the job—yet even they admitted they were totally unprepared for this murder investigation.

Lieutenant Moody called DeSanti and Goodwin away from the classroom with a unique and peremptory command. "We've had seven murders in the last two months in the prison at Florence. The governor is real concerned. You two are assigned to prepare a report on prison gang violence. You report directly to the governor. Another inmate, Waymond Small, has been killed today in the tag plant. The governor wants you to find out why we have wholesale killings in our prison. He wants to know how this has happened, why it happened, and to make sure it doesn't happen again. He's tired of front-page news about another prison murder every other day. You're to jump on this with both feet. You have the full support of DPS, from the director on down. The governor's emergency fund is a hundred percent at your disposal."

"When do we start?" asked Bart Goodwin, who looked the part of an archetypal boot-camp drill sergeant right down to his piercing gaze, square jaw, rugged face, barrel chest, defined musculature, above-average height, and close-cropped chestnut mustache.

"Yesterday. The governor wants your first report within eight hours," Lieutenant Moody exclaimed as he picked up the phone that never seemed to stop ringing that day. No official act by the state of Arizona could have been more urgent or more earnestly begun. Arizona had declared war on its prison gangs, and it was determined to win.

When DeSanti and Goodwin arrived at the Arizona State Prison gate in Florence, they found that the governor's writ wouldn't carry them far—and that not every apparatus of the state had yet declared war on the same enemy. They were met by Pinal County Deputy Herb Padilla.

Sheriff Frank Reyes's right-hand man, Padilla was a large, dark-skinned Hispanic Indian with a burr haircut and an intense edge. Padilla knew why DeSanti and Goodwin were there, and he didn't like it.

"John, there's a problem," Padilla told DeSanti, for the two were well acquainted and respected each other. "Warden Cardwell and Frank don't want to let the Department of Public Safety investigate this crime scene. Frank is sheriff, and this is his county. The governor can order you anywhere he wants, but Frank's still the highest law enforcement official of this county, and until we get this issue cleared up, he doesn't want you at the crime scene." Padilla was correct. Arizona sheriffs possess complete control over law enforcement in their counties. The State of Arizona and its agencies do not have original jurisdiction to investigate crimes.

It took a few minutes before the sheriff and the governor agreed, in classic political style, to a joint investigation, with the Pinal County sheriff's department receiving booty and more funding. Politics intruded into the investigation from day one, but this confrontation quickly receded as Goodwin and DeSanti smoothed the ruffled feathers of their investigative counterparts within the Pinal County sheriff's office and the Department of Corrections.

The sun was setting before DeSanti and Goodwin were escorted by the prison's chief investigator into the industrial yard of the prison. "As if today wasn't bad enough, the shitter's gone South," prison investigator Capt. Dale Davis grumbled as the trio walked past four inmates digging a six-foot by six-foot by six-foot hole to reach a main junction in the sewer lines. "We've got a complete sewer blockage on top of all this but, hell, it's not the first time." The trio assumed the sewer problem was a coincidence with the murder. Two months later they would know better.

DeSanti and Goodwin visited the tag plant and learned what they could from the on-scene investigators, assuring themselves that the tag plant would remain locked and secured until they could thoroughly investigate the scene themselves. Then they drove back to Phoenix with a knife, a hammer, and Small's body for an autopsy.

The next morning, Dr. Heinz Karnitschnig, Maricopa County's chief medical examiner, found that the prison-made knife fit neatly into the hole in Small's chest that had punctured with surgical precision all four ventricles of his heart. The doctor pronounced Small's skull so thick that the hammer blows, though cutting two divots into the scalp, would have hardly caused a headache.

Once the scene was inspected, diagramed, and photographed the next day, the routine portions of the investigation were completed and now DeSanti and Goodwin's wild ride was about to begin. When a crime occurs in prison, none of the standard rules apply, and the detectives' usual bag of tricks is useless. DeSanti and Goodwin were about to find out what happens when sixty eyewitnesses to a murder—and 1,800 potential suspects—are the cream of the criminal crop as chosen by Arizona's finest judges. To make matters worse, prison has its own language. "Kite," "run," "fish"—what do they mean? DeSanti and Goodwin didn't know. Prison has its own mores and culture, too. "Do your own time." "Don't get involved." Even prison guards don't want to testify about what they see in prison, since they have to go back to work amidst the same prisoners every day. DeSanti and Goodwin had never investigated in an environment where the victims and eyewitnesses were natural accomplices and accessories after the fact. They had a lot to learn.

Upon rational grounds, the investigation of murders inside prison walls seems to be simple. The administration knows who was in the prison and where they were supposed to be; the body is found before the corpse is cold; witnesses who saw the crime are plentiful and easily detained. In fact, any witness can be locked up for security purposes and his privileges and good time taken away just as easily as any suspect. Prisoners have plenty of scores to settle, and finding out who is on the outs with whom is child's play. Convicts start with plenty of reasons to rat on each other, and a creative administration can stir up simmering antagonism into full-blown wars with a few well-placed leaks, a few well-chosen perks gratuitously withheld or granted. Maybe slip a few lines to a talkative queen to fit someone out with a snitch jacket.

Surely the same rational assumption applies to the prosecution of prison crimes—once solved, the trial seems a certain winner. What chance does the inmate have before judge and juror? Either will naturally believe the defendant guilty of the worst charges imaginable and will have not a shred of sympathy for the pathetic and misguided accused, with whom jurors feel they have nothing in common and whom the judge abhors, having sent so many of his kind away already. All inmates' alibis must come from the mouths of other inmate witnesses, thoroughly impeached before they take the witness stand by the life of crime that brought them to prison in the first place.

And suppose the administration doesn't know who did the crime from day one? No problem. Just keep an ear to the ground, Captain Davis, and the secret will be yours, for there are no secrets in the pen. While inmates are doing their own time and not prying into someone else's affairs, they remain fundamentally human, so gossip spreads every petty detail.

Outside, a man looks to society and the rule of law for his security; the young, the weak, the infirm, the sick—all are equally protected. Inside the walls, in an environment where the social contract is so loosened, a convict survives as long as the prison culture permits or as long as he can protect himself, or if he's too weak, for as long as he can buy protection. The prison venue offers a virtually unassailable bastion of defense against prosecution: a Darwinian axiom dictated by each prisoner's dependence on his fellow inmate's dispensation for his very survival. Do your own time. A corollary flows from this axiom, and every prison prosecution must overcome its force: Never snitch off another inmate to the man.

DeSanti and Goodwin quickly learned that the inmate code of silence stood as a nearly unbreachable barrier to prosecuting Small's murderers. Their instincts told them, "Begin with the blacks, they hate the Aryan Brotherhood. They're tired of the killing. They'll realize, 'If Small can't protect himself, no one can.'" With the prison securely locked down and every inmate in his cell, the investigators could play their cards however they chose. Call every inmate with an AB tattoo into the office? Every inmate at the tag plant? Every black inmate who had worked in Small's corner the day of the killing? Which way to play it? Where to start?

Captain Davis began the very day of the crime at the most logical point—talking to the blacks assigned to the packing room along with Small. A subtle form of racial segregation permeated prison job assignments. While all races were mixed in the tag plant, the separate tasks maintained barriers for mutual protection in the racially charged Arizona State Prison. Small's coworkers were black—Ronnie Jones, Robert Toney, Billy Banks.

Banks began to talk, but then he froze up, as noted by Captain Davis in his report: "Banks states Small was working in the back of the tag plant at the paint machine. He and Small had been working in the carpenter shop but they had a lot of heat from white inmates. They requested work assignment change to the tag plant. Banks was working at the press about 50 feet east of the victim's work area. The only thing Banks saw was the victim chasing a white inmate with a hammer. Then the victim went down. Banks stated that Small was first hit with a hammer. At this point inmate Banks froze up and would not give any more information."

The investigators ran smack into another obstacle: getting coherent information from illiterates who spoke in a combination of street rap, prison slang, and jive talk that was all but incomprehensible to those on the outside. But it did cut across racial lines, for the ignorance, poverty, and the welfare/ghetto milieu that begets the idiom paid no heed to a man's color. Putative prison enemies—the general of the Aryan Brotherhood and his Mau Mau counterpart—understood each other, but outsiders never would.

DeSanti's and Goodwin's assignments were to solve a prison murder, bring its perpetrators to trial, explain to Gov. Wesley Bolin the hows and whys of the gang problem, and suggest its solution. Their wide-ranging tasks meant they needed to talk to virtually everyone at Arizona State Prison—inmates and guards alike.

Starting with the guards at the scene of Small's murder, they quickly realized that common sense and mental acuity were not job requirements, and the guards' instinct for self-preservation made them less than enthusiastic about becoming witnesses for the prosecution.

The entire prison population of 1,800 inmates was locked down for as long as DeSanti and Goodwin needed for their investigation. This wasn't much of an inconvenience for the cons, who had nothing but time, and DeSanti and Goodwin quickly learned the inmates were only too happy to string them out. They also realized they couldn't just call out the inmates they really wanted to question; they'd have to interview the inmates in large groups so that no one would feel singled out—an expediency required by the unique prison environment yet hardly an efficient use of time. During the protracted process of calling out the prisoners, the sixty inmates working in the tag shop all gave monotonously identical interviews.

"Were you in the tag plant on November 30 when Small was killed?"

"Yes," each inmate would respond.

"Did you see anything?" the duo would ask.

"No" was the universal refrain.

For their own amusement, Goodwin began following up with a satirical, whimsical query, "Would you tell us if you had seen anything?"

"No" remained the consistent, and far more honest, answer. But the effort at humor showed that DeSanti and Goodwin were hip to the convicts' games. As a gauge of honesty, Goodwin invented a winnowing device. He would ask the inmates, "Are you guilty of the crime you're here for?" Anyone who answered "yes" merited more time and attention. Those answering "no" were quickly ignored as unbelievable.

The twenty or more inmates awaiting their turn outside the doors of the Parole Board Hearing Room—now converted into a full-time interrogation room—served as the prisoners' eyes and ears, obsessed by the all-important question: "Who might be talking?" So the investigators standardized the process to keep the prisoners guessing. They settled on a standard length for interviews. Even if the inmate would say nothing, they would detain him in the room, outside the eyes and ears of the waiting inmates, for exactly the same length of time as anyone else. If they had kept anyone too long, the prisoners would have assumed that the prisoner had snitched, and that prisoner might have been found dead the next morning. If an inmate was cocky and arrogant, DeSanti and Goodwin turned the tables to make it seem as if he'd snitched. As DeSanti walked one such reprobate out of the parole hearing room, he put his arm around his shoulder, patted him on the back, and said, "Thanks a lot. We appreciate your time." Realizing the setup, the inmate screamed, "I didn't tell you guys nothing!"

Interviews were constant mind games: who's going to talk? But there was one major and inviolate constraint: DeSanti and Goodwin could never lie—stretch the truth maybe, but not outright lie—and anyone who cooperated in the least could never be burned. Either blunder would doom their credibility and assure zero future cooperation. The most powerful lever DeSanti and Goodwin had in their effort to crack the prison code of silence was the most obvious of all, and the one that worked: the race card. For decades Warden Cardwell, like Warden Frank Eyman before him, had used the race card to run Arizona State Prison.

In the tag plant, work groups were segregated by race for their mutual protection, because the inmates would protect one of their own from attack by another race even if they didn't like each other. Small had been surrounded by other blacks in the portion of the plant where the tags came off the conveyor belt. They had obviously witnessed his murder and knew the identity of his white assassins. Surely one of them would give up the killers if the right buttons were pushed.

Willy "Bang Bang" Banks, who'd worked next to Small, came into the interview as hostile as any inmate. He wouldn't shake hands with DeSanti or Goodwin. "Don't touch me, white honky motherfucking peckerwood," he shouted, injecting for the sake of emphasis a profane litany commonplace among prisoners. "No white man's touched me in five years, and you ain't about to," he snarled as he sat handcuffed.

Goodwin pushed back. Banks was seated, isolated and alone, as Goodwin and DeSanti sat behind the horseshoe-shaped desk. "Okay, you don't want to cooperate. We've got a plan for you. We know you were there. We know Waymond got stuck, and you saw who did it." Goodwin then began to wing it, making up eyewitness statements he didn't have and convict cooperation that had not been forthcoming—demarking the furthest extent to which the investigators could lie to the convicts without destroying their own credibility and undermining their investigation, for if they were ever to succeed, this momentary lie eventually had to become a permanent truth.

"Toney's told us what he saw. You were right beside him. You're a material witness, just like Toney. If you don't cooperate with a criminal prosecution, then the judge can lock you up in county jail as long as he likes."

"You honky lying son of a bitch. There ain't no shit law like that," Banks protested.

"You're going to find out," Goodwin threatened. "We'll call you back tomorrow, and if you're not going to cooperate with me, you're going to county jail. I'll have a court order."

Banks had never heard this line before. "Well I don't know. I ain't sayin' nuttin' to you shits."

The next day, DeSanti pulled the race card on Banks, who came in more cooperative, since an overnight conversation with a jailhouse lawyer had convinced him there really was something to this "material witness" line. Curiously, prison inmates hate the county jail more than state prison. In county jail they are the highest-risk prisoner and get the most severe lockdown and no privileges—a form of solitary confinement and indefinite lockdown with no work, no diversions, no coffee, no exercise, and no friends to shuck and jive with.

"You tell me, Bang Bang, why don't you want to cooperate with us? You let a white man kill a black dude right in front of your nose, and you didn't do a goddamn thing about it?"

"Naw, man, I didn't see nothing," he still protested.

"We know the whites did it. Why didn't you off them yourselves when you had the chance?" This needle pricked. It was the very question the blacks had heatedly been asking themselves.

"I mind my own business. I don't see nothin'," Banks shot back as DeSanti and Goodwin poked and stoked the fire of Banks's black rage against the man, the system, the whites, the Aryan Brotherhood.

After turning up the heat, DeSanti shifted gears, talking street with Banks, making connections. Who did Banks know that DeSanti knew? Who'd done favors for Banks? Banks was from Avondale; he knew John DeSanti's father, who'd run at various times the local grocery store, the pool hall, and the taxi service. Banks remembered the time DeSanti's father gave his mother a free taxi ride to the hospital. As a means of solving the murder of Waymond Small, the genuine kindness that DeSanti's father had extended to this black man's family may have counted for more than clever tricks or manipulative ploys.

Banks broke, but with a twist. Starved for information, DeSanti and Goodwin agreed to his terms. Banks agreed to steer them the right way, but he wouldn't testify. Tape recorders were turned off, note pads laid aside. Banks faced some indisputable, cold, unyielding facts. As an eyewitness to the crime, his life was already at risk, even if he said nothing. As a material witness, he could be locked down indefinitely in county jail. As a black man, he hated and feared all whites. An organized white-supremacist gang like the Aryan Brotherhood was simply an overt expression of the enmity he felt every white institution—including the prison administration—would hold against him until his dying day.

A routine began. Captain Davis fed guard reports and bits and pieces of gossip to DeSanti and Goodwin. Inmates would walk by guards in the kitchen and whisper, "That's the guy." After running the prison like a fiefdom for twenty-five years, Warden Cardwell and his lieutenants Cordova and Avenetti manipulated a seamless web of anonymous snitches that penetrated into every crevice. DeSanti would then run down a scenario about how he thought the murder had happened. Banks steered the investigators through the tidbits they'd gleaned from snitches. "You got that right. That's right, guys," he'd coach when the scenario jibed with reality; "No, that ain't right," he'd caution when the information veered off course.

DeSanti and Goodwin worked on other black eyewitnesses as well.

Ronnie Jones started out far less hostile than Banks; he just wanted no part of it.

"You were sitting right next to Small and you let this happen?" Goodwin tore into Jones.

"No I wasn't."

"You were there. You were working right next to Small."

"Well, I was sitting out back playing cards," Jones shot back.

Getting madder, Goodwin bore in. "So you're playing cards out back, so you're seeing what's happening inside the shop."

"No, the door is shut."

"Bullshit, Jones. Impossible. There ain't no door on the shop. You had to see it."

"Didn't see nuttin'."

"Get out of here, Jones," Goodwin shot back. "There ain't no damn door. It's open. You ain't playing cards all the time. When do you work, anyway?"

Jones dodged the parry. "I works when I wants ta work, and I don'ts work when I don'ts wanna work." Twenty years later, Goodwin and DeSanti still remembered this black con's dodge, delivered in a slow, drawn-out slur, as the funniest laconic one-liner they heard throughout the tedium of 650 inmate interviews.

Less hostile than Banks and weak minded, Jones was more susceptible to pressure. "You're black, Jones. You're right next to Small and Banks, banging out plates. You're going to let two white guys come into a black shop and kill this black brother and ain't nobody seen nothing or done nothing about it? Or gives a shit about it? What's the deal?"

"Don't want no snitch jacket," Jones finally admitted.

Now came the other side of the coin. Could DeSanti and Goodwin really deliver on any promise, being from outside the prison? "Listen, we can move you out of here today if you're willing to testify truthfully. We ain't talking no bullshit, Jones. You can't change your mind and say you were outside playing cards or some shit like that when the time comes. If you're willing to testify," Goodwin bargained, "we'll get you out of here today, move you someplace where they're not going to know where you're at and won't be able to get to you. Then we'll move you out of state to ensure they're never going to get to you. But we're not buying shit. You were there when it happened. Now, what have you got? And it better be good, because you gotta pass the lie box, too."

Jones worried about his kids. He wanted to be closer to them and his mother in New York. He didn't want his kids following in his footsteps.

"How you gonna make a better world for them, Jones, if you won't testify?" Conscience swayed Jones.

Working up the second black eyewitness required a different approach. Robert Toney was a tough young kid from Tucson who was in the joint for a second-degree murder conviction picked up at age eighteen. A theft for drug money went macabre when Toney burned the victim's body. DeSanti and Goodwin got Toney talking about his crime. Toney passed Goodwin's basic credibility test when he described his crime in graphic detail. Goodwin took a lighthearted approach to its grisly details.

"You did what to the body, Toney?" Bart jived. "Come on, man, you didn't burn him. Lit him on fire? What made you do that?"

"We fucked up, man. I don't know. Ran across this drunk out on Old Benson Highway. We took his money, just burned his body. I don't know why."

Goodwin noticed Toney had a chipping fingernail. "Nice chipping nail, Toney," Goodwin nodded with approval. His two-inch-long pinky nail allowed Toney to shovel a little more of the heroin his way as the guys cut it amongst themselves. When the cutting's done, Toney would have an extra sniff for himself off the nail.

Toney loosened up to Goodwin's display of knowledge about Tucson street life, drug talk, and Toney's old cronies. Toney wanted to know he'd be safe. "We can roll you up and have you out of here before the sun sets, but you have to pass a polygraph, you have to be truthful, and you have to give us the whole thing," Goodwin coaxed Toney along.

The jiving steered back to Small's murder. "We know you were there. You want this cleared up, don't you? You goin' to let this happen to a brother? You're not even going to tell anybody about it and shit?"

"I ain't going to be no snitch, man," Toney shot back.

"You won't be snitching. You'll be helping us with information." The spin softened the witness's resistance. To snitch was to be lower than a woolly worm's navel, lower than bug shit. Once you're a snitch, the jacket never leaves you.

"You want to help us, you want to keep someone else from getting hurt," Goodwin reasoned with every black witness to gloss over their snitch rap.

"Here's poor Waymond, sitting there doing his job, and a honky mother comes up and kills him. Do you think that's right? You ain't gonna do nothin' 'bout it?"

Each time around the block with "You were there. We can roll you out of here," butting against the convict's rejoinder, "I don't want to be a snitch," Toney would expound a little bit more about what he knew, but he needed to be careful since he had to live inside the system forever. Though convicted of only second-degree murder, the brutality of his crime had earned him a sentence of sixty years to life.

Learning the con games quickly, DeSanti and Goodwin knew the identities of Small's killers within three days. When Jones finally agreed to testify, DeSanti and Goodwin segregated Terry Lee Farmer and Ernest Goff in custodial lockup. Identifying Small's assailants yielded only a bare-bones case and didn't penetrate the conspiracy to kill Small. DeSanti and Goodwin had to have it all. That would require witnesses willing to testify from the inside, and that took long enough for the Aryan Brotherhood's code of violence to turn upon its own and leave a few so isolated that snitching to the man would become their only alternative to death. That took less than two months.

Did he not recall, Goodwin and DeSanti wondered, or did language problems make Ronnie Jones's account of Small's murder seem so incomplete, so hazy? The investigators realized that Jones's memory of events lacked clarity and precision. Candid assessment of this key witness's ability to testify left the investigators feeling uneasy. The trial jury would not expect the State of Arizona to ask for a murder conviction based on a flaky eyewitness. To see with your eyes is to be certain and to be able to tell what you saw. Anything less makes "eye witness" an oxymoron.

Jones's work station placed him within spitting distance of Small; both worked at the tag plant on the conveyor belt near the roller coater. Why didn't he recall more? say more? sound more certain about what he saw? The decision to lock down Farmer and Goff was made after Jones identified them from a photo lineup in Captain Davis's office nine days after the murder. DeSanti and Davis showed Jones the lineup, six passport-sized pictures of inmates from their prison records but with their names and inmate numbers blocked out. He picked out Farmer and Goff. This was evidence sufficient to prosecute, but would it be enough to convict?

Perhaps Jones would recall more if he were hypnotized. Certain pros-
ecutorial techniques — the rack, the Star Chamber, rubber hoses — have
enjoyed a period when they were in vogue, only to fall out of favor. As
with the demise of far less subtle forms of persuasion during bygone
days, news of hypnosis's imminent fall was slow to filter down to law
enforcement in the field. The ultimate demise of hypnosis as an investigative technique in Arizona resulted from the supreme court's concern
that a witness's memory might be tainted by suggestions of the hypnotist,
leaving the witness confused or unable to distinguish between his honest
recollection and the memory implanted through hypnotic suggestion.

Little did the prosecution know at the time, however, that hypnosis
of eyewitnesses to crime was due for a complete and rapid fall from judicial grace, and they called a professor of psychology at the University
of Arizona in Tucson. "Dr. Lindsay, can you help me?" Goodwin asked.
"I've got a witness to a murder at Arizona State Prison, a black man. He
saw another black man murdered right in front of his face and he's willing
to testify in court, but he gets confused easily. I'm afraid he won't be as
strong a witness as he could be. The killers stood not six feet away from
him, casually talking with Jones and the victim just before the attack. Do
you think hypnosis could help?"

Dr. Lindsay encouraged the attempt, and Goodwin brought Jones
to Tucson for a session with Dr. Lindsay and his colleague Dr. Russell.
Jones, however, was apprehensive about the hypnosis. "There's nothing
magic about it?" he asked.

"Have you ever been reading a book or doing something and been so
intent on what you were doing that somebody said, 'Hey Ronnie I've been
talking to you five minutes.' Have you ever had that state of concentration?" asked Russell, assuring Jones that hypnosis was soothing, deep
concentration that feels like the "twilight stage" before falling asleep.

"So there's nothing magic about it? There's no magic spell that can
be interrupted if you move or if you wants to scratch your ear and you
don't have that magic pendulum and all the Hollywood stuff that's all
bullshit?" Jones asked.

"We're not interested in any part of your life except what has to do
with the killing that went down," the reassuring Dr. Russell continued. "I
would say most times under hypnosis the concentration in a way becomes
so intense that you can recall clearly. Just as if you see it on the screen.
Things you might have otherwise forgotten. Just this morning we had an

assault victim who couldn't do much better than a description. But under hypnosis she began to describe the ring on his finger in great detail. So this is why they brought you down here. There's nothing magic about it. It does help us to recall. Why this is, we don't know."

Having firmly suggested the efficacy of his technique, Dr. Russell proceeded, "I'll start out giving you some progressive relaxation."

"Can I call you Ronnie?" Dr. Lindsay took over. "If you're willing to enter hypnosis, what we would like to do is take you back to the day that it happened and you would actually see it happen. Do you think that will upset you?"

"No," Jones assured.

"Please sit in this recliner," Dr. Russell motioned. He then suggested to Jones that he visualize a peaceful forest setting beside a brook, with warm yet pleasant sunshine bathing his body in white light, clouds floating peacefully through the blue sky, wind blowing through soft pines. Jones was invited to progressively relax each muscle in his body with soothing instruction. Once Jones was relaxed, Dr. Lindsey suggested that Jones could now answer questions with his fingers moving all by themselves and that he could watch his fingers tell him the answers to the questions.

"Now I'm going to show you something very interesting about hypnosis. I'm going to ask you questions and instead of you answering 'yes' or 'no' you're going to answer with your fingers. They'll move all by themselves. You won't have to move them. And you just watch and see what the answer is. But now I'm going to talk to your subconscious and you let your subconscious mind answer the questions. Dr. Russell is going to talk to you now and he's going to explain to you how you will be able to see what took place at the prison on a movie screen that we have here on the wall and all about how it works."

Dr. Russell then explained to Jones, "There will be a magic television screen up here, and when I count to three you will see the television screen light up and you will see a very interesting documentary film. This documentary film will show clearly, and with great detail, everything that took place in the tag plant and afterwards having to do with the stabbing. You will be able to see everything in complete and vivid detail. But because you know that you are presently on the third floor of the Tucson Police Department surrounded by police officers that you are perfectly safe and of course you are perfectly comfortable in that chair.

"When I count to three we'll light up the screen. This documentary was made with a very special camera that you and I can control, so we can stop the film or speed up the film. We have a special zoom lens so we can focus on any particular scene. We can reverse the film. We can do anything we want.

"When I count to three the screen will light up. Will you tell me everything you see?"

Jones nodded.

"All right. One, two, three. What is happening, Wednesday, November 19th at approximately 1:15 p.m. in the afternoon? You're there with a man named Small. Now tell me what's happening on the screen."

"We're sitting on the machine, looking at tags when these two white guys setting in the back. . . . I really didn't pay too much attention to them," Jones answered.

Not liking this tack, Russell intervened. "Let's stop the camera right there." Suggesting something Jones never mentioned, he said, "There's one white dude and he's raised his hands up, and now you're looking at the other white dude. Zoom in that camera. Do you see his hands?"

"Can't see his hands," Jones responded.

"Okay, can you describe the dude?"

"Blonde hair."

"What about his hair. Is it parted or is it straight back?

"Parted."

"Parted, where?"

"On the side."

"Which side?

"Right side."

"What about his eyes?"

"Gray."

"Anything else about his face? Any scars, whiskers, growth of beard, mustache?"

Jones never responded.

Russell instructed Jones to open his eyes and look at a photograph of Terry Lee Farmer, which Goodwin had brought to the session: "Okay, I want you to open your eyes right now, Ronnie, and take a look at that picture and tell me if that is the person."

"Yes," Jones conveniently confirmed.

Dr. Russell directed Jones to look again at the screen and to return from a conscious to a hypnotic state of mind in an instantaneous twinkle.

"Do you remember the number of this dude? Tell me the number."

"36922."

Suggesting again something Jones never said, Russell ventured, "Now I want you to focus in on the camera, look up at the screen, and you'll see the other dude *and he's got his hands raised. What's in his hands?*"

"A hammer."

"Describe this dude."

"Pointed nose, eyes brown."

Russell then broke back to the "conscious" by asking Jones to "look at this picture, is this the man?" Goodwin had brought William Goff's photo to the session, too.

"Yes," Jones answered.

"Now, you can close your eyes if you want. What was the number on that man? Could you see the number on his jacket? on his shirt?

Jones didn't respond.

Russell tried again, "Look at the picture on the wall and tell me, is there any number you can see?"

"36922."

"Now what happens? We'll start the camera again."

"I yell to Small, 'Look out,' but by that time he had gotten hit. Small jumped from the stool and bent down and picked up the hammer and started chasing him and I jumped off my stool and ran and they hit him again."

"Do you see the knife in his right hand?" Russell then suggested for a third time "upraised hands" and "weapons" before Jones mentioned any such thing.

"Yes."

"Describe it."

"Small, something wrapped around it."

Dr. Russell brought in Dr. Lindsey, who asked—again suggesting details never mentioned by Jones in the session—"Ronnie, let's go back to the place where these guys and Small are right in front of the wire screen that separates this place from the other shop. When you see the knife in the guy's hand. Can you tell me what hand it is in?"

"Right hand."

"Which guy has the knife?

"The blonde hair."

This answer is ambiguous, so Lindsey seeks to aid Jones, "The guy with the hammer or the blonde guy?"

"I don't know him."

With Jones's answer going from bad to worse, Lindsey attempted to begin anew, adding more suggestions about what had transpired, though they were never mentioned by Jones during the session.

"Now, Ronnie, let's back that picture up until you're sitting across from the table from Small and this guy is standing beside Small with this hammer. Now, does he hit Small on the head with a hammer before the other guy did something to him or after?"

"Same time."

"He's punching him in the side of the arm, in the back, or in the chest?" Lindsey asked.

"In the back of the shoulder," Jones offers.

The two hypnotists huddle and turn off the tape recorder before again starting anew. Jones is asked to remember the number "on the other person."

Jones does no better than "36" before Lindsey prompts, "36, 9, and 22. Now describe the other dude."

"Man," is all Jones offers before Russell has him again open his eyes and look at Goodwin's prison picture of Goff.

"What was the number on this man," Russell asks again, knowing Jones hasn't yet uttered Goff's prison number, only Farmer's. "Do you see the number on this guy?"

"36," Jones started and stopped.

Russell reset scenes of Small and Jones running, and asked for more. Jones sat in silence or said only "yes."

"Describe the knife."

"Long," replied Jones, contradicting his earlier answer of "small."

"I'm going to let Dr. Lindsey ask you some more questions," Russell said.

"Which guy has the knife?" asked Lindsey.

"Blonde hair," Jones responded, contradicting his prehypnotic statement to investigators that Goff wielded the hammer, not the knife.

Realizing the error, Lindsey implored, "Now, is that the one with hair that hangs over his forehead? The guy with the hammer or not?

Jones fell silent again.

Lindsey changed tack, now placing the hammer in the blonde's hands, contrary to what Jones had just said. "Let's back up the picture. This guy is standing beside, behind, beside Small with this hammer. Now, did he hit Small on the head with the hammer before the other guy did something to him or after?"

"At the same time," Jones repeated.

"Which hand is it in?" Lindsay asked.

"Left hand," Jones said, contradicting his earlier "right."

Trying to remedy this new difficulty, Lindsay offered, "It's his left hand. It would be the one on your right, right?"

Jones didn't answer, so Lindsey asked again where he punched Small.

"In the back of the shoulders."

The hypnotists led Jones out of prison and back to the forest again, for another conference, before trying again.

"We're going back to the prison for a few minutes," Dr. Lindsay directed Jones while showing him photographs of the tag plant. Dr. Lindsey suggested that Jones saw those two men in the morning for a few minutes in the tag plant before guards told them to get out of there. Having set this new scene, Dr. Lindsey asked, "Do you remember that?"

"Yes."

"Did you notice the numbers on their jackets?" Lindsey tried for the fourth time.

"9 and 18 and 36, 9."

With this failure, the doctors gave up. "OK. Let's leave all that prison stuff and let's go back to the pine forest"—a place investigator Goodwin most assuredly now wished he could go, for this day had been a disaster. Jones remembered less under hypnosis than before. Worse, his hypnotically induced recollections contradicted earlier statements. Under Arizona's rules of disclosure, the defense lawyers would receive copies of the tape-recorded hypnosis fiasco. They had only made the prosecution's case weaker.

"How do I tell the governor our star witness knows even less now than we thought?" Goodwin wondered as he drove back to Phoenix. "Why did I ever get stuck with this case?" he asked himself, not for the first time.

The string of stabbings and murders at Arizona State Prison in 1976–77 and their increasing prominence in the news accounts of the day had flashed repeated warnings to Arizonans that their correctional system was running amuck. The Government Operations Committee of the Arizona House of Representatives, through its "Report on Organized Crime within the Arizona State Prison," issued a formal public indictment of investigative journalism's accusation that prison gangs controlled Arizona State Prison and that this gang warfare had spilled outside to the streets. The committee's fifty-eight-page report, issued December 29, 1977, fleshed out the indictment. William C. Smitherman and Raymond P. Herand, the lawyers for the House Government Operations Committee, made the following conclusions in the report, which the *Arizona Republic* fed to an incredulous public:

> Highly structured gangs within the state prison do exist.
>
> Murder, assault, bribery and extortion will be used to further their aims.
>
> Control of these organizations will be obtained only through concerted action by law enforcement, legislative direction, and vigorous prosecution.
>
> Any system of criminal justice and punishment cannot be permitted to be subverted by the persons who are the objects of that system, in this case the inmates of our penal institutions.

The report's chronology began with the March 1975 murder of Charles Schmid, stabbed forty-seven times by two bikers who were members of "the Highwall Jammers," predecessor of the Aryan Brotherhood, and climaxed with a tenth murder, Waymond Small's, on November 30, 1977. With all ten homicides, the murders were either unsolved or the perpetrators received a plea bargain and concurrent sentence from the Pinal County attorney's office. All were attributed to gangs—the Mexican Mafia or the Aryan Brotherhood, "the largest and most powerful organized groups within the prison." Forty other armed assaults were sandwiched among the murders, all attributed to prison gangs.

The threat of these gangs had increased in recent months. Although "in the past hostile and antagonistic towards each other," the two gangs had reached a truce in July 1977 "for economic reasons," which increased their strength. The truce divided rackets along racial lines. The Mexican Mafia agreed to release its few white members recruited as enforcers and to prey only upon Mexican and black inmates. Its white "punks" were released to the Aryan Brotherhood. The AB agreed to extort and attack only Anglos and blacks. If a Mexican Mafia member had a grievance against any Anglo in the prison for any reason, he must take his grievance to the Aryan Brotherhood to take the necessary steps. Like any business deal between equals, the Aryan Brotherhood reciprocated. Blacks were fair game to both of the parties to the truce.

In the report's chronology, though it predated the supposed truce, the murders of Tony Serra and Gary Carel were explained by this modus vivendi, with enforcers provided by the group of the victim's heritage. Relying on documents found by Captain Davis during a shakedown of William Steven "Red Dog" Howard at Arizona State Prison on November 8, 1997, the report outlined how the Aryan Brotherhood financed its operations. The document described the gang's methods of collecting and spending money. Red Dog, the gang's minister of finance, acted as the accountant and comptroller of its illegal businesses, as follows:

"Front Money"—If a brother or anyone else has the connections for scoring drugs, then the brotherhood will front them the money to score with. In the case of a brother or anyone that is on good terms with the brotherhood, this is the arrangement that will be made with them. The money will be sent to where ever it is required with a bank receipt being proof that money was sent. When delivery of the drugs takes place, they will be handled as follows: Before all else, the original investment will be repaid. After this is done, the remainder of the drugs will be split 50–50 between the brotherhood and the man who scored. The brotherhood will take its 50 percent and from it make every effort to sell enough to match the original investment. Once that is done, the remainder will be given out to all members to use as they see fit.

"Loan Sharking"—All business transactions must go through the Minister of Finance. But the brother who actually makes the loan to the borrower is responsible for collecting and seeing that the money gets to the bank. The Minister of Finance will keep track of all accounts loaned and the due dates. Anybody may borrow money, but there is a fee of 50 percent on each loan. The man who borrows the money has two weeks (14 days) to pay back the loan in full, plus interest. If in two weeks time he does not have the money to pay back the loan, he must at least pay the interest on the loan in order to extend it for another two weeks. This type of payment can be carried on indefinitely, so long as the interest is paid every two weeks.

"Stores"—There is to be at least one store in each building and in cell blocks a store should be set up on each side of the building. This is also true for dorms that are split into two or more sections. A brother will be chosen to run the store by the building officers and for this effort he will receive $10.00 worth of store each week for his own use. The brother running the store will keep accurate books and must be able to show the building officers what is loaned out, how much is owed in, and what the weekly profits are. All items in the store will be sold at a 2/3 basis. That is to say that if 2 packs of cigarettes are loaned out, then 3 must be paid back. This is to hold true for all items in the store. After the store has been built up to a satisfactory level to take care of its side of the building it should begin to show excess profits. These excess profits are to be converted into cigarettes and cash, which will be turned over to the Minister of Finance for other uses.

"Football and Sports Tickets"—A brother will be selected by the Minister of Finance to arrange the odds for all sporting tickets. This man must be able to set odds properly and he should be the best known brother in the field of sports knowledge. This man will be given 25 percent of all profits made from all tickets sold, but in the case of a losing week he will not be held liable for the 25 percent of the total debt. The brotherhood will absorb all losses for the tickets. The building Officers will select a runner for each side of their building, who will handle tickets for his area. This runner will receive 25 percent of all profits made from his tickets, and he will not be responsible for any costs on a losing week. The remaining 50 percent of all profits will be held by the Finance Minister and will be considered brotherhood profits. The runners will use the cigarettes they take in, to pay off any winning tickets at the end of each week. In the case where a runner owes out more than he takes in, they are to see their building Lieutenant who will notify the Captain. The Captain will contact the Minister of Finance so as to obtain the necessary cigarettes to pay off the runner's debt. The runner will be given a certain number of tickets, for which he will be held accountable to his building Officers, who at any time they may deem proper, check the runner's records.

"Jacking up and Bulldogging"—As of the 1st of September, 1977, all new or old fish that get bulldogged after this date, will have 25 percent of their payoff turned over to the brotherhood. If he is bringing in dope, 25 percent goes to the brotherhood. If he is bringing in cash, then 25 percent goes to the brotherhood. If he is giving up store, then 25 percent (in cigarettes only) will go to the brotherhood. This 25 percent will be delivered to the Minister of Finance and will be considered brotherhood profits. The brother who has the guy jacked up will keep 75 percent of the payoff for himself. If the guy who is jacked up should move to another building, then the brother who has him shall notify the building Lieutenant of where the guy moves to, and the Lieutenant will assign him to a brother in that building. This is to be on an equal sharing basis and these guys are to be distributed evenly. Anyone that you have jacked up prior to 1 September, 1977, will remain a brother's private property, unless the brother gives the guy to the brotherhood.

All profits from all these businesses that have been discussed, are to be turned over to the Minister of Finance at the earliest possible time. The Minister of Finance will make sure that these profits are reinvested in an appropriate manner.

The rules could be changed, but they would be enforced:

This list of Financial rules is submitted to you as the basis for how our finances should be run. It will be up to the General and the three Captains to make a final decision as to its approval. These rules may be changed in the future, so as to be more accommodating to members of the brotherhood. Such as higher or lower interest rates for borrowing and individual profits. But all changes must have the approval of the General and his Captains. It will be the duty of the Captains and Lieutenants to see that all of these rules are carried out in the exact manner indicated.

The Aryan Brotherhood's financial document mirrors many business school style principles and sound business practices: delineate a clear business plan, articulate an organizational purpose, create an organizational hierarchy, provide for a division of profits, offer piecework and commission-based incentives to the labor force, and announce enforcement mechanisms. Nonetheless, the rules foretell that this enterprise would fail because it contained flaws that commonly undermine many legitimate small-business startups: undercapitalization, over-reliance on leverage, and undue optimism.

Having outlined the problem, the Smitherman and Herand report suggested an inadequate and simplistic solution: "We therefore strongly recommend the passage of legislation giving the Attorney General the power to prosecute all crimes committed by persons committed to the custody of the Department of Corrections," thereby assigning the state's highest priority to prosecuting these crimes. "We also recommend that mandatory consecutive sentences be given to any person under the custody of the Department of Corrections who commits a new crime while under that custody."

With publication of the report, the successful prosecution of the Waymond Small murder became a top priority of Arizona's legislature. No more creative means of eradicating prison gangs was entertained than vigorous prosecution and consecutive sentences for prison assault and murder. The legislature quickly acted on the second proposal. In short order, aggravated assault by a prisoner carried a new punishment: a sentence of twenty-five years without possibility of parole to be served consecutively with any other term already imposed. An assault by a prisoner became nearly as serious a crime as first-degree murder.

The attorney general's office twice experimented with the prosecution of prison crimes: the Waymond Small and Bobby Phillips murders. After those failures, the attorney general's office lost interest in this expansion of its authority. In later years, the legislature adopted its final solution: it poured millions of dollars into concrete and rebar to build more cells, prisons, and ultramodern super-max facilities in which to isolate the totally incorrigible convicts from the more lethargic, compliant, and manageable prison masses.

8 The Preliminary Hearing

Since I had not yet started working as a prosecutor in Pinal County when
the preliminary hearing began, I never observed those proceedings in the
courthouse. I suspected the prosecution's effort jumped the tracks early
in the game, but until I read the preliminary hearing transcripts in 1997,
I didn't know how farcical and inept those first court hearings were. As
I read, I could see that the preliminary hearing unraveled from the outset
and disintegrated further each day until it ended in utter futility—with
nothing accomplished by the state and all advantages from the wasted
effort accruing to the prisoners. It need not have turned out that way.

Perhaps the attorney general discounted the Pinal County lawyers as
ill-equipped to defend the case. Perhaps the attorney general assumed that
with eleven men facing the death penalty, some defendants would cut a
deal and switch sides, making their job easier with each desertion of gang
allegiances. Both assumptions turned out to be false, but one conclusion
is evident: The attorney general's office bungled when it chose to begin
the most complex criminal case in the state's history with a preliminary
hearing before a justice of the peace.

The defense began its task with no captain of the ship, no team leader,
no "lead counsel" for the accused. The defense was not a team; it was
eleven completely independent, court-appointed lawyers representing
eleven defendants. The court had no power to assign a lead role. With
each defendant facing identical charges, each lawyer had equal standing
and claim to center stage, with complete freedom to fashion a defense
as he saw fit without regard for the consequences for any co-defendant
or disagreements with co-counsel. Each defendant might have interests
antagonistic to his co-defendants, and each might decide to make his own
deal, run his own course, even switch sides and snitch if the state offered
a good enough deal.

From the opening day of the preliminary hearing, a natural sorting of
roles among co-counsel began, with the only rule being "every man for
himself." When the curtain rose, the play began and the cast of lawyers

sorted itself out into a hierarchy, setting apart the competent from the lazy, the infirm from the vigorous, the mediocre from the memorable, the ridiculous and miscast from the confident and ready. Among the eleven lawyers, hard drinkers outnumbered social drinkers and teetotalers; two were admitted alcoholics who had seen death's door before their instinct for survival returned them to the path of sobriety.

The eleven defense lawyers knew each other well enough that their roles in the Small murder case were predictable if not automatic. In the role of respected elder dean, all would cast Harry Bagnall, who had practiced law in Coolidge for thirty years. He was a handsome man with a full head of white hair, an elegant tan, a rotund but pleasing paunch, and a sunken chest befitting his middle-aged station as a man who made his living with his mind, not his physical strength. Harry's legend as a man of nine lives flowered from his near-death brushes with drinking and driving.

The role of champion fighter would have been assigned to attorney Michael Tidwell. I first saw Tidwell at the arraignment of three prison inmates charged with an Aryan Brotherhood stabbing. I sat in the back of the courtroom along with a law school classmate and fellow prosecutor in the Pinal County attorney's office. In a whispering, disdainful tone, he pointed out Tidwell to me as "one of the enemy, a real prick, a first-class jerk"—for he viewed all effective defense lawyers as pariahs, reprobates, or worse. Tidwell dominated the proceeding that day—sartorially as a dandy in a baby blue, pinstriped, three-piece suit and professionally as a determined advocate who spoke in behalf of his client with authority and zeal. Obviously, Tidwell would be a burr under the state's saddle.

At the preliminary hearing, Tidwell became the dominant figure for the defense. Just thirty-six years old but bearing himself with the dignity and presence of a fifty-year-old, his jet black hair betrayed not one strand of gray. Michael approached every courtroom battle with indignation that the state had to prosecute his client—as if an act so misguided boggled the mind. The sentiment was not feigned; he felt it every time and remained so confident of victory that his demeanor never betrayed doubt.

Though intellectually and morally miles apart, Michael and the inmates shared a mentality, a psychic space—both distrusted wealth and privilege. Tidwell had a deeply ingrained identification with the plight of the accused and a near-paranoid fear of the power of the state. He would forever identify with the poor and distrust the rich while tenuously aspiring from his teenage years to acquire sufficient wealth to live modestly well and retire permanently at an early age. Born in Scottsdale one week before the bombing of Pearl Harbor, Tidwell's life began in as much ruin as the Pacific Fleet. His father divorced his mother before he was born, and his alcoholic grandfather committed suicide. Raised of hard necessity by a working mother who was helped by a grandmother, he never identified with the smug and comfortable norms of white, middle-class Scottsdale.

The ideal trial lawyer is expected to zealously and single-mindedly take to his bosom the cause of his client alone. The lawyer's personal interests, his desire to stay on the good side of the judge before whom he must try the next case, and his reluctance to alienate the leading elements of the community by espousing unpopular causes can all divert the lawyer from his duty, but the lawyer's creed requires surrender of all self-centered motivation to the cause of fervently representing the client. Few lawyers have accepted this ethical challenge more completely than Tidwell in his representation of prison inmates.

In Pinal County, trial lawyers faced a special dilemma. With only three judges—T. J. Mahoney, E. D. McBryde, and Robert R. Bean—burning one's bridges with any one judge became the lawyer's equivalent to Arctic exile with only one match left to start a fire: Arizona law gives the lawyer just one request to change the trial judge assigned to a case. In a large county like Maricopa, with fifty superior court judges, alienating a judge comes at a small price. But in Pinal County, many lawyers compromised zealous representation in favor of staying on the judge's good side, the better to fight and win the cases that were more important to their careers.

Even in Pinal County's small club of lawyers and judges, Tidwell knew few bounds to his zeal, as he showed when he stood up to senior judge T. J. Mahoney on the day he denied a procedural motion Tidwell had filed in the prosecution of Tony Serra's alleged murderers. While just beginning his practice, Tidwell received a court appointment to represent Don Dilski, one of four prisoners accused of the January 1977 murder of Tony Serra, cohort of land fraud king Ned Warren. The murder occurred at 10:00 a.m. while Serra was at his job in the sign shop. Although it happened in front of at least sixty inmates, all predictably followed the code: they had seen and heard nothing. Tidwell filed a motion for a new determination of probable cause, so the prosecutor would again have to present his case to the grand jury before Dilski faced trial.

Still drinking heavily at the time, Tidwell knew a fellow alcoholic when he saw one. On Monday morning Judge Mahoney assumed the bench for the brief oral argument of Tidwell's motion sporting a three-day growth of beard, bloodshot and tired eyes, an exceptionally florid complexion, even for so ruddy a man as he, and no socks under his black lace-up shoes, as Tidwell's convict client pointed out.

Mahoney permitted oral argument. Tidwell knew his motion was solid. His ten-page brief explained the law, but Tidwell knew early on this Monday morning that Mahoney was hungover, tired, and suffering. Tidwell spoke, but his attention was on Mahoney's condition. As one alcoholic reading the body language of another, Tidwell knew that Mahoney would overlook the nuisance of reading and understanding a ten-page brief. Tidwell's face reddened and he became visibly upset as Mahoney breezily denied the motion. Venting in hushed tones, Tidwell grumbled to defense counsel, causing a low-level commotion in the courtroom.

"What's your problem, young man?" Mahoney demanded, asserting his dominance over the insubordinate lawyer.

"I've got a concern with your ruling, Your Honor," Tidwell shot back. "You never read my motion or my brief."

"I've been on the bench thirty years. No one talks to me like that. I'll see counsel in chambers!"

In his private chambers, Mahoney planned to administer an ugly humiliation upon this upstart, but Tidwell seized the initiative. "Before we begin, Your Honor, I'd like to put on the record, so the court reporter will have it on her transcript, that you called me a son of a bitch as you left the courtroom," Tidwell coolly held ground.

After ten minutes of remonstration and rejoinder, Mahoney backed down. "I'll withdraw my earlier denial of your motion and I'll read it. I'll reset it for hearing next Monday and tell you my ruling." One week later, Mahoney was none too pleased with Tidwell. "I've read your motion, son. I didn't enjoy reading it. I didn't like one thing about it, but I'm going to grant it anyway."

After this victory in his first murder case, Tidwell cemented his reputation among prisoners and prosecutors through his defense of four of the Florence Eleven in the Waymond Small murder and conspiracy prosecutions.

It seemed like a good idea at the time to hold a preliminary hearing instead of simply indicting the eleven men charged with the conspiracy and murder of Waymond Small. Though the attorney general could have gotten the eleven indicted with thirty minutes of white snitch Dominic Hall's testimony before a grand jury — a proven fact, since three months later that's exactly what happened — the state would enjoy one major advantage if the murder prosecution began at a preliminary hearing instead of with a grand jury.

Felony charges are prosecuted in Arizona's Superior Court after the state establishes probable cause to believe that a crime has been committed and that the defendant is the one who did it. The state has its choice of two vehicles by which to establish probable cause: in public at a preliminary hearing or in secret before a grand jury. A preliminary hearing is held before an elected justice of the peace, often a layman untrained in law, who decides the probable cause issue. Grand juries meet in secret, with only the prosecutor and his witnesses present, and return an indictment if a two-thirds majority vote of the sitting grand jurors believe probable cause exists.

By and large, the secret grand jury route is far easier, surer, and quicker for the state. Best of all from the viewpoint of efficiency, the prosecutor is the master of the domain, in total control, for the defendant has no right to participate or to even be told that the grand jury is considering his fate. Not without justification, defense lawyers derisively consider grand juries anything but grand, a rubber stamp for the prosecutor being a more apt description in their eyes.

A preliminary hearing carries one advantage for the state. That the state sought this advantage amounted to a damning admission — an admission of the state's loss of control over its prisons and jails, an admission that public hysteria about prison violence had infiltrated up to the state's highest level of law enforcement and the attorney general's office, an admission that the Department of Corrections no longer was equal to its most basic task, keeping prisoners from killing one another.

The state's sole advantage for proceeding by way of a preliminary hearing in public, as opposed to a secret grand jury, stems from the defendant's presence at the preliminary hearing and his representation by a lawyer who questions the witnesses. The defendant's Sixth Amendment right to confront and cross-examine his accusers has been satisfied. For this reason the witness's testimony at a preliminary hearing can be read to the jury at the trial if the witness is "beyond the subpoena power of the court." If the Aryan Brotherhood were to find a way to eliminate the convict-snitch witnesses Jones, Toney, Farrell, or Hall after they testified at the preliminary hearing, their testimony would nonetheless have been preserved and potentially used at trial, since dead men are always beyond the subpoena power of the court.

By the state's choice, the preliminary hearing began before Justice of the Peace Roy Nowlin, who had retired from a career as a prison guard. When the attorney general filed charges against the eleven prison inmates for conspiracy and murder, Judge Nowlin faced the most challenging and tumultuous hearing of his judicial career, and the defendants became known as the Florence Eleven. Judge Nowlin's fifteen minutes of fame, richly earned as it was, did not come from presiding over the Florence Eleven's preliminary hearing; his fame, forever memorialized in the pages of *Playboy* magazine, came later, for his solicitation of an act of prostitution from an undercover vice squad officer during his lunch hour. Presiding as a visiting judge in Mesa, he thought he had been removed from the gossiping, all-seeing eyes of his rural constituents.

During the Small preliminary hearing, Judge Nowlin proved unable to manage a courtroom with three prosecuting attorneys, eleven defense attorneys, and eleven hardened convicts charged with first-degree murder. This task would have challenged the skills of any jurist. Justice of the Peace Nowlin's elected domain gave him experience with misdemeanor assaults, DWIs, and civil cases with less than five hundred dollars in controversy. To say Nowlin was beyond his depth understates the obvious. The attorney general's office failed to foresee this hurdle when it grasped for the slim advantage of a preliminary hearing.

A hurricane roared from the moment Nowlin announced, "Court is now in session." Defendants and attorneys interrupted each other with objections and requests, one after the other. Before the judge could tell the first lawyer to sit down, another popped up.

Convict Ernest Goff took one look at his lawyer, C. William Gorman, a white-haired, frail, elderly man so infirm of mind and with legal notions so unusual that senility alone seems to explain his incompetence. "If he is my attorney, I do not wish him to represent me," Goff gruffly demanded upon seeing Gorman.

"I'm going to appoint him to represent you—regardless," Nowlin snapped.

"I don't feel he is qualified to represent me. I feel I should have proper counsel to represent me."

"Your Honor," Gorman interjected, "I suggest you do appoint somebody else to represent him because he is dissatisfied. This is the type of case that we ought to at least give him that one chance."

Nowlin refused to relieve him, so Gorman returned the favor by immediately making a motion that betrayed his inadequacy to the task at hand. "Very well. At this time I have a motion to make. I move the preliminary hearing be continued so I can talk to my client about the charges."

"When do you think I can get all eleven lawyers back into this courtroom?" Nowlin replied, " Motion denied."

Harry Bagnall, defense attorney for Michael Belt, asked Judge Nowlin to order the prison guards to remove the defendants from their shackles—a torturous, clanging apparatus of manacles clasped around the hands and feet and interlocked with chains that encircle the waist and bind the wrists to the navel area, preventing any stride longer than a baby step.

Then Bill Haus, Stretch's lawyer, moved to exclude the public from the hearing because the testimony "could be detrimental to other trials that are pending," referring to the backlog of cases from Arizona State Prison's carousel of stabbings and murders.

"I would like to join in the motion," chimed defense attorney Phil Glen. "I have a murder trial starting June 6th. Testimony introduced here will be very detrimental to that case. The publicity that surrounds this prison is just very intense, and I do not believe that anything that comes out of here should hit the papers before that murder trial starts."

Judge Nowlin ordered his bailiff to clear the courtroom to take up this matter and determine, at the prosecutor's suggestion, if all defense counsel agreed to this unusual exclusion. All did. For no discernible reason, Goff's elderly attorney chose this precise moment to interject, "I move you to dismiss on the ground that the charge of murder is unconstitutional." Well satisfied with himself, Gorman sat down, saying no more for the rest of the day.

Assistant Attorney General Wayne Ford objected to releasing the prisoner's manacles. "There are security precautions here with eleven inmates involved. We request that restraints be held on the inmates at all times."

"It is impossible for a competent defense attorney to communicate effectively with his client in chains," Glenn implored. "They have to sit at the table with us and take notes to assist us in the defense. I request the court at least remove the hand chains from my client. There are a number of guards here, all with loaded guns. If something happens, I'm sure they'll be able to take care of it."

"There are fourteen guards here for eleven inmates, which would be ample," observed William Hackenbracht, attorney for inmate Russell "Rusty" Harbin. "It's absolutely imperative that I be able to talk to my client during the proceedings so I can properly defend him."

Nowlin ordered the hand chains removed, but the leg irons stayed on.

After Nowlin denied eight motions to continue the hearing so that defense lawyers could prepare, defense attorney Glenn moved the court to supply daily transcripts. "I believe that would be impossible," Nowlin demurred. "Had you wanted that, I should have been notified well in advance to get two or three other court reporters here to take fifteen minutes and then be relieved and somebody else come and take fifteen minutes. I'm not going to ask this young lady to work all night long to prepare a transcript for you for tomorrow."

Unsure whether he'd blundered, Nowlin took a recess to ask the advice of Judge E. D. "Bud" McBryde, the presiding judge of the superior court. Fortified with McBryde's guidance, Nowlin reconvened the hearing and confidently barked, "I just inquired as to the expense of these daily transcripts and I was told the superior court doesn't allow this, so I won't either. And the state is going to give each attorney transcripts."

Bewildered by Judge Nowlin's confusion of hearing transcripts with witnesses' statements," Harry Bagnall asked, "Transcripts of what?" Showing he too was confused, Judge Nowlin answered, "Of the statement they made." Since the defendants had said nothing and only the state's snitches had given statements, Assistant Attorney General Galen Wilkes helped the judge by interjecting, "What we have here, Your Honor, are the statements of the witnesses that are going to testify. We also request that the attorneys not send these inside the prison wall. They can work on them with their clients, but that they not go into the prison wall area."

The unusual condition upon disclosure puzzled and surprised the defense attorneys. "Is that in the form of a court order, that I cannot give a copy of the transcripts to my clients?" Glenn asked.

"Yes it is," Nowlin confirmed.

"We haven't heard from Mr. Wilkes about what possible reason he could have for such a ridiculous order in the first place to keep us from giving copies to our clients," William Hackenbracht broke in.

Admitting the state's inability to run its own prisons, Wilkes argued, "Some of the testimony contained in here will probably be detrimental to the well-being of some of the other prisoners in there, and we fear the repercussions that will occur should these [transcripts] be circulated among the general population."

"Each of these eleven men are in lockup, and there is no way for these statements to get away from their possession inside of a prison," Attorney Bagnall objected.

"For the protection of the general population at the prison, I will deny that motion. I will request that no copies be made and released to the defendants," Nowlin ordered, as he betrayed yet again his predilection to sustain the state.

The impracticality of the state's demand quickly sank in. How were the defense attorneys to do their job if their own clients couldn't possess and review the statements of their accusers? Since the order apparently would not allow those documents to go inside the prison walls, Harbin's attorney requested the defense team be given "a transportation order to bring all these defendants over here to the courthouse, so then we can go over these things bit-by-bit to ascertain exactly what our clients can help us with in their proper defense."

"The state would object," prosecutor Ford responded. "There are ample facilities inside the prison for counsel to confer with their clients, to take these documents in to show them to their clients and let the clients read them, but not to leave the documents in the possession at all of any of the individual defendants."

"The state has never denied these men are in protective lockup," Bagnall objected. "These documents would remain with them and not be passed out into the general prison population. I can't see any reason for the order."

"Your Honor, point of order," Glenn bellowed, shouting down prosecutor Ford as he tried to interrupt Bagnall. "Motions are being made and the other attorneys are not being given a chance to speak. When a motion is made, I think the other attorneys have the right to be heard on that motion, and I would like to speak to Mr. Bagnall's."

"We are being paid thirty dollars per hour for our representation,"

Glenn continued. "If I have to go into that prison and sit there for a full day while my client fully understands these lengthy documents, it is going to be a big waste of time. If he is able to take the statements with him and read it on his off hours and have his questions written out for me, then I can go over there and we can go over these particular points much more speedily and save the state one heck of a lot of money."

"I agree, Your Honor," added Michael Beers, Red Dog's attorney, with a commonsense plea. "Not only are we denying the defendants their rights, the court is wasting its time with the order. They are going to read it and know everything that is in there. And if the prosecutors are that worried about the rest of the prison population finding out what is in it, I don't see why they don't move to not let them see the statements at all."

"We are precluded from going over to the prison and spending all day with our clients anyway," Harbin's attorney interjected, bringing up another practicality. "Visiting hours for attorneys are between 9:45 and 11:30 in the morning and 1:30 to 3:30 in the afternoon. The first afternoon I went there, they took until 2:30 to bring my client to me. If I have to go over there and get to see my client one hour each day, we are going to have to continue this case forever, and ever, and ever."

"I'll withdraw that order," Nowling declared, "and I will check with the administration at the prison. I will reserve any order until I can talk to Warden Cardwell or Captain Avenetti. If they can assure me that these transcripts will not be reprinted and given to the general population, then I will permit the inmates to have them. Are we ready to proceed?"

"One more thing," Mr. Beers asserted, not letting the state off the hook so easily. "If you are going to make this decision by talking to the authorities at the prison, I would like the opportunity to cross-examine and find the basis for your decision."

"All right," Nowlin conceded.

After taking roll call to ascertain that all eleven defense counsel joined in the collective motion, Nowlin was finally permitted to announce "Call your first witness"—these words appearing on the thirty-eighth page of the court reporter's transcript of the first day of the preliminary hearing. And so the case went on for three years and three months, from May 18, 1978, until August 26, 1981—a torturous path from the first day of the preliminary hearing to the last day of the fifth and last trial for the murder of Waymond Small.

On the first day, the prosecution chose to start on what seemed a strong point, calling as its first witness Robert Toney, the twenty-three-year-old black inmate who had stood next to Small at the roller coater when he was attacked on November 30, 1977. Yet Toney never seemed to be up to the seemingly simple task of telling what happened in front of his face in broad daylight. On the day of the murder, Toney had talked to Small outside the cafeteria over lunch, in a huddled group with other black inmates Billy Bangs, LeRoy Smith, and Richard Bangs, one of the leaders of the black supremacist gang the Mau Maus. Small told the group that the Aryan Brotherhood had a contract out on his life. "Why don't you go to lockup, then, like the man says?" Toney asked Small.

"I'm gonna show them ABs I'm not scared of them," Small retorted.

After lunch, Toney saw two whites walk into the tag plant, go to the tool room, then walk up to Small, who laughed and talked with them, being friendly. Toney turned away. When he turned back, Small was reaching for a hammer as Crazy stabbed him with a homemade shank in his left hand. Then the whites ran away.

The prosecutor asked Toney to stand and identify the man he'd named as Crazy, the blonde, the one who had stabbed Small. He made the identification by reading off the prisoner identification number "36918." Had Toney goofed? He'd identified Goff, not Farmer, as Small's principal assailant. The attorney general compounded the damage with the very next question: "Did the brown-haired individual, did you see him do anything at the roller coater?" No," Toney answered. Cementing the damage, Toney stood and formally identified for Judge Nowlin that the "brown haired" guy was Farmer. The preliminary hearing had just begun, and according to Toney the murderer Terry Lee Farmer had done nothing wrong.

Phil Glenn's fourth question on cross-examination provoked a fifteen-minute recess in which the defense lawyers debated amongst themselves whether to take an immediate appeal to the supreme court if Judge Nowlin didn't require Mr. Toney to answer the question "What are your parents' names?" This seemingly innocuous question forced the lawyers and the court to tackle head-on the key strategic reason why the attorney general had chosen to hold a preliminary hearing. "This transcript will be admissible at trial if something happens to Mr. Toney," Glenn argued. "I have to have clear, wide-ranging, full cross-examination."

Tidwell proposed a solution. "We ask the state to enter into a stipulation to allow us to take the deposition of the witness at a later date."

Prosecutor Ford couldn't give up the sole reason for a preliminary hearing — the state's right to use the snitches' testimony from the preliminary, even if later they were killed by the AB or simply changed their mind about breaking the convict code by testifying at trial. "We are going to go ahead with the prelim," Nowlin ruled.

Initially, Toney had given investigators DeSanti and Goodman the brush-off, claiming he had seen and heard nothing during the attack on Small. Defense counsel confronted Toney with this inconsistency. "Why would you tell him that?" Glenn asked.

"At that time I didn't want to get involved in anything," Toney admitted.

"Why did you walk from the small press over to the area where the fight was going on?" Glenn asked.

"At that time it looked to be more than one-on-one. It looked to me as being two-on-one. So I was going to help Small, if possible."

"But you just said you did not want to get involved?"

"I didn't want to get involved with a statement or sending nobody to the gas chamber," Toney explained.

"Have you been promised anything for your testimony?"

"Protection. Nothing else."

"At what point in time did you decide to tell the different story?"

"After I noticed that the two people that I seen attack Small, they were not locked up. Nothing was done with them. They were still walking around the yard." So when called out for a second round of questioning, Toney told the investigators he had seen the attack on Small.

So ended the first day. Not one defense lawyer had completed his questioning.

The second day began with a blizzard of defense requests and motions dreamed up over a four-day hiatus. "I expect this preliminary hearing to last five days, the way we are going," Judge Nowlin groaned upon hearing the first of the motions. Defense lawyers wanted the state to provide a list of the names and prison numbers of the inmates Jones said were also standing around the roller coater when Small was attacked; they wanted the state's second investigator, Bart Goodwin, excluded from the courtroom; they wanted all the turncoat prison witnesses to be sworn at once and the state to be ordered to segregate them until the hearing ended so that they couldn't discuss, and thereby coordinate, their testimony — a procedure known as invoking "the rule on sequestration of witnesses." Once "the rule is invoked," the trial judge calls all the witnesses before him and gives them two admonitions: "Do not discuss your testimony with any other witnesses while the hearing is in progress" and "Wait outside the courtroom until after you are called and finish testifying."

But how does a court sequester witnesses who are incarcerated twenty-four hours a day in adjoining cells, as was the case here with the state's star witnesses? The defense suggested the court order the state to house the testifying inmates at separate institutions; the court refused to do so. On the other hand, the court now agreed with the state's request to with-hold copies of all witness statements from the eleven defendants out of fear their testimony would become known throughout the prison via the grapevine and thereby endanger the witnesses and their families.

With the procedural wrangling over, Tidwell began his cross-examination of Toney. From that moment on, Tidwell evolved into the acknowledged first among equals within the defense team. Though only three years out of law school, Tidwell never paused in his questioning, never gave the witness time to relax or feel in charge of the course of events. His questions were crisp, short, and perfectly clear. Each question moved forward in small steps, from which no orderly retreat by the witness was possible.

By late morning, Ronnie Jones, a second black eyewitness to the attack on Small whose memory had been enhanced through hypnosis, had been called to testify. Twenty-four-year-old Jones was serving a six-year sentence on heroin selling charges after selling one twenty-dollar balloon to a narc. Jones admitted to being a junkie with a sixty-dollar-a-day habit at the time he was busted, but he maintained he was "no big pusher." Jones said that on the afternoon of November 30, while sitting on a stool next to Small, he saw two out-of-place white inmates walk up. One was dark-haired, the other blonde. The dark-haired prisoner went to the tool shop and returned with a claw hammer hidden inside his coat, which he drew overhead in both hands, striking Small's head from behind as the blonde jabbed Small from the front.

"Look out, Small," Jones yelled. Small slumped forward onto the roller coater as the two whites fled, the dark-haired one dropping the hammer. Small picked up the hammer, screaming "I'm going to get you motherfuckers" as he chased the pair. Jones gave chase behind Small. Small caught up with the dark-haired one and fought, trying to hit him with the hammer, before he fell to the ground and the pair escaped out the shipping room door.

Jones claimed to have seen the prison numbers of the pair on their clothing during the chase and "so the number I had written down, I didn't want to get involved because it would look like the black guys had something to do with it. So I tore up the numbers and throwed it in the trash as they took us outside and shook us down." During his interview with investigator John DeSanti, he hadn't been so sure of the numbers. Having again volunteered this twist during the preliminary hearing, prosecutor Ford asked Jones, "What numbers did you write down?"

"I wrote down 36922 and 36918," Jones answered without hesitation.

"I seen them on the guys' pants, below their waist, and seen them on the back of their coat, their blue Levi jacket."

In the courtroom, Jones proceeded to identify the dark-haired one with number 36922 as Farmer and the blond with 36918 as Goff. Since Goff and Farmer lived in CB-3, Jones had seen them many times before the murder and many times afterward. He could easily have grafted the knowledge of their correct prison numbers to their faces without having seen prison numbers on their clothing when they fled the murder scene.

In cross-examination, Phil Glenn thought to ask if Jones had taken a polygraph or been hypnotized. Jones confirmed that both examinations had occurred. Yet the prosecutor had given the defense lawyers no written records or recorded statements of Jones during those examinations. Glenn demanded that the court order their immediate production.

Assistant Attorney General Wayne Ford was caught in a dilemma. He stalled. "I believe in talking with the investigators that there was a tape made with the procedure with the hypnosis. . . . The investigators have informed us that the tape is unintelligible. We told them to get that tape and provide it to us. And when it is provided to us, we will provide it to counsel." Ford was on even shakier ground with the polygraph. The defense had been given a form showing that the examination had taken place, but the results weren't attached. He promised to remedy this deficiency. After talking to DeSanti, Ford went farther out on a limb concerning the hypnosis. "There was a tape made. The investigator has listened to the tape, and we can put him on the stand now to find out the evidence, the facts surrounding that tape. The officer says he does not know where it is at this time, but he might be able to find it. That is why I suggest putting the officer on the stand to get this information from him."

The defense demanded a continuance of the hearing until the polygraph report and tape of the hypnosis session were produced. Investigator Bart Goodwin, when sworn to testify, wasn't so emphatic, saying merely, "The quality of the tape is not that well." Nowlin called the bluff, directing the state to produce the tape on Monday "to where all of you can listen to it with me at four o'clock in the afternoon in my office." The state produced the polygraph result, however, before defense questioning resumed.

The defense cross-examination impeached Jones with one inconsistency: He said a claw hammer was used in the attack on Small. However, he told investigators Goodwin and DeSanti that the weapon had been a slug hammer. Jones knew the difference; he drew diagrams of the two types of hammers: one with a ball on the end for pounding; the other, a claw to pull out nails.

The day's proceeding ended early because the state had not produced the tape recording or a transcript of the hypnosis session. Before cross-examination of Jones could finish, the defense lawyers needed to see this material. The day closed with the state being given four days to produce the "unintelligible" tape recordings so that the court and defense lawyers could hear it for themselves.

When produced four days later, the state's bluff failed. Jones's voice came through loud and clear, along with the prodding suggestions of his hypnotists. "This is inaudible?" Nowlin growled as his mind slowly grasped the enormity of the state's deception. Eleven defense lawyers gloated; two assistant attorneys general hung their heads. DeSanti was livid but did his best to show no emotion. The eleven convicts enjoyed a good old time, because the prosecutors and investigators all looked like liars.

Being fair and honest himself, Judge Nowlin assumed that Wayne Ford, an assistant attorney general for the state of Arizona's criminal division, always knew and spoke the truth. Disillusionment followed disappointment, and Nowlin's predilections followed suit. Once the state fell from the pedestal of infallibility, Judge Nowlin became receptive to arguments of the defense attorneys, especially Tidwell. The deception permanently tarnished the credibility of the attorney general and Department of Public Safety's chief investigator, John DeSanti, in the minds of the eleven defense attorneys. They never forgot this subterfuge; they were forced to assess their strategy and actions from that time forward with the foreknowledge that the investigators, in their zeal, were not above manipulation, sleight of hand, or terminological inexactitude. Through five trials, normal trust levels were never fully restored between the prosecution and defense sides of the courtroom.

Whenever a court hearing resumes after a few days' hiatus, creative legal minds have had time to think of new causes with which to cavil. With eleven minds working for the defense, the probability of newfound objections increased exponentially. So it was upon resumption of the preliminary hearing seven days later. The prosecutors had a complete copy of the preliminary hearing proceedings thus far. New defense attorney Robert Brown had his copy. Now all the other defense lawyers wanted a copy, too, or else the state should have its copy taken away "so that they don't have the advantage of this material in the future," Glenn argued. "It is fundamentally unfair that the attorney general has possession of these articles in order to rehabilitate their witnesses when the defense attorneys do not have copies of them in order to cross-examine the witnesses." Seeking a simple expedient, Judge Nowlin took the prosecutors' copies from them. "No one is allowed to use Mr. Brown's except Mr. Brown," he added for good measure.

Peace still did not reign. Attorney General Ford spoke up: "If Mr. Brown is able to use his copy for the purposes of impeaching either of the two witnesses, the state certainly has the right to either use their copy or to use his copy to make sure he is making the right statements." Judge Nowlin simply bulled ahead, ignoring the conundrum created by all this lawyer posturing that he was unable to decipher or untangle: "All right, Mr. Glenn, are you ready to cross-examine?"

Ronnie Jones was recalled. Defense lawyers worked, but new concrete information was hard to come by, though all is not lost even when hard facts prove elusive. While observing Jones testify, the lawyers assessed his personality and his ability to tell his story. Jones's testimony powerfully portrayed the racial warfare of prison life. After the chase scene ended beside Small's collapsed body, Jones explained how blacks at the roller coater "were cussing with each other" for allowing Small to be killed: "After he got hit, you know, like everybody was upset, you know, and like he ran up and says, 'What's wrong with you motherfuckin' niggers?' You know, 'You all let these white motherfuckers off in here and take the dude and whip the dude off like this here,' you know. And I said, 'Well, look here, shit happens so fast, you know, nobody didn't know what was happening no way, you know.' And then that was it."

"Was anything else said?" Tidwell asked.

"Yes, a few more cuss words and shit, you know."

"By whom?"

"Both of us."

"Why were you upset with him?"

"I wasn't upset with him. I just didn't like the way he said it, you know, like there were a few of us sitting over there, you know, like we supposed to have been babysitting the dude or something, you know."

A new level of testiness entered the proceedings, the first bitter fruit of the imbroglio over the "unintelligible" Jones hypnosis tapes. In cross-examination, Tidwell discovered that Jones had been shown a photograph of the tag plant and of the shank recovered at the scene during his interviews with investigators Goodwin and DeSanti. Jones also gave Captain Davis a piece of paper with the prison numbers of the attackers he remembered. Tidwell wanted these three items produced on the theory that they were part and parcel of Jones's "written" statement.

"I'm amazed by the attorney general's confusing himself, in my mind, as being the judge rather than the prosecutor. If the attorney general wants to do away with cross-examination, then perhaps he should go to another place to practice law," Tidwell chided.

"Your Honor, I would like that stricken from the record," retorted Ford. "I'm getting sick and tired of him making statements and accusations, and counsel here is being as devious as possible. I'm getting sick and tired of personal comments."

Tidwell demanded the "devious" comment be stricken. The court sided with the defense and ordered the paper with the prison numbers and the photographs of the scene and shank be produced the next day — if they still existed.

When asked if he was ever concerned that he might be accused of Small's murder, Jones answered, "I had a few doubts. I didn't have no concern that I be accused, but just by the way it went down, you know, it looked like some black done it, you know."

"Was one of your concerns the fact that everybody around Mr. Small in this area was black?"

"Yes."

Jones said he decided to "give up his statement" to Captain Davis and identify Small's attackers to avoid a race war, because the blacks had decided "something had to be done," in light of the "cold way" Small had been killed.

The day ended with fevered accusations flying when Tidwell asked inmate Jones, "Where are you staying right now?"

"They want to try and find out where he is so they can pass the word through their sealed mail to other people at other places to where they can get it." Ford argued.

"Your Honor, at this point I would like to have the remarks of counsel for the state stricken from the record on the grounds that he is implying that we are trying to elicit this information in order so we can have the witness bumped off. As an officer of the court, I do not appreciate such an insinuation," Glenn argued.

"I would like it kept in the record, Your Honor, for future use," Tidwell interjected.

"It will not be stricken," Nowlin replied. "We will stand at recess."

The next day began with tussling over cross-examination about the whereabouts of the state's inmate witnesses in protective custody. Ford asserted that the bounds of proper cross-examination are limited when the "personal safety of the witness is at stake." "The specific reason that Mr. Small was killed was because he was providing testimony. He was scheduled to go before the Senate Investigative Committee on December 1 and give information. He also promised to testify about three prior occurrences at the prison. That is the basic reason that he was silenced in this case. One of our witnesses was stabbed seven times in prison because the Aryan Brotherhood was worried that he was going to testify. He was stabbed seven times and thought dead by the man who stabbed him. All the inmate witnesses are personally afraid for their own safety and for their families' safety if this evidence is revealed. Past testimony has shown these gentlemen are being incarcerated for their own protection. Their whereabouts should not be revealed under any circumstances."

"The threat has to be real, not conjectural, Your Honor," Tidwell protested. "I have participated in other murder cases at Arizona State Prison. Never has anybody been taken out of the prison, put in protective custody, and their life been endangered. We have a right to know where they are.

Absent a showing of an actual threat, any right to cross-examination shall not be limited under United States Supreme Court cases."

"I'm going to deny your motion," Judge Nowlin announced. "This is a very special case."

The judge's ruling didn't stop the arguments, as the eleven defense lawyers found new ways to advance the same points.

"Your Honor, I move the court to order the prosecution to disclose this information to the lawyers outside the presence of the defendants and off the record so we may send investigators out to find out if they have cell mates, or whatever. If we give our word to the court that we will not disclose this information to the defendants, I can see no possible prejudice to the state's witnesses. Your Honor, I move for a hearing to establish what prejudice or possible harm will come to the witnesses by a confidential disclosure to counsel," Hughes added.

The rest of the day was spent tediously cross-examining Ronnie Jones and Robert Toney. The defense questioning suggested that inmate Jones (1) wanted to leave Arizona State Prison because of unpaid gambling debts, which he denied; (2) contrived his recollection of Crazy and Goff's prison numbers on their clothing since he could not remember the prison number of any of the hundred other inmates in the tag plant on November 30; and (3) knew Crazy and Goff's prison numbers because Captain Davis showed him their prison pictures and file jackets with their numbers right next to the pictures. The defense proposed a test of Jones's ability to recall numbers by giving him random numbers to memorize and asking him to recite those numbers five minutes later. Judge Nowlin wouldn't permit the test. Jones attempted to deflect questions by saying "I had my own problems at the time." Jones was asked "hypothetically" if there was testimony "the people that went over there to do the stabbing didn't have any numbers on their uniforms" whether they would "be lying." Jones said that would be a lie.

The defense got another crack at cross-examination of the second black eyewitness, Robert Toney. Toney's memory of the fight scene began with Small bending over to pick up the hammer from the tag plant floor and running after Goff and Farmer. He saw Small and Crazy "scuffle" by the restrooms at the end of this chase, adding that "by the time Small was swinging at this cat with that hammer, man, everybody seen it, that wasn't just horsing around. Toney admitted that at first he had told investigators that he'd seen nothing, but he "changed his mind" two weeks later and told investigators "everything" after he was promised "protection."

On June 2 the hearing began without preliminary motions and wrangling among the lawyers, but as the day wore on quiet distrust disintegrated into open confrontation. The defense lawyers had learned that Robert Toney's incarceration arose from a mutilation murder. Toney persuaded the jury that the mutilation had occurred at the hands of his "fall partner" and co-defendant, and as a result, he was convicted only of second-degree murder. Now on the stand Toney declared that he saw no prison inmate numbers on Goff's and Farmer's clothing at the time of the attack and that he hadn't seen the shank until after Small had collapsed dead by the restrooms, the hammer on the floor a foot from his limp right hand. Toney first gave a statement to investigators admitting knowledge of Small's death after "they done kidnapped us off the yard," putting Toney in involuntary protective custody on January 20, 1978.

Toney's testimony graphically showed the ease with which DPS investigators manipulated the prisoner's code of silence to coerce statements out of snitches like him. Toney had been moved to protective custody before he had made any statement, but simply being placed there was enough to convince other prisoners that Toney had already snitched. As Toney saw it, the administration had "put him up on Front Street already," where "everybody out on the yard is going to think we done already give it up."

"So once they locked you up, you were labeled a snitch?" Tidwell asked.

"Yes," Toney replied.

"And, in fact, you had told everybody that you knew nothing about the case at the time?"

"Yes."

"Why were you afraid of being labeled a snitch?"

"That is a hell of a jacket, man, to be walking around the yard with on your back."

"Why?"

"A lot of people don't appreciate that, man."

"You were afraid of more than just they wouldn't appreciate it, weren't you?"

"Yes."

"Weren't you afraid your life was in danger?"

"It could have been if I would have went back to that yard, yes."

"And did you ever think about the possibility of you going out in the yard and being killed?"

"It had crossed my mind."

"Was it a regular thought?"

"To tell you the truth, when I heard on the news that Cowboy had got stuck, and I seen his cell mate come into P.C., the thought crossed my mind what would happen to me if I went back on the yard."

"At this time you had told no one anything about the murder of Waymond Small?"

"That's right."

"But, yet, you were in a position where you feared for your life?"

"Yes."

"'And that was because of what the administration had done by putting you in protective custody?"

"Yes."

So Toney had decided to talk and never went back on the yard.

The day's first blowup again came over the defense's right to cross-examine the snitches about the locations where they had been housed since turning state's witnesses and who they may have talked to in those jails, including guards.

"Do you remember the guard's name that you've asked to [relay messages to other jail inmates]?"

"Your Honor, I object to disclosing names which might lead to a disclosure of where the witness is being held," prosecutor Ford pleaded.

"I'm prepared to bring witnesses in here [who will] testify this man's life is not in danger," Tidwell countered. "Mr. Toney says his life is not in danger. He is secure. If I can't know who this man has talked with since this incident, we might as well fold up our books and go home now. We are going to be back here in several months and do it again if we don't have the right to cross-examination. In all probability, we already know where they live. I have a good hunch where they live just from reading the material the state provided me. If they can convince you that they have some legitimate fear that Mr. Toney's life is in danger, fine.

"They can transfer people from this jail to that jail. As soon as this man comes off the stand, they have at least fifty jails in this state that they can transfer him to. I guarantee you that they can have him somewhere else tonight. But knowing where he is now, and who he has had access to, and who he has talked to, and how he may or may not have been coaxed, or violated the court's ruling, is very material," added defense attorney Robert Brown.

"One thing we have brought out in the past two days is that the court's orders are being violated," Bohm interjected. "The witnesses are not segregated. They are able to communicate. They have been transported together. The attorney general's office has made statements that witnesses have been instructed that they are not to converse, and we have had these witnesses come on and say that they have never received these instructions and have conversed with each other."

Judge Nowlin dismissed the argument and Toney's questioning continued until a second blowup occurred over the state's destruction of the hand-drawn diagram of the tag plant Toney had prepared while giving his first tape-recorded statement to investigator DeSanti

"All handmade drawings that were utilized in discussions with these prisoners during interviews were torn up afterward," prosecutor Ford conceded.

Defense lawyer Brown exploited the new opening. "I move to strike the testimony of this witness on the grounds that written statements have been intentionally destroyed by the prosecution."

Tidwell moved to hold Assistant Attorneys General Ford and Wilkes in contempt of court. Bohm moved for sanctions. Tidwell waded into the fray with a demand that DeSanti be questioned about this destruction of material evidence. Attempting to stem the tide, Judge Nowlin announced he was denying every defense request.

"I formally move that an evidentiary hearing be held to determine whether the diagram has been intentionally destroyed," attorney Brown persisted. "If so, then the motions for sanctions will be renewed."

Judge Nowlin acquiesced, and under questioning by Tidwell, DeSanti justified his destruction of Toney's diagram because he "didn't consider that evidence."

As the other defense lawyers each took their turn, another gem dropped. Clothing removed from a sewer had been destroyed two weeks after the murder and before DeSanti learned its connection to Small's murder. Captain Davis, accompanied by Warden Cardwell in the courtroom, took the witness stand to explain the clothing debacle. The defense objected to the warden's presence since he, too, might become a witness about the clothing's disappearance. When Judge Nowlin asked Cardwell to leave, attorney Bagnall couldn't resist a parting shot: "We finally got rid of the Bayou sheriff."

Davis testified that torn-up denim clothing had been removed from a blocked sewage line twenty-four hours after Small's murder. "I had no knowledge at that time that it was tied into this case. It was covered with feces" and had no numbers.

"The testimony I heard this afternoon indicates if any evidence was destroyed it was by pure coincidence and with no intention of destroying it to keep it from the defense counsels," Judge Nowlin reasoned, thereby denying all defense requests.

The day ended on a gloomy note as Toney portrayed the grimness of Arizona State Prison. He had seen fourteen other stabbing incidents of every possible inter- and intraracial permutation during his three years at the prison. Most of those fights had been between blacks over petty gambling debts. Small's killing marked the first time he'd told authorities what he'd seen.

By day seven of the preliminary hearing, the defense team's endurance for cross-examination and continuing objections had worn down the last vestige of the attorney general's hope for a rapid conclusion to the hearing.

"Mr. Tidwell, did you finish your cross-examination of Mr. Toney?" Judge Nowlin asked as the day began, hoping for a "Yes."

"No, Your Honor, I didn't."

By afternoon, Tidwell and the other defense lawyers still weren't finished with Toney, now on the stand for the third day. The ordeal, however, produced valuable concessions from Toney: He didn't see Small being hit with a hammer or stabbed; he saw nothing until he heard Small's shout and Small began chasing two white men in the ensuing scuffle; Small, armed with a hammer, had the "upper hand in the battle" over the one unarmed white man, whom he caught up with by the bathroom area. Toney had a motive for testifying against the Aryan Brotherhood since Small had witnessed the stabbing of his "foster" brother, Timothy Malone. After Small's killing, Toney heard rumors that black inmates let Small be killed since he had agreed to testify about prison gangs. Blacks around him "didn't go out of their way to try to put a stop" to the hit, because "it was probably a good thing that Small was not going to talk."

Curiously, the state produced for the first time the scale diagram of the tag plant prepared at investigator DeSanti's direction one hour after Small's murder. Later that afternoon, the state also produced its prize witness, Dominic Hall, who testified that he had orchestrated the murder of Waymond Small on orders from Aryan Brotherhood leaders. Now he would finger everyone who had helped, ordered, or carried out the hit. The day ended, however, with Hall barely beginning his tale. He was constantly interrupted by a withering fire of foundational objections (How does the witness know what he's talking about?) and relevancy objections (Do we really need to know this fact to decide the case?) from defense lawyers to every new question the attorney general wanted to ask Hall. Judge Nowlin overruled each time, but the torrent of lawyerly objections would not stop.

If the hearing were ever to end, Judge Nowlin had to curtail defense objections once rulings were made. Judicial assertiveness only grows from confidence gained through experience either as a trial lawyer or a judge. Lacking both experience and a law degree, Nowlin couldn't stem the tide. He didn't know where the law of evidence drew its lines in the sand or where permissible objections by the defense lawyers should begin or end. Who could blame Nowlin? No one had a right to ask him to do any better than he did. But obviously someone had.

Judge Nowlin had ordered the court reporter to prepare transcripts of the first two days of the preliminary hearing. When the hearing resumed on June 7, the prosecutors had copies, but defense lawyers had not been given copies, despite their requests. Now it emerged that the prosecutors had given a copy to a Phoenix television and radio reporter, Kathryn Smith of KOOL Radio and TV News. After harsh squabbling, Nowlin got in his first word of the day. "At this time we are going to stand at recess. I'll rule on the motion tomorrow at 1:00 o'clock." The preliminary hearing had reached a standstill.

The next day, however, Judge Nowlin did not get to rule on either motion. The defense had begun the day with a new peremptory attack, further bogging down the hearing: "Under Rule 10.1, Arizona rules of Criminal Procedure, I request the court bring in another judge to determine whether the court can continue in a fair and impartial manner," announced Glenn. His tangent was unpopular, and no other defense attorney joined in the motion.

"I'm going to deny the motion," Nowlin firmly announced, sensing by the refusal of defense lawyers to join the gambit that he was on strong ground.

"Your Honor, I don't think you have the power. Rule 10 provides, 'Promptly after the filing of the motion, the presiding judge shall provide for a hearing on the matter before a judge other than the judge challenged.' It's mandatory language."

Defense lawyers now backed up Glenn.

"If I may be heard, Your Honor," defense attorney Michael Beers interjected. "I'm afraid Mr. Glenn is right. I don't think this court has the authority to deny the motion to bring in another judge to hear this motion."

"Judge, the grounds arose yesterday," Glenn continued, announcing the substance of his complaint. "At that time it was discovered that Your Honor had provided to the prosecution those transcripts without giving the defense a chance to be heard on the matter. I had no prior knowledge this case could not be heard before this judge in a fair and impartial manner, and I filed the motion promptly upon reconvening of this court."

Nowlin jumped in, confident the gambit would fail through his foresight. "Mr. Glenn, I would like to read to you something that I wrote down purposely for this," he began. "I'm going to deny your motion to dismiss because at no time was there ever an order made to prevent you or any of the other defense attorneys from reading the transcripts Mr. Brown obtained from the court reporter. I did not at any time imply that the news reporters could not obtain one from the court reporter, nor did I make an order not allowing the state to read the transcripts provided for them. I took the transcripts from Attorney General Ford only to prevent him from being able to refer to it during the testimony of Mr. Toney and Mr. Jones."

Glenn held his ground. "This court has no power but to turn this matter over to the presiding judge of the county for assignment to a judge for hearing on the matter."

Genuinely perplexed, Judge Nowlin turned to the prosecutor, "Is this correct?"

Having no choice, Wilkes conceded the point.

Nowlin acquiesced, in resignation and disgust. "We will turn it over to Judge McBryde."

The preliminary hearing was now detoured until Judge E. D. McBryde, presiding judge of the superior court, could rule. But before then, the defense withdrew the request for a change of judge on June 21, believing the essential issue of entitlement to witness statements was already preserved for review by a higher court.

On the tenth day, the state's key witness, inmate Dominic Hall, the Aryan Brotherhood captain who had reluctantly orchestrated Small's murder, finally got to the meat and potatoes of his tale, casting a net large enough to ensnare all eleven defendants in a charge that Waymond Small died at the hands of a wide-ranging conspiracy of the Aryan Brotherhood.

From the outset, Judge Nowlin had shown noticeable pique with defense motions and objections. "Objection overruled," he trumpeted at once when Tidwell broke into the prosecution's first question for Hall.

"Would it be possible for me to state the reason for my objection, Your Honor?"

"No. We are going to get on with this preliminary hearing."

"I think I have a right to state the legal grounds of the objection," Tidwell asserted.

"Sit down, Mr. Tidwell, we are going to cross-examine this witness. I am not going to mess around today."

"Your Honor, I am not asking you to mess around, I am asking you to let me state on the record the reason for my objection."

"Go ahead and state your objection, but I have already ruled on it."

"Well, my objection is on the grounds that the question calls for hearsay. There is no foundation as to where the statement came from or how he found this information out. I would also like to add that I have never been in a situation where the court rules on an objection before I stated my argument."

With the day off to a rough start, Hall told his story, often interrupted by defense objections—all identical and routinely denied. Hall told how Farmer and Goff had worked in the print shop along with him. The day Small was killed, he saw Farmer leave, then return after lunch. Farmer told Hall, Farrell, and Belt that he'd stabbed Small and Goff had hit him with a hammer, then they went back to work. Hall saw Belt "trying to flush something down the toilet." Belt told Hall he'd cut up the clothes and flushed them, "but the pipes got plugged up." Belt had stashed in the restroom the clothes for Farmer and Goff to wear during the hit. Bilke asked Hall for the key to the padlock to the tag plant gate so that Goff and Farmer could more easily get back and forth. After the killing, back in the cell block, Breshears told Hall he'd supplied the hammer and "got rid" of the gloves Goff had worn. The killing had been planned since November 15, when Breshears, Hall, Bilke, and Farrell had discussed Small at the athletic field. Hall had discussed killing Small with Richard Compton and Farrell in the Catholic church on two Sundays, November 15 and 27. Compton, the "acting general" of the Aryan Brotherhood while Stretch was locked down, told Hall he had to "take care of Small and Gomes" or his own life "would be in danger." After the hit, Compton told him, "Good job."

While they were in lockup, Troy Killinger had sent "three or four" kites to Hall. Red Dog had sent "two or three," and Rusty Harbin sent two. The kites repeated the order to kill Small. There were two problems with Hall's testimony about these kites. Hall had never seen Troy's, Rusty's, or Red Dog's handwriting; he assumed all the kites were from them simply because James "Watermelon" Waltman, the porter who had brought them to him, had said so. After he read each kite, he threw it away.

Judge Nowlin cut off all objections and allowed Hall to tell what these handwritten notes said. "Why is Small still walking the yard? You better take care of it," was the gist of all seven.

Hall further testified that he had joined the Aryan Brotherhood in August 1977 as a soldier but was promoted to lieutenant and acting building captain. Captains and officers made the decisions. Stretch was the general, and Puff Huey, Troy, Compton, Burger Red, and Frank Farrell were the captains. The rules were that "You stuck up for each other, you washed each other's back, you obeyed all orders, respected all of your officers, and there was no way out other than death."

Some of the conspirators had met in the print shop during the workday on November 28 and 29 to perfect their plan. At Hall's request, inmate MacDonald ground a lump of steel into a shank for the hit, wrapping tape around the crude blade to fashion a handle.

With these bare essentials on record, prosecutor Wilkes announced that his examination was over.

The eleventh day brought the state's star witness back to the stand for cross-examination, undertaken entirely by Tidwell, now ascendant as lead defense counsel. Tidwell began on safe ground, laying out Hall's criminal history, beginning in California in 1969 at age twenty-three and escalating in severity over time, all of it fueled by heroin addiction and the need for quick money for the next fix. Hall drifted to Tucson, Arizona, where he was convicted in April 1976 for forgery. The plea agreement dismissed "three or four additional forgeries" and sent Hall to prison until he honored America's Independence Day by declaring one for himself and escaping from Fort Grant over the holiday. His liberty lasted three days until he held up a store using a toy gun. With this escapade and convictions for escape and armed robbery, Hall earned his first serious prison sentence: ten years.

The artful examiner pursues no obvious pattern with his questions, keeping the witness on edge as the topic changes, then returning to key themes, asking the same questions in new ways. Thus, Tidwell repeatedly asked Hall about his place of confinement and cell mates, the better to learn the names of everyone Hall might have talked to about this case.

The gambit showed that the state's key white witnesses, Hall and Farrell, were cell mates, at their request, and shared a strong, perhaps even intimate, bond. This suggested that the two were cohorts in a new conspiracy: to tell all about the Aryan Brotherhood to earn protection and become perpetual cell mates, for indeed they'd been each other's only cell mates since their removal from Arizona State Prison.

Farrell and Hall had been cell mates in the Pima County Jail for six weeks in 1975. Farrell had made the evening news as the "Cowboy Bandit" for his habit of wearing a cowboy hat during his heists. Farrell and Hall again celled together for three months in Arizona State Prison. Two months after Small's murder, on January 27, 1978, Farrell "got a hit on him by the Aryan Brotherhood." Hall heard the sounds of a struggle and attack at 3 a.m. from his adjoining cell and was "pretty upset" because he considered Farrell "his best friend." The stabbing convinced Hall to "give up the AB" the next day, immediately earning transfer to protective custody.

As Hall stated, after Farrell "got stuck on the twenty-seventh, they called me to the warden's office about 9 a.m. I don't know to this day why they called me in, but I told them right then that I was going to give up the Aryan Brotherhood." Before the DPS investigators asked any questions, Hall "told them that I was glad that he called me over because I had something to tell him." They asked Hall if he knew the AB had a hit on his head. Hall knew because Warden Cardwell had told him that inmate Schumaker, Hall's cell mate on January 27, was supposed to have killed Hall at the same time Cowboy was hit. Hall's story left the unmistakable impression that the administration and the Department of Public Safety investigators had arranged to use the convict code to turn him into a snitch, as had been done with Robert Toney.

After Farrell got out of the hospital from the attack, Hall and Farrell were again cell mates and naturally talked about the Small killing. Tidwell dug for specifics. "What did Mr. Farrell tell you about this incident?"

"He just said he was going to give it up," answered Hall. "He was going to testify because they stabbed him . . . they did him wrong and there was no reason for it. He was just really, you know, disappointed in the whole Aryan Brotherhood trip and said that he had nothing to lose. They already attempted to take his life and his life was in danger right now and he's living on borrowed time. He said the Aryan Brotherhood was a 'bunch of bullshit.'"

In Hall's first conversation with Captain Davis, he didn't talk about the Small murder but later agreed to talk about the killing once he was told he wouldn't be charged.

When Tidwell learned that Hall's January 28 statement had been tape recorded, he asked for a copy. Then he learned that Hall's January 30 statement, which lasted twelve hours, had been tape recorded as well. With this revelation, he called a halt, declaring, "Your Honor, I find it impossible to go on at this point if they have twelve hours' worth of conversation with this man regarding this killing." Tidwell became indignant: "I can recall two additional times that the prosecutors have not provided the relevant discovery. Today I have found two more times. I can't effectively cross-examine this man without his prior statements. They've had since January 30, 1978, to find out about this tape recording, a twelve-hour tape, and they come forth before this court [today] and say, 'We don't know anything about it.'"

Judge Nowlin tried to seize control, ordering the attorney general's office to provide the tape recording to defense counsel. The hearing was then postponed indefinitely for the attorney general to comply by finding the tape recordings and having them transcribed.

Prosecutor Wilkes announced that only Farrell remained to be called as a witness. Even so, could the state ever bring the hearing to an end?

In two days Judge Nowlin reconvened the preliminary hearing. He had read a transcript of Hall's statements, excised portions not dealing with

Waymond Small's murder, and given defense lawyers the redacted document.

The defense wasn't buying. Phil Glenn asked, "Do any of the statements that the court has read pertain to the Aryan Brotherhood?" Nowlin conceded the point, so Glenn protested, asking for the entire statement.

Prosecutor Wilkes had no objection if the statements were sealed for any further proceedings and so long as the defendants at the preliminary hearing only received "those portions which the court has found to deal solely with the Small matter."

Attorney Brown immediately confronted Judge Nowlin with his logical inconsistency. Nowlin had admitted general testimony about the Aryan Brotherhood's practices and so had determined that this type of information was "not relevant and material in these proceedings. Now it either wasn't material two days ago and it wasn't relevant and it shouldn't have come in, or it's still material and it's still relevant and I am entitled to this statement on that subject."

Judge Nowlin wouldn't yield, but he didn't proceed either: "I can't give you this stuff because of the fact of the contents. I wish I could but it pertains to stuff that I will just not—if you get it you will have to take special action to get it in the superior court. In here is, each of you, a copy of the material here, and this court is at recess until further notice."

On June 20, the thirteenth day of the hearing floundered in futility as the preliminary hearing sputtered with its last signs of life. How else to characterize a day in which not one shred of testimony was taken, the state refused to give defense counsel a transcript of Hall's twelve-hour statement to investigators about the Aryan Brotherhood, the judge sided with the attorney general, and the eleven defense lawyers split into shifting camps vacillating between whether to accept excised transcripts or to take another appeal by special action to the superior court.

Prosecutor Wilkes indicated that investigator DeSanti was keeping the twelve-hour tape as "intelligence tapes, separate and apart from the Small investigation" because they dealt with other matters, so they need not be produced. Release of the entire tapes would provoke "threats to witnesses, threats to inmates, families, children, wives, and jeopardize certain prison officials and civilians." Defense lawyers wanted the entire statement. "The question involved here is not whether cross-examination will be limited attorney Brown insisted, but whether effective cross-examination will be permitted."

Seeking another compromise, Judge Nowlin inquired, "Would any other defense counsel like to be heard? If not, then I will ask that the attorneys all go in chambers with me, and this will be gone over to prove to you that this should not be disclosed," hoping defense counsel would acquiesce if they could read the transcript of the twelve-hour interview themselves, though not obtain copies. "Mr. Brown, we will go in chambers without the court reporter, and one of you attorneys can read it aloud to everybody there."

"I for one don't want to go off the record. Whether in chambers or in open court, I demand that it be on the record," Glenn interjected, with a show of emotional outrage.

Prosecutor Wilkes objected even to this, claiming, "Some of the contents are so sensitive it is the state's position it cannot even be read to the defense counsel," stymieing Judge Nowlin's attempt at compromise.

"Last week the attorney general was directed to provide a copy of all of the relevant material. [Instead] they have given us five or six paragraphs of a twelve-hour tape recording," Tidwell chimed in, pointing out that the state was attempting to maneuver out of the court's direct order.

Judge Nowlin cut in, saying, "I would never provide this statement for you in writing and have the prison population get a hold of it. But if you would like to go in chambers and read this, not in its entirety, but you may read only the portions that would not be harmful to someone, and you will probably get to read 90 percent of the statement."

Realizing that Nowlin might be giving the defense a no-lose straddle, defense lawyers broke ranks. Lawyers Tidwell and Brown announced after recess they were interested in following up on Judge Nowlin's compromise offer to read the transcript of the tape recording, but the other defense lawyers disagreed, preferring instead to seek a recess and file an immediate appeal by special action to the superior court and to ask that court to order production of Hall's twelve-hour statement. Straddling the straddle, some of the defense lawyers further split, saying they'd be interested in reading Hall's statement now, with the understanding that they could join in the special action to obtain a transcript of the full statement.

Anarchy reigned. No one knew the next move, prompting defense attorney Beers to lament: "I don't want to take a special action. I want to know exactly what is going to happen here." A second recess ensued at the request of defense lawyers, with Brown then announcing, "It is my understanding that at this time we are willing to proceed with the hearing as outlined this morning."

Prosecutor Wilkes called DeSanti as a witness, eliciting pat responses utterly lacking in specifics. The excised portions of Hall's statement did not "relate to the Small matter," DeSanti said, but revealing them "would jeopardize ongoing investigations" and lead to "potential harm." Nothing was specific. No cross-examination was afforded to defense counsel, and all defense lawyers got a five-page, excised copy of Hall's statement.

The thirteenth day of the hearing had been an unlucky one for the state. Defense lawyers had another round loaded, and ready to fire, to stop the hearing in its tracks. They could file another special action any time before the state completed its case, bringing another halt to the state's convoluted attempt to establish probable cause to bring the defendants to trial for their lives.

The state's patience may have broken on June 22 when Harry Bagnall, Belt's lawyer, began the next day with a motion to recess the preliminary hearing during his upcoming three-week personal vacation. Judge Nowlin readily agreed. The proceeding began with attorneys Bagnall, Glenn, and Beers requesting that Judge Nowlin exclude guard personnel from the courtroom because they were the source of vicious rumors circulating in the prison, some of which were "just out of this world." The rumors in turn were leading to "threats on the lives of these defendants." "Threats have been made on prisoners and their families," said attorney Bohm. "It has been accepted by this court that certain members of the general public's lives have been threatened. To allow threats and possible violence to be carried out upon the families of the prisoners is just as great as a threat upon the families of the guards and of the witnesses." Prosecutor Wilkes objected: "We are entitled to the security of these guards."

Tidwell joined the fray, "I don't think anybody in their right mind objects to security. My objection, and I think Mr. Bagnall's objection, is who is providing the security? There are six people in the courtroom who are employees of the Arizona State Prison Department of Corrections that answer to the administration officials, and the administration officials have been on television and stated various things. Warden Cardwell has been on TV saying he wants the death penalty for all of the defendants. I think that the possibility of the information that goes on in this courtroom getting back to the administration officials is great. I am asking you to replace these guards with five or six deputy county sheriffs."

"I will not remove the guards from the courtroom," Judge Nowlin decided. Yet in his growing sympathy with defense requests, he added, "but I will talk to the sheriff's office and see if he will provide employees down here when we reconvene in July." The defense wasn't satisfied. Bagnall requested that the guards be admonished not to repeat any of the testimony heard in the courtroom.

"This is a public hearing — public record," Wilkes objected. "They are not witnesses. An order directing them not to discuss what they heard in here would 'not be within the realm of the rules. . . . not authorized by law.'"

"Your Honor, relevant discovery material has been kept from us on the basis of Mr. DeSanti's vague allegation that it is going to result in threats to unknown people," Michael Beers continued, hoisting the state upon its own petard. "We have come in here and given specific reasons why these guards, if they go back to the prison and are talking to the prisoners, it will result in specific threats against these specific defendants and their families. If Mr. DeSanti's avowal to the court, or whatever it was, is sufficient to keep relevant disclosure from us, then what we have said here today has got to be sufficient to give this court the power and right to admonish these guards not to talk about this case with anybody."

"I will take this under advisement and talk to Judge Platt and we will work on it from there," Nowlin intoned, conceding yet again and seeking a delay to get help with yet another thorny conundrum beyond his analytical domain.

More wrangling was in store as Tidwell broached a new subject: "I would like to get one thing on the record. If anybody from the prosecution, DPS, or a guard wants to talk to my client about this case, I would ask that they come to me beforehand and not consult with my client without talking to me."

Judge Nowlin tried to mollify Tidwell with common sense, "You should so instruct your client."

"My problem is," Tidwell continued, "that my client is hardly in a position to argue at length with the prison administration or DPS. They have a very unique position; they can chain the man and then talk to him without my being there, and I don't want it to happen. If they want to talk to my client, they have a duty to come to me and not approach him without my permission; I want that on the record. And if violated, I am going to raise Cain."

"Show that all of the counsel feel the same way as Mr. Tidwell," Judge Nowlin noted as ten heads bobbed in unison with Tidwell's growled warning.

The questioning of Hall resumed, but it became snarled by yet another failure of the prosecutors to provide Hall's written statements. Hall testified that he had prepared a list of all members of the Aryan Brotherhood and their ranks for DPS investigators.

"Your Honor, once again, for the umpteenth time, written statements by the witnesses were not provided to myself prior to my cross-examination, as directed by Rule 5.3," Tidwell railed in fury. "The court ordered that I be provided a copy of the statement and I would ask that the court order them to provide me with a copy."

"We haven't been able to find it," came Wilkes's tired answer. "This was a list of names. Maybe if counsel would like, he can ask the witness here if he can give him a list that was there."

"I would ask the court to direct him to provide that to me before I continue my cross-examination," Tidwell demanded. "This is the heart of one of the charges. Who was in the Aryan Brotherhood? Who, according to Mr. Hall, had power to order things within the AB?"

"I don't know what happened to it," Wilkes repeated. "We are trying to find it. We have attempted to locate this, and I cannot, Your Honor."

"Your Honor," added Bill Haus, making his first comment in fourteen days. "I would even suggest that the disappearance of the piece of paper that would purportedly show the names and rank of the members of the Aryan Brotherhood is more than just coincidental. I think it very possibly could have been deliberate. I think Your Honor has every right and should positively order the state to bring that list forward now, so we can properly effect our cross-examination, to possibly show that certain persons, my client being one of them, could not in any way have been involved in this conspiracy; it is very vital to my case, Your Honor."

The judge tried to bull ahead. "The state has indicated that it is not available at this time and they are looking for it. We will proceed right now."

"Is the court not ordering them to provide the information?" Tidwell asked.

"It is unavailable. There is no way they can produce it," Nowlin growled.

"I think they have an obligation to put Mr. DeSanti on the stand and testify that it is unavailable," Tidwell parried. "Mr. Wilkes's statement that it is not available does not suffice as far as I am concerned. If they have lost it, fine, let them come forth now and tell us how they lost it, or where they last saw it. I want somebody under oath to say 'We lost it.'"

Tidwell's point carried the moment. Investigator John DeSanti was again called to the stand. DeSanti was evasive. Yes, Hall had made a list of the Aryan Brotherhood membership, but, no, DeSanti didn't know where it was and couldn't be sure if it had been destroyed or lost, or might still turn up someday even though DeSanti personally placed the list in a safe at the Arizona State Prison security office when he obtained it four months ago. From the safe, DeSanti moved the list to his desk drawer, but he'd never looked for it there.

"No real effort has obviously been made to locate this list," Brown objected upon hearing DeSanti's admissions. "I blame the DPS, for they haven't done what they should have done to produce this statement. I would therefore move that, until the state can satisfy us that they have made some effort to locate it, that the testimony of this witness be held in abeyance."

Nowlin had heard enough. "Mr. Brown, I'm going to deny your motion, we will call a witness now and start with our proceedings." The examination then became a test of memory. "What names did you write on the list?" was the subject for several hours.

After morning recess, Stretch Hillyer attempted to fire Haus. In a quivering, meek voice, Stretch told Judge Nowlin, "I have a conflict of interest with my lawyer, and I would like to represent myself and have him dismissed. I don't see how we can go on with him sitting here and just not doing nothing."

"That's curious," Tidwell thought to himself as he listened. "This man is supposed to be the general of the fearsome Aryan Brotherhood, but he's obviously nervous standing up and talking in this courtroom."

Nowlin rebuffed Stretch, "If Mr. Haus is to be dismissed, it will be in superior court and not in this court."

The balance of the day was spent proving that the brotherhood didn't operate much like an army. Officers' ranks changed willy-nilly. Hall was designated "acting captain" by Puff Huey, not Stretch, the supposed general. Though every member of the AB supposedly had an equal vote on who would be a member, and all decisions would be made by a majority vote, no vote occurred over the decision to hit Waymond Small. Nonetheless, as Hall admitted, he went ahead with it anyway.

At the next recess, Stretch upped the ante on his bid to rid himself of his unwanted lawyer. Haus filed a written motion for his removal, signed by Stretch. Nowlin denied the motion again and offered to allow Haus to stay as advisory counsel if Stretch wished to represent himself.

"Judge, I would like Mr. Haus gone off completely, and not as advisory counsel," Stretch answered. "I don't know if Mr. Tidwell could do it or not, but I would like to ask him if he would help me along."

The court permitted Tidwell, Haus, and Stretch a recess to talk.

"I don't see any conflict if I represent Hillyer and Killinger and both men agree," Tidwell told Judge Nowlin. Tidwell had already represented Stretch on a previous murder charge. Nowlin consented; Haus was discharged; Tidwell now had two clients.

As the questioning of Hall resumed, Tidwell plumbed new ground. Though also ordered to hit Destiny, Hall did nothing and suffered no consequences. When ordered to hit Woodstock the day after he was sworn in, Hall didn't attempt the hit, and he suffered no punishment. In fact, Hall testified he sent a kite to the administration in August 1977 concerning the hit but didn't sign it for "fear that the administration might front me off or somebody might have seen me or seen the kite in the yard office."

"What does 'front you off' mean?" Tidwell asked.

"They might have just called me out," Hall explained, "and talked to me in front of other brothers and stuff and somebody in the yard office—one of the inmates there might have seen the kite."

Sending such a kite would be a violation of AB rules: "It's the same thing as snitching. You don't go to the man for anything like that," Hall said. Hall testified he had sent two kites to the prison administration warning about the AB hits on Small and Gomes. He did this after he got the hit orders from Troy.

"What did they say?" Tidwell asked.

"They better get Small and Gomes out of CB-3 because there is a hit on them," Hall answered.

According to Hall, he had done everything possible to keep from killing Small prior to November 28, and even before that, he had participated in a vote on a previous AB hit. "Red Dog, myself, Puff Huey, and Stretch Hillyer sat in the kitchen, in chow, and discussed what we should do to Greek," Hall testified. "We talked it over and I had said I thought Greek was a good dude and I didn't have anything against him," and "Puff said that he would take any responsibility if it was later found out that Greek had been snitching or doing something behind his back, he would watch Greek," and so "it was decided not to hit him." Stretch had wanted to make a hit on Greek, but Puff Huey talked him out of it. "Stretch said, 'Did you hear about Greek?' And we didn't know what he was talking about, and he explained to us that he was in PC and he knows a lot of information and you know, knows — you might as well hit him."

Hall recruited Belt, Bilke, Farmer, Goff, and Rooster into the AB and admitted them on his own "say-so," without getting Killinger's or Stretch's opinion, because he had been told he could do so by Puff Huey. Hall began to fear a threat to his own life from the Aryan Brotherhood when he failed to carry out a hit on Destiny: "I began to think that the odds would be pretty good, because Destiny was still alive." He wrote a kite to Stretch about the hit, using a code, but he never got an answer.

"How did the code work?" Tidwell asked. He then learned Hall had written for DeSanti how the code worked, and Tidwell asked for the document.

"Your Honor, I don't think we have that written piece of paper," Wilkes droned in dread of another diversion. "If we have it we can bring it back whenever we reconvene. The state will make every effort to get it here for them," he promised.

"Let's continue until they produce the code and the other statements that Mr. Hall gave them," Tidwell countered. "This is getting a little absurd. They have lost clothing, they have lost diagrams, they lost evidence, they've misplaced almost all of it, and finally find parts of it. Perhaps we should recess long enough to let the attorney general's office go back and find all this material, then we can start again. They have had six to eight months to do it."

Nowlin quickly agreed and ordered the court to recess for at least three weeks. The state, however, didn't wait that long to abort its own stillborn creation. The hearing never resumed.

The locals of Casa Grande, the largest city in Pinal County, learned of the state's decision to abandon the preliminary hearing while sipping their morning coffee and reading the *Casa Grande Dispatch*:

Eleven inmates charged with the knife and hammer slaying of another convict pleaded innocent today after weeks of legal proceedings which have cost taxpayers close to $40,000.00.

A preliminary hearing for the inmates began May 18, but was supplanted last week when a special grand jury returned indictments against the convicts which were handed down after about six hours of testimony.

Persons charged with crimes can be bound over for trial in two ways, either by indictment through a grand jury or by a preliminary hearing.

Originally, a hearing was chosen for this case so that testimony given could be admitted at later legal proceedings in case some of the witnesses were unavailable.

However, after six weeks lapsed at high cost to taxpayers, the prosecutors asked for a grand jury, reported Superior Court Judge E. D. McBryde.

Fees totaling $41,522 had been paid to defense attorneys by Arizona's taxpayers because every defendant was indigent. The citizenry had also paid the prosecutors, investigators, prison guards, judge, court clerk, and court reporters. However, the "high cost to taxpayers" did not explain why the state had given up on the preliminary hearing that had been covered for six weeks by Arizona's newspapers, radio, and television media. The prosecutors' concern for expense was prattle for public consumption and political camouflage for their failures. Bungling of evidence by prosecutors and investigators had dealt a fatal blow to completion of the preliminary hearing. Besides, another legal thicket reared its head during the hearing, offering prosecutors Ford and Wilkes a pretext to abandon the effort.

Inmate Carl Eugene Mixon stood charged with the prison murder of convict Roy Ropeter. Mixon told his lawyers that he was an Aryan Brotherhood member and that "General" Stretch Hillyer had ordered him to kill Ropeter. Phil Glenn and Robert Brown had been appointed as Mixon's lawyers. They also represented Farmer and Goff in the Small murder. The two defense lawyers asked prosecutors Wilkes and Ford to interview Mixon to see if he could also help the state prosecute the Small murders.

The street-smart Mixon knew he held a trump card he could play to his own and other convicts' advantage. If he could testify for the state in the Small case, he'd help himself get a shorter sentence for the Ropeter killing, but he'd also disqualify Glenn and Brown from representing Farmer and Goff in the Small murder. If Glenn and Brown were disqualified, the state would have to start all over again with the preliminary hearing, with Farmer and Goff getting new lawyers.

When the prosecutors talked to Mixon, he knew enough to intrigue and tantalize them. They told Glenn and Brown they would use Mixon as a witness in both the Ropeter and Small murder cases. In exchange, Mixon got a reduced charge and beat the death penalty. Had Mixon gamed the system while playing both sides and helping old friends? Or had Ford and Wilkes found in the discovery of this new witness an excuse to abandon the preliminary hearing? Ford and Wilkes knew that saying the state intended to call Mixon as a witness would compel attorneys Glenn and Brown to withdraw. A lawyer cannot represent both a criminal defendant and his accusers at trial.

When Glenn and Brown asked Judge Nowlin the next day, June 29, 1978, for permission to withdraw, their request had to be granted. The endless preliminary hearing would have to start over—or the state could go to a grand jury for a rubber-stamp indictment.

The media never questioned the attorney general's performance or decisions. The public never knew the truth. But the prisoners knew the scorecard now read: Convicts, 1; State of Arizona, 0. The state never called Mixon as a witness at any of the five subsequent trials of Waymond Small's accused murderers, leaving the impression that the prosecutors had used Mixon as a face-saving device to drop the preliminary hearing. Undoubtedly, the state inflicted upon itself incalculable damage from holding the preliminary hearing. Owing to their inexperience with the vagaries of prosecuting prison crimes, Arizona's attorneys general failed to foresee those consequences. On each of the fourteen days of the preliminary hearing, the eleven defendants were assembled together, in one place, where they heard the state's case in detail and—in spite of the presence of prison guards—agreed on a clever defense playing to racial prejudice and stereotypes.

Transportation of the eleven defendants to court created a surfeit of opportunities for clandestine conversation. Once guards removed each convict from his isolation cell, the Florence Eleven had to be placed together in one holding cell, and no guard remained in their midst.

Once assembled, the Florence Eleven were chained together in one long train. Consequently, all eleven enjoyed another chance to powwow in hushed tones. Assembled closely together throughout the day, passing kites became incredibly easy, on the bus, in the court, or in the holding cells. While inside Pinal County Jail, situated across a narrow alley from the courthouse, the conspirators enjoyed easy communication among themselves, for the jail lacked segregation facilities and was already was filled with its usual patrons. Riding on the bus to and from prison, even though the distance was less than two miles, convicts sat inside the buses for anywhere from thirty to sixty minutes each way, giving them time for a daily postmortem on the proceedings. For security reasons, prison guards were not be positioned amid the prisoners on the bus rides. Making matters even easier, racist prison guards sympathized with the Florence Eleven. They made no effort to enforce silence among the unruly bunch and put forth little effort to intercept their kites. Warden Cardwell gave no marching orders to the escorting contingent of guards to thwart the convicts' efforts to talk among themselves. In fact, the norm inside a prison cell block is an incoherent cacophony of voices. Prisoners shout over one another to carry on separate conversations above the din. The decibel level inside the typical prison makes the noise level of howling monkeys and screaming birds emanating from a teeming African rain forest seem like a calm prairie day. Habituated to such bedlam, guards and prisoners alike expected the bus ride to and from court to be no different. Underneath the incoherent babbling drone, prisoners made themselves well understood to each other as they planned their clever defense against the state's case, courtesy of the state's ill-conceived decision to hold a preliminary hearing instead of obtaining rubber-stamped indictments in secret from a grand jury.

9 Breaking into Prison

Two weeks after their indictment, the Florence Eleven still may have hoped that the political spotlight on the prison would blow over and the Small homicide would be dealt with in the usual way. Until Sunday, July 30, 1978, the legislature, the governor, and the Department of Corrections thought news from Arizona State Prison couldn't get any worse. But it did. It got much worse. That day, convicted murderers Gary Tison and Randy Greenawalt escaped from Arizona State Prison in a daring breakout, aided by Tison's three sons. The violence had now spilled out of the prison's walls—every citizen's nightmare. The victims were no longer prisoners, they were white, middle-class, innocent, and all-American.

Dorothy, Gary's wife of twenty-one years, and his sons—Ricky, Raymond, and Donald, aged eighteen, nineteen, and twenty—visited Gary in Arizona State Prison every single weekend. While other boys spent their weekends with friends or in school and church activities, the three brothers joined their mother on weekly pilgrimages to Florence and the prison, for Dorothy worshipped this armed robber and murderer. She inculcated into their sons her belief that their father had been wrongfully sentenced and imprisoned—a shibboleth fed into juvenile minds for so long by a manipulative, sociopathic father and an emotionally stunted mother that the three sons believed it as an article of faith and a fact of life. The family's mission became breaking Dad out of prison, and Gary manipulated his sons and wife to be tools to seize his freedom regardless of the price to them.

The prison administration and guards treated Gary Tison as a favorite, which was strange because Tison had committed a truly unforgivable crime from the point of view of any guard or warden. He had murdered a prison guard hostage during one of his numerous escapes. The guards supervising visitation recognized the family from their weekly pilgrimages. This familiarity dulled the guards' normal caution, assuring the success of Tison's bold gambit on this particular Sunday, when the sons came to visit Gary one more time.

Ricky, Raymond, and Donald smuggled three shotguns into the visiting rooms of the medium-security area of the prison, locked two guards in a locker, walked out the front door with Gary and another convicted murderer, Randy Greenawalt, and simply drove away—all without an alarm being raised or a single shot fired. "We had ample security for a breakout, but we weren't adequately prepared for a break-in. We were vulnerable at the front door," Warden Cardwell told the *Arizona Republic*. Before this break-in, visitors weren't searched for weapons when they entered the prison. Thirteen days after Tison escaped, Warden Cardwell assured the public they now would be.

The group's escape vehicle, a black 1966 Lincoln Continental licensed to Tison's brother Joe, had no spare, and the four tires on the vehicle were bald. Loaded down with five passengers and a trunk full of camping and escape gear, one of the Lincoln's tires blew late at night, thirty-six hours into their escape and two hundred miles from the prison in the solitary fastness of the Mohave Desert. Though the gang was stranded, its whereabouts remained a complete mystery to Arizona law enforcement.

Marine Sgt. John Lyons, traveling with his young family, stopped to aid the stranded motorist on the desolate road. The Tison gang rewarded his act of compassion with lead. To commandeer the Lyons' small Mazda, the gang herded the family into the Lincoln, where, as they huddled in abject terror, wondering their fate, the dimwitted Gary and cowardly Greenawalt executed their benefactors, discharging countless shotgun blasts into the car. This mindless slaughter ended the lives of Sgt. John Lyons; his wife, Donelda; their twenty-two-month-old son; and their fifteen-year-old niece, Teresa Tyson. Tison and Greenawalt weren't even competent executioners. After the gang departed, Teresa Tyson, no relation to her similarly named killers, lived long enough to drag her tortured body a quarter mile from the Lincoln, back toward Highway 95, before she died from massive bleeding.

Intense media coverage had already been shrill and incessant from the day of the daring escape, but now, after a passing motorist discovered the grisly scene in the Mohave Desert, Arizona's radio and television stations, and newspapers were flooded with news of the Tison gang's horrible deed. Amazingly, worse news was still to come.

Four days later, law enforcement nearly captured the Tison gang in Flagstaff, but they had otherwise remained clueless as the psychopaths aimlessly wandered the back roads of the Four Corners area. After thirteen days, Gary's homing instinct got the better of him, and he returned to his hometown roost, a mere thirty-five miles from the prison. The exhausted gang stumbled into a roadblock on the Papago Indian Reservation, twenty-five miles south of Casa Grande, near the Indian outpost of Chuichi. The roadblock had been set up at this unlikely spot on the chance Tison would be foolish enough to return home, then make a run for Mexico at an isolated border crossing. Tison behaved true to form—on every other escape he'd returned to Casa Grande, the town that held maximum peril because nowhere else on earth was he so infamous.

Donald Tison, driving a van with Texas plates, died in a hail of bullets. Ricky and Raymond Tison and Randy Greenawalt scampered from the disabled van to find cover in the desert before meekly surrendering, still clutching the weapons they dared not use. Gary, however, gave it a go, escaping into the desert. The four square miles of the surrounding desert was searched meticulously on foot, horseback, and helicopters, but Tison evaded the manhunt by hiding less than a mile away, under dense brush in a hole beside a desert wash. Eleven days later, circling buzzards and the overwhelming odor of a rotting corpse led to the discovery of Tison's last hiding place, beside the Tat Momoli Mountains. Rather than surrender, he had died a horrible death from heat exhaustion and thirst under the brutal August desert sun.

The Texas plates on the getaway van were traced back to newlyweds Mr. and Mrs. James Judge of Amarillo. The honeymooners had last been seen in the San Juan Mountains outside South Fork, Colorado. Though the Tison gang was never tried for the Judges' murders, no doubt exists that they claimed their fifth and sixth victims when stealing the Judges' van. The bodies of the newlyweds were found near Chimney Rock, Colorado, close to Highway 160, the Tison's route of flight.

Unbelievably, the coda to the Tison story nearly became a replay of the original. While in the Pinal County jail awaiting a court hearing on charges arising from their father's prison escape, Ricky and Raymond Tison themselves escaped. Theirs, however, was a far less dramatic enterprise than any of their father's. Within twelve hours, bloodhounds had found the fugitives hiding in irrigated fields not far from the jail. The Tison boys have never seen the outside of a jail or prison wall since that day—and probably never will.

The public was clamoring for blood to avenge the prison's serial outrages. With this latest incarceration fiasco, it was a sure bet that the murderers of Waymond Small would pay a price. Now there could be no letting up on any prosecution of prison crimes. The politicians, the warden, and the prosecutors urged death penalties for the Florence Eleven and the surviving members of the Tison-Greenawalt gang.

Rep. Peter Kay (R-Phoenix), House Judiciary Committee chairman, told the *Arizona Republic* that the Tison-Greenawalt case "abundantly demonstrates the need for the death penalty in Arizona. It is just tragic that the U.S. Supreme Court has been so equivocal in its divided opinions recently. They have done a great disservice to the people of the United States." ·

Sen. Jones Osborn (D-Yuma), Senate Judiciary Committee chairman, said that the death penalty was justified "if it can be proven that the fugitives murdered the Lyons family. I think it's tragic that these inmates could have broken out of prison so easily. It's inexcusable. I want to see a full investigation of this."

Rep. Peter Dunn (R-Phoenix) expressed outrage that Tison and Greenawalt escaped from a medium-security section of the prison. "An immediate investigation should be undertaken of the prison-classification system," Dunn declared. "Incredibly, prison officials were notified this year by law enforcement officials that Tison was planning a breakout, and officials left him in medium security. Whoever is responsible should be fired immediately." That person was Warden Cardwell. Inmate Bobby Tuzon had notified him beforehand of Tison's escape plan, and the *Arizona Republic* now let the public know Cardwell had been warned.

In this charged and poisoned political environment, the Florence Eleven awaited trial for the conspiracy and murder of Waymond Small. What Las Vegas bookie would have given odds of one thousand to one that any of the Florence Eleven would receive a fair trial, much less an acquittal, from the jurors of Pinal County, the home of Arizona State Prison, the cesspool where society threw its rejected losers to be isolated and punished?

PART III THE TRIALS

10 Severance

In a single indictment, the grand jury charged the Florence Eleven conspirators with murder and conspiracy to murder Waymond Small. In so doing, the state proposed to try all eleven men at one time, repeating the fiasco of the preliminary hearing, but the judge possessed the procedural power to grant separate trials.

Predictably, the trial judge faced eleven defense motions for severance of trial. Constitutional grounds afforded the most logical point of beginning for Judge William E. Platt's decision matrix as he decided how to rule on the severance motions. The Sixth Amendment to the U.S. Constitution affords the criminal defendant the right to confront and cross-examine his accusers. Under rules of evidence developed over centuries in the English common-law tradition, the out-of-court statement of an accused is admissible against him to prove his guilt. Confessions or admissions of guilt or complicity in a crime are the most straightforward examples of these out-of-court statements the jury may hear.

When two or more criminal defendants are tried at the same time for the same crime, one defendant may have given a confession or made an admission that damaged both himself and his co-defendant. However, the Fifth Amendment to the Constitution's protection against self-incrimination means that no criminal defendant can be forced to testify during his trial. Separate trials are often required to preserve each criminal defendants' Fifth and Sixth Amendment rights when one defendant has made a statement that damages his co-defendant. How can one co-defendant cross-examine his accuser—in this case his own co-defendant—when he cannot force that co-defendant to take the witness stand? A joint trial at which the prosecution seeks to admit a statement of one co-defendant to convict the other creates irreconcilable contradiction between one co-defendant's Sixth Amendment right and the other's Fifth Amendment right. In *Bruton v. United States,* 391 US 123 (1968), the U.S. Supreme Court created the constitutional remedy for this conundrum: separate trials.

The Bruton principle meant that Stretch Hillyer, the general of the Aryan Brotherhood, because of his confession to having ordered the Waymond Small hit, would have to be tried separately from all other defendants. In its fall-back position, the attorney general proposed three trials, agreeing that the Bruton principle required a separate trial for Hillyer. The attorney general requested that Terry Farmer, Ernest Goff, Richard Compton, William Howard, Russell Harbin, and Troy Killinger be tried first; Michael Belt, Mitchell Bilke, Willard Breshears, and James McDonald be tried second; and Jerry Hillyer be tried last and separately.

The rationale for the attorney general's first two groupings arose from the Fifth Amendment self-incrimination problems arising from Farmer's and Goff's statements, given to defense investigators, which cleared co-defendants Belt, Bilke, Breshears, and McDonald. Since in their statements Farmer and Goff had denied they'd acted with the assistance and cooperation of any other co-defendant—in short, because their statement denied that a conspiracy had existed—the attorney general agreed that those co-defendants would want to call Farmer and Goff in their defense. Moreover, the attorney general agreed they could not do so if their trials were joined because of Farmer's and Goff's Fifth Amendment privilege against self-incrimination.

However, the attorney general didn't believe that the kite senders were entitled to separate trials, since their defenses were not "on a single collision course" with one another. Compton, Howard, Harbin, and Killinger were "free to say that they never sent the orders and Farmer and Goff can testify it was self-defense" at their trials.

The Florence Eleven requested eleven trials; no one agreed to be tried with any other co-defendant. Taking the most aggressive tack, Harry Bagnall, the lawyer for Michael Belt, asked not only for a separate trial but also for a grant of immunity for any inmate who testified on Belt's behalf and for "all of the remaining ten defendants [who would testify] on his behalf and in the trial of his case."

Stephen Bogard, Goff's attorney, laid the groundwork to ensure that Goff and Farmer could not be tried together, because of Fifth Amendment problems. "Defendant Terry Lee Farmer has previously made a statement which in effect exculpates Defendant Goff but he will not take the stand at a joint trial with Defendant Goff and Farmer but rather assert his Fifth Amendment privilege to remain silent so as not to jeopardize his own defense at the expense of exculpating Defendant Goff. Therefore, Defendant Goff submits that he should be tried separately from Defendant Farmer."

Robert Boehm, Richard Compton's attorney, wanted a separate trial for his client to avoid "guilt by association." "In the opinion of Defendant Compton, the evidence against several of the defendants is great, with there being both items of physical evidence and witnesses to their alleged participation. On the other hand, the evidence against defendant Compton and several other defendants consists only of the unsubstantiated statements of two unindicted co-conspirators. Defendant Compton fears that the evidence against other of the defendants will sway the jury and that he will be found guilty because of their guilt."

Leonard Sowers, James McDonald's lawyer, had different reasons why his client should get a trial all his own:

"Co-defendants Belt, Bilke, Goff, and Farmer are in a position to offer exculpatory testimony as to defendant McDonald" but would "wish to assert their Fifth Amendment rights during the joint trial involving McDonald." Therefore, "McDonald is clearly entitled to a severance of his trial from that of the other individuals." McDonald's attorney wanted the court to "grant use immunity to a co-defendant willing to give exculpatory testimony on behalf of defendant McDonald. . . . Since the government has given immunity to Hall and Farrell for their testimony, the court has the inherent power to grant use immunity to another individual in order to make his testimony and evidence available to the defendant.

William O'Neill, attorney for Willard Breshears, raised "antagonistic defense" as his grounds for a separate trial. Breshears "will want to comment upon his nonmembership in his defense while all other defendants may want to . . . prevent the prosecution from presenting evidence concerning the Aryan Brotherhood."

Resolving these competing positions as best he could, on March 14, 1979, Judge Platt came up with his own severance package, which separated Hillyer from all other defendants and separated Farmer and Goff from one another so that each could testify in behalf of the other yet remain silent at his own trial. He separately grouped the "higher ups," who had ordered the hit and did not consolidate them with either Farmer or Goff, so the Aryan Brotherhood officers could call the foot soldiers in their defense. Judge Platt had done as much to benefit the defense through this alignment as any defense attorney had any right to expect:

First trial: Belt, Breshears, and Goff, beginning April 3, 1979; to be
    followed immediately by the second trial
Second trial: Bilke, Farmer, and McDonald
Third trial: Compton, Harbin, Howard, and Killinger
Fourth trial: Hillyer

This resolution survived one week, until Bilke created another can of worms by insisting on his constitutional right to be his own lawyer. Once Judge Platt granted Bilke's request to represent himself, on April 10, 1979 — a request that could not be denied if the defendant insisted on it — the court was inevitably forced to afford one more severance. No competent lawyer will ever permit his client to be tried along with a co-defendant acting as his own lawyer. Naturally, Farmer's lawyer objected to any joint trial since Bilke was "going to be acting as his own attorney and Bilke has expressed his intent to make no use whatever of any advisory counsel appointed for him."

Thus, the final alignment was the following:

First trial: Belt, Breshears, and Goff, beginning on April 3, 1979, to
    be followed immediately by the second trial
Second trial: Farmer and McDonald
Third trial: Compton, Harbin, Howard, and Killinger
Fourth trial: Bilke
Fifth trial: Hillyer

Though not as envisioned by Judge Platt's pretrial scenario, five trials occurred. No two were alike, however, except in their futility.

11 Self-Defense

While the first trial of the Waymond Small case unfolded in the Pinal County courthouse, I worked each day in the building as a deputy Pinal County attorney. Along with the other nine prosecutors in the office, I took a casual interest in the case and used breaks in my daily routine to observe the trial. I still remember the closing arguments, especially the earnestness of youthful attorney William O'Neil in defending Willard Breshears. The Waymond Small murder case received more than passing attention since the case had been taken away from our Pinal County office by the big boys from the Arizona attorney general's office. Naturally, we wanted to see how they'd do with a case that rightfully belonged to our office. Our track record suddenly looked better after the Florence Eleven thoroughly trounced the attorney general during the first trial of the Waymond Small murder, with Goff, Belt, and Breshears winning acquittals. As I casually watched snippets from that first trial, I had no inkling that I'd ever become involved in the case.

Leonard Sowers obtained an acquittal for James McDonald at the second trial. While I was practicing law as a Pinal County attorney in 1978 and 1979, Sowers was carrying on a small, mundane private practice in Kearney, Arizona, and accepting court appointments to represent indigent defendants charged with crimes in Pinal County. He seemed to me then a low-budget oddball whose legal talents were so meager that he could only survive by practicing in a rural backwater like Pinal County, and in one of the county's smallest towns at that. My regard for Sowers increased immensely, however, when I reviewed the trial transcripts in 1997 to learn how he walked McDonald.

Sam Withers, whose office was in Tucson, became the first out-of-county lawyer appointed in the defense when he replaced Farmer's first lawyer, Phil Glenn. Having already represented Farmer on the charges of murdering Kathleen Herman and Tilfred Oso, which had sent him to Arizona State Prison, the appointment was akin to Terry having his own personal lawyer to take up the baton the second time he faced a first-degree murder charge.

In this case, Withers decided to ask Judge Platt for a Rule 11 examination to determine if Farmer was mentally competent to stand trial. Rule 11 examinations occur only if requested by the prosecutor or criminal defense attorney. In asking Judge Platt to have Farmer examined, Withers filed a "pleading"—legalese for a written request for the court to do something—explaining why he thought Mr. Farmer's mental condition needed evaluation: "Based upon interviews with the defendant, it is the undersigned's opinion that defendant manifests both physiological and behavioral symptoms of a personality aberrant in the extreme. His perceptions of reality deviate, at least periodically, substantially from the normal. A telephone conversation with the defendant's parents substantiates a history of mental illness in the defendant beginning with brain damage at birth." Faced with this showing of need, Judge Platt had no choice. To be sure of Farmer's competence, he appointed three psychiatrists to examine him independently and provide their written opinion.

Dr. Otto Bendheim, a renowned seventy-year-old psychiatrist responsible for developing the "psychiatric autopsy"—a retrospective head shrinking of the deceased to decide if his mien and reputation were sufficiently terrifying to have caused his own death by provoking the accused's act of self-defense—was the first to evaluate Farmer. Although he found Farmer competent and sane based on a one-hour interview, Bendheim's report expressed genuine reservations:

> We are dealing with a disturbed, psychologically distorted human being who, since earliest childhood, has lived in fear for his life, has always been on the defensive, has always run scared and has felt it necessary to strike out, attack and kill out of a terrible inner fear, a pressure which he cannot explain, as though acting in self-defense. This young man has been unable to control his impulses and to conduct himself in a lawful and socially acceptable manner, since early childhood. Despite the serious distortion of his feelings, I found nothing to indicate that he was suffering from a psychosis in the narrower sense of the word, and that he was legally sane, if I understand this concept correctly.
>
> I consider it most unlikely that the alleged offense would have taken place if the defendant had not suffered experiences in early childhood

which led to antisocial, defensive, aggressive attitude and an almost delusional fear for his own life.

As Bendheim noted, Farmer's body bore testimony to a life of trauma, and he explained the derivation of his prison nickname, "Crazy":

> Congenital key hole pupil of left eye, with poor vision in that eye, good vision in the right eye. This pupillary deformity may have been inflicted in early childhood or it may have been "congenital" as he says. There is a traverse, self-inflicted scar on the left lower arm, a suicidal gesture or attempt. Several tattoos on both arms. Facial expression: scared, depressed, hardly ever smiling, tense and preoccupied.

Farmer's family history explained the origins of the psychiatric aberrations:

> The history was partially given by the defendant but also learned through the material which was made available to me by Mr. Withers. Indicates extreme deprivation, cruelty and neglect in early childhood, with resultant behavioral difficulties, attempts at counseling in correction in Florida, but finally resulting in various aggressive acts, at first directed against his adoptive parents, later against others. Not much is known about his natural parents.

Bendheim explained Farmer's mental state in these words:

> When I asked him about reality contact, he almost cries and tells me that occasionally there are voices and also visions. He then draws me a picture in a rather shaky, tremulous hand of a prison door and next to it a large eye with tears coming out of it.
>
> He tells me that he feels scared, he never has felt secure in his life. He never felt really loved. He always felt he had to defend himself. He has terrible nightmares and sometimes, even in the daytime, he feels he is being shot or being stabbed and he has to defend himself. He does not know who does the shooting and the stabbing but he can feel it and he can sense it. It is then that he strikes out. There is pressure. He can't control it and he does things which he cannot quite account for, he states. "I can't really explain it. It is a terrible pressure. I even attacked my mother and my father. I tried to strangle my mother. I had a fist fight with my father. I always felt I had to look out for myself and my safety. No one really wanted to take care of me."

Though sympathetic, Dr. Bendheim concluded that Farmer was "competent to stand trial. Not insane under the McNaughton test." (Mc-Naughton is the name of an old English case deciding when insanity is a legal defense to a crime; it is still followed in Arizona and many other states.)

Two other psychiatrists made less effort but agreed with Dr. Bendheim. Dr. Michael Cleary painted a picture of a morbidly depressed, suicidal person. Dr. Maier Tuchler found Farmer a habitual drug abuser, an "abrasive individual," and an "antisocial personality."

With these examinations out of the way, Withers had done his job as well, for besides representing the client, the criminal defense lawyer's duty is twofold, with one aspect paramount to himself and the other all-important to the judicial system. The lawyer must do his job so as to protect himself from claims of neglect and incompetence. In so doing, the lawyer also assures that society obtains a valid and sustainable conviction. The record was now "protected." If convicted, Farmer couldn't later claim his lawyer should have asked to have his mental competency tested or should have tried to "get him off on insanity."

The only other motion Withers filed in Farmer's behalf before allowing him to go on trial for his life was for a separate trial from his co-defendants. Since every other lawyer filed the same motion, Withers needn't have bothered.

During jury selection for Farmer and McDonald's trial, each side had an unlimited number of challenges to any potential juror "for cause," meaning legitimate reasons why a juror is unable to serve fairly, competently, or impartially. For example, a person who is deaf cannot sit as a juror, nor can someone whose answers to specific questions about his thoughts, opinions, or life experience show he is biased about the case.

Each side also had a limited number of "peremptory" challenges, meaning the potential juror would be stricken on request. The state was afforded six peremptory challenges, as were Farmer and McDonald, whose challenges were to be exercised jointly.

In 1979, Pinal County created a pool of citizens from which jurors were called. Members of the pool were called to sit on trials over a three-month period, creating the possibility that some members might serve on several juries, while others might never serve at all. In fact, during jury questioning one woman indicated that only two weeks before, she had been a juror in Stretch Hillyer's trial for the murder of Bobby Phillips, which was unsuccessfully prosecuted by Assistant Attorney General Wayne Ford. This was enough for the prosecuting attorneys to decide to strike her off the panel. So many jurors had already served on juries that had found defendants guilty of prison crimes that the defense didn't have enough peremptory challenges to dislodge them all. In the end, these fourteen jurors were impaneled:

Dennis Boatman, of Kearney, a truck driver for Kennecott who four weeks earlier had returned a guilty verdict against two Aryan Brotherhood recruits for the prison murder of white inmate Bobbie Phillips.

Raul Alvilez, of Kearney, a miner for Kennecott who sat on the same jury with Dennis Boatman.

Anthony Ramirez, of Florence, a journeyman who sat on the same jury with Dennis Boatmen and Raul Alvilez.

Eleanor Brown, of Eloy, a housewife whose husband had returned a guilty verdict for second-degree murder against Blackbird.

Jerry Boales, of Maricopa, a measurement technician for El Paso Natural Gas who returned a guilty verdict against Aryan Brotherhood recruit Freberger for the prison murder of white inmate Bobby Phillips.

LaVerne Bonner, of Kearney, a diesel mechanic for C & H Transportation who sat on the same jury with Jerry Boales.

Henry Bribiascas, a boilermaker for Kennecott Copper who sat on the same jury with Boales and Bonner.

David Buffington, a planner and surveyor for the U.S. Department of Agriculture who sat on the same jury with the Boales, Bonner, and Bribiascas.

Margaret Bayles, of Casa Grande, a homemaker.

Ila Thompson, of Whiterock, a homemaker who returned a guilty verdict on drug charges against prison inmate Benny Williams.

Rosa Sauceda, of Eloy, a teacher's aide.

Thelma Bell, of San Manuel, a housewife who served on three juries, all returning guilty verdicts.

Mary Aguero.

Angelita Arroyos.

With this jury, how could the state possibly lose? Seven jurors had already heard cases presented by these prosecutors concerning Aryan Brotherhood hits at the prison and had returned guilty verdicts. Bobby

Phillips was white; Small was black. Beyond that, the cases were roughly similar, with the state's case dependent in both instances on snitches, turncoat informers who had been part of the Aryan Brotherhood at one time and who had conspired to kill each victim. Adding to their probability of success, the prosecutors had the benefit of lessons learned from the loss of the first Waymond Small murder trial, when Goff, Breshears, and Belt won acquittals.

To prepare for this trial, prosecutors and investigators interviewed previous trial jurors to learn their reasons for acquitting Goff, Belt, and Breshears. Samuel Withers, Terry Lee Farmer's defense lawyer, and Leonard Sowers, William James McDonald's defense lawyer, did not bother. Though they could have obtained the entire transcript of the first trial for the asking, Withers and Sowers had not done so, depriving themselves of this invaluable resource for learning the tactics and strategies successfully used by the defense lawyers during the first trial.

All the advantages of a second trial—a second bite at the same apple—accrued to the state. That the state had changed tactics for the second trial was evident from the first day, because the first witness in *State of Arizona v. Farmer and McDonald* was Aryan Brother snitch Dominic Hall. Prosecutor Stanley Patchell asked Hall to educate the jury about the routines of prison life, the layout of the prison, and the prisoner's everyday activities of working, eating, and exercising. The jury then heard about the prisonwide strike leading to a complete institutional lockdown for two or three months; the disciplinary write-ups for rules infractions and how those regulations prohibited socializing among inmates; and the ways in which prisoners socialize (and plan more crimes) at "either the church or movies or the athletic field or work."

Every prisoner who had gone on strike lost his job in the industrial yard but could earn it back "if we didn't get into any riots, if we behaved ourselves, we could get our jobs back. So everybody had to go to the gun gang [farm labor] for thirty days." Hall returned to the big press in the tag plant for a week before fighting and being sent to the hole for twenty days, where he lost all privileges, including access to TV, radio, reading materials, and visitors. After he was released from the hole, Hall went back to the lowly life of working on the gun gang until September 1977, when he first heard about the Aryan Brotherhood from Goldie Watkins. Watkins recited the Aryan Brotherhood's rules to Hall, who explained the paramilitary organization as a "gang of white supremacy that was supposed to protect our own race."

Hall began recruiting on the industrial yard where he was the only member of the Aryan Brotherhood. He recruited Danny "Cowboy" Farrell, Mike Belt, Paul Bilke, Rooster Cannon, and Greg Halligan. Any inmate who had paid protection was "considered a weak individual from the start" and therefore could not become an AB member. Sometimes protection was extorted from an inmate's family members. According to Hall, the letters would read, "You send so much — X dollar to this address or we will kill your son. Things like that was going on all the time."

Sexual exploitation was also part of prison life. Gangs "would take real young individuals and make a punk out of him. A punk is an individual who is somebody that comes to the joint; is real weak, has no income. He can't pay protection, you know, by money or anything of value. They make a homosexual out of him. They rape him; do whatever they do. They sell him for a different amount of money to different people." Hall told the jury "the Aryan Brotherhood was organized so the white people wouldn't have to become punks or kids or anything like that. They would pay us protection. We wouldn't rape them. They would pay the little they could and we would protect them. That's kind of the prison rules."

At this point in Hall's testimony, Patchell said, "There is another word that I wanted you to define for the jury, if you would. And that is 'hit.'"

"It means to kill," Hall deadpanned.

The state's beginning of the second trial was head and shoulders stronger than the first. But the jury was also discovering, in graphic detail, that survival in prison required protection to avoid predation. As the trial continued, they learned that Small was one of the predators.

Dominic Hall's second day of testimony revealed Compton's order in church to silence Small because he was scheduled to testify before the legislature. Hall recounted the events leading up to Small's death: the Koolaid and Malone stabbings; how Small tried to choke Little Ritchie in chow line with a guitar string; and Small's willingness to identify the four AB members who stabbed Malone.

Hall received "eight to ten" kites from Watermelon, the building porter, and Cal the Barber, with orders from Killinger, Howard, and Harbin to kill Small so he couldn't testify. Red Dog's kites told Hall "Watch over my kids for me." Red Dog was worried about his ten kids in CB-3 and told Hall it was his responsibility to "take care of" Waymond Small.

Hall developed a plan to hit Small, working with the few ABs who avoided the lockup dragnet of November 3: Farrell, Bilke, Belt, Breshears, Rooster Cannon, and the Greek. "Willard Breshears said that Waymond Small was pretty tough," Hall said, "and that it would take more than one guy to down him, to hit him. He suggested hitting him with a hammer and somebody else stabbing him. He had a hammer over there where he worked in the shipping room that would do the job." Breshears and the Greek were supposed to help Goff and Farmer "in case something happened with the blacks jumping on them. They were going to help them out." The plan advanced when Farrell told Hall that a fish named Goff had asked if he could become an honorary member of the Aryan Brotherhood for killing a guard, and Farmer asked Hall if he and Goff could do the hit on Small.

Goff wanted to clear up an incident. Booger Red had approached him and asked to "borrow" a cigarette. As Hall explained, this was "one of the techniques they use to approach somebody and get him into paying protection." Goff feared the convicts would interpret the cigarette he'd given Booger "as paying protection rather than as a loan." So Goff asked Hall if his participation in Small's murder "would be able to clear up that matter with the Aryan Brotherhood as far as him having to pay protection. I told him 'yeah.'"

Hall explained McDonald's motivation for making the shank to kill Small. McDonald didn't join the Aryan Brotherhood but wanted to get "on the right side of Stretch Hillyer" over a loan of $160 for heroin to Jon Watts, one of Stretch's kids. After McDonald pressed Watts to repay, Stretch told Mac, "You're burned, you're not getting your money." "To have Stretch Hillyer mad at you wasn't a very pleasant experience at that time because of his authority," Hall said. MacDonald kept asking Hall whether Stretch was mad at him and how he could still get his money back. Hall asked McDonald on November 28 to make the shank since he was the maintenance man and had access to a grinder. If he did so, Hall would "talk to Stretch" and see if something could be worked out about his money.

Hall and Farmer talked about the hit on January 24 or 25, 1978, in the administrative lockup areas of CB-3. By that time Farmer had been identified as Small's killer and locked up. Hall and Farrell "were both locked up because of a kite which was apprehended" with Hall's name on it. Farmer "ran down again" how he'd killed Small. Hall told Farmer "he could consider himself a brother now."

Hall then discussed how he had avoided orders to conduct other Aryan Brotherhood hits. The disobedience began when Hall avoided Puff Huey's order to kill Destiny Celenza, an act of defiance that ultimately led to the stabbing of Danny Farrell, Hall's friend, which in turn unwound the Small conspiracy when Hall agreed to tell all. "We didn't feel that Destiny Celenza did anything wrong to be killed. Puff Huey said that Destiny is the one who snitched him off and got his mule busted. His 'mule' is a guard who brings drugs into the prison. I told Cowboy Farrell that Puff just ordered me to kill Destiny, and I said, 'Get Destiny rolled up, get Destiny out of the yard. Man, get Destiny put in the hole or something, but don't tell Destiny that there is a hit on him.' So Danny Farrell did. We did the best we could to get Destiny moved away. They shook down Destiny's cell and found a syringe and some marijuana seeds. They wrote up Destiny for that, and then Destiny was put in the hole and out of harm's way."

"Why is it that you became a member of the AB?" Withers asked Hall.

"There was a lot of friction between the different races in the joint and protection was going on, and I figured that if I join some type of organization, I would be better off, so I joined. I wasn't really in any personal fear. It's just that in Florence at that time a lot of people were getting hit up for protection by different gangs, especially the Mexican Mafia. And if you didn't belong to anything or you didn't belong to anybody, you were liable to be approached and forced to pay protection, or get involved with some type of fight."

Withers then asked Hall about the anomaly of his taking an oath of allegiance to the AB and then immediately refusing to follow orders. "Why didn't you want to hit Woodstock?" Withers asked.

"I didn't want—first of all, Woodstock has never done anything to me. I never knew Woodstock. I didn't feel that I was, you know, somebody can come up to me and tell me right after I get into the organization, walk up to me and give me a knife to kill that guy for no reason at all, do it. Well, you know, myself, I react personally. I don't believe in that, and I can't see taking a man's life for no reason at all," Hall answered.

"Okay. Let me ask you this, then. Did you know Small or did you have any reason to have anything against Small?"

"No."

"But you did participate in the alleged conspiracy to kill Small?"

"Yes."

"So, in other words, you thought differently about Woodstock from the way you thought about Small?"

"I did my best to prevent Small from being killed."

"Did you send a kite to the administration?"

"Yes."

"Did you send a kite to the administration about Destiny Celenza?"

"Yes."

"Was there a hit on Mr. Gomes?"

"Yes."

"Were you ordered to hit Mr. Gomes?"

"Originally, yes, we were ordered to hit Gomes and Small."

"Did you hit Gomes?"

"No."

"Did you do anything to try to prevent the hit on Gomes?"

"No, Gomes was moved out of the building right away. As soon as he moved to CB-3, he was moved within a few days out."

"You say that you did send a kite to the administration regarding the hit on Waymond Small?"

"Yes."

"Probably about a week before he was killed?"

"Yes."

"But your testimony has been that you were already planning the execution of the plan to kill Waymond Small. Were you not?"

"Yes."

"And, in fact, you continued your plans—by your own testimony, you continued your plans all during that week following the time you sent the kite?"

"Yes."

"Up until the moment Small was killed?"

"Yes."

With this background, Farmer's lawyer impeached Hall with his preliminary hearing testimony that he hadn't done anything to plan or organize the hit until November 28. His questioning had danced around the edges but hardly elicited any major contradictions or inconsistencies in Hall's story.

McDonald's attorney, Leonard Sowers, got Hall to repeat his admission that McDonald wasn't directly told the shank would be used to kill Small, and then he suggested that Hall had a personal vendetta against McDonald. This theme became an important defense.

On day three, Danny "Cowboy" Farrell backed up Hall's story about the hit on Waymond Small and his own stabbing for failure to carry out the hit on Destiny Celenza. As Hall's best friend, he'd been present during the planning of the conspiracy, acting virtually as Hall's right-hand man. Farrell said he had put two and two together: combining Goff's willingness to kill a guard to get honorary Aryan Brotherhood membership with Goff's friendship with Farmer, who in turn volunteered to kill Small to join the AB.

Farrell recounted how the conspirators had come into possession of keys that unlocked virtually every gate inside the industrial yard. Farrell and Hall got the key from Destiny — a shadowy, mysterious, enigmatic character. Always as nervous as a high-strung weasel and busy as an alley cat chasing eight rats, Destiny was so notorious a homosexual that every convict and guard used the pronoun "she" when referring to him. As a sexual pervert and notorious homosexual, Destiny's natural place in the prisoner's hierarchy was on the lowest rung, but he compensated and assured his prison survival using the skills of a con man and fraud artist that had earned him a lengthy sentence. He was a man without scruples who would swindle his own mother.

Destiny "had a lot of pull in the prison," though Farrell gratuitously added, "Why, I don't know." Nonetheless, the master manipulator had a ring of keys that fit doors and gates throughout the prison. "Celenza got locked up, put in the hole, sometime around the beginning of November. And before he left, he handed me the ring of keys." Bilke used those keys to open the gate for Farmer and Goff to more easily leave and return from the tag plant.

Disclaimers aside, Farrell obviously did know why Celenza had pull. He was adroit at smuggling drugs into Arizona State Prison using corrupt prison guards. Farrell and Celenza were tight; they had been cell partners, bonded through drugs and sex. While cell partners, Celenza got busted and sent to the hole — once for making an "unauthorized phone call" that undoubtedly related to smuggling logistics, and the second time for having "an outfit, a homemade syringe for narcotics and some other contraband." Celenza took the rap by claiming the outfit, sparing his cell mate Farrell from the beef.

On day four, the jury heard the shaky contributions and contradictory tales of black inmate eyewitnesses Ronnie Jones and Robert Toney about the murder scene. As if to settle and calm his witness, Prosecutor Ford took great pains with questioning Jones about trivialities before asking him anything of importance. Still, Jones incorrectly identified Goff as Small's assailant with the shank. And when Jones claimed to have identified Farmer and Goff by the prisoner numbers on their clothing at the scene, he contradicted Hall's testimony that co-conspirator Michael Belt had flushed "black-out clothing" down the toilet.

Describing Small's murder, Jones told the jury he'd seen "a little object" wrapped in "beige tape" sticking out from Goff's pants. Goff dropped a license plate on the floor. When Small reached down to pick it up, Jones "seen Crazy with a hammer—a claw hammer—in his hand . . . and he hit Waymond Small in the head with it." Then Jones saw Small pick up the hammer and "started chasing behind Crazy," yelling, "I am going to get you, motherfucker."

Jones ran along behind, then saw Small, armed with the hammer, fight "another figure" armed with a shank. Standing beside Small's crumpled body, Jones and inmate Banks got into an argument. "You motherfuckers stood up over here and let these honkies come and kill this dude," Banks chastised Jones, who then wrote down the first two numbers off the attackers' clothing—"a 35 and a 36"—and just as quickly tore up his note when he heard an inmate yell, "Everybody pretend you're working."

Jones knew Goff and Farmer from the cell block where they all lived. When they came back there after the strip search, Jones wrote down their numbers again, this time on a matchbook cover. "I had a pencil in my hand and a matchbook cover, 'cause I knew the individuals lived there. So that's why I was writing the number down." Jones kept the piece of paper in his cell. "I left it on top of my locker under some stuff. I kept hearing the rumor from the black guys that something had to be done about this here, you know. So the next day, they called up over to the Yard Office where Captain Davis and a couple other DPS Officers was there. 'Well, Jones, where were you working?' I told them where I was working. I told them I was working on the conveyor belt during the incident when Small was hit. So he said: 'Well, what did you see?' I said: 'I didn't see nothing.'" Two weeks later, Jones snitched and gave the matchbook cover to Captain Davis.

Jones said that the black inmates thought Small had been a fool. "My new lead man in charge of that roller coater there—Shot—one day, he was standing up and he was talking with Willy Solomon. I overheard the conversation. He said: 'Yeah, well Waymond Small is a fool. He is out to get it. He is still got his ass out here working. He needs to go get away from the industrial yard. I would say he was a fool for not going to PC [protective custody], you know. Get some kind of protection.'"

In another conversation, Jones saw Banks, Green, Toney, Joe, and a few other black guys rapping with Waymond Small. "They were going to knock the head off this thing before anything gets started. What I mean, they was telling him: 'We might as well get the shit started now before anything happens.' So Waymond had said, 'Well, I'm going to let them make the first move.'"

Defense attorney Leonard Sowers's only area of cross-examination was the height of simplicity. Was the beige tape similar to masking tape? Yes, Jones admitted. Sowers asked Jones to point out something in the courtroom that was "beige": the same color as the tape he'd seen around the object protruding from Goff's pants. When Jones pointed to the ceiling, every juror knew the tape introduced by the state—a piece of silver duct tape—was definitely not the color that Jones had identified.

Black inmate Robert Toney, who at twenty years old had already served five years in Arizona State Prison, began his testimony with an astonishing embellishment he had never before disclosed. He said many blacks—himself, James Green, Joe Garret, Billy Banks, Richard Briggs, Willy, Jones, Leroy Smith, Shot—had talked to Small on four occasions on November 30 about his going into protective custody. Small told the group that the prison administration had told him "the hit was on him and it was supposed to come down today, on the thirtieth." But, "Waymond told us he wasn't worried about it, because a couple of his friends told him the hit was off. We asked him who, and he pointed to some white guys standing outside the building. He just pointed to that general direction and told 'my friends over there' with 'close ties to the group that he was supposed to testify against.'"

"Did he mention who the group was?" asked the prosecutor.

"Yes," answered Toney.

"Who was it?"

"The Aryan Brotherhood."

"Do you know whether or not when he pointed to the group of white people that the defendant Farmer was one of them?"

"Yes."

"Was he?"

"Yes, he was."

"And do you know whether or not Mr. Goff was one of the people in the group he pointed to?"

"He was also."

Toney told the jury that he talked to Small in the tag plant just minutes before his murder.

Shot said, 'That boy is a fool to be staying out here on the yard. Somebody is going to try and take him out.' I told Small that everybody was getting a little leery. They don't know what was going on. That he was going to have to bring the situation to a head somehow and confront them to see what was going to be done. He heard from one source, there was to be a hit on him. He heard from different sources it was off. And we, as being black members of that inmate population, we wanted to know what was going on. I felt—a lot of people felt—if anything was going to be done, it had to be Small to do it; to confront them in a talking manner or whatever seemed fit. He said he was going to let them go ahead and make the move. He was not going to PC. He was not going to do nothing but wait and see what they do. He was going to show the Aryan Brotherhood they just could not stab every black inmate they saw because they wanted to; that there was going to be some kind of retaliation about it, and his way was going to court and testifying.

Toney had seen Goff and Farmer "three or four different times" in the tag plant during the morning. He saw Goff, Farmer, and Small talking in the tag plant around 1 p.m., but Toney turned away. When he looked back, Small "picked a hammer up and started chasing Farmer and Goff. Goff was in front. He ran past me. Farmer was being chased by Small. Farmer turned toward the restroom area, and Small was chasing him with a hammer. They both went into this restroom area and stopped by this wall. And at that time, I lost clear sight of them."

John Watling, a fingerprint examiner, was in one sense the most important witness confronting James McDonald. Of all the defendants, only Mc-Donald was tied to the crime by objective physical evidence. McDonald's fingerprints were discovered on the tape wrapped around the shank found in the tag plant. Watling told the jury that John DeSanti gave him the shank on November 30. The next day, using forceps, he peeled back the gray tape in stages, examining it for latent prints. He had found four. Watling took photographs of the shank and tape to record its location. Two latent prints matched McDonald's, one being his left thumb, the other his left middle finger.

How could defense attorney Leonard Sowers explain away McDonald's fingerprints on the death weapon? First, he established that two latent prints not matching McDonald's fingerprints were nonetheless sufficiently clear to be identifiable. These were on the adhesive side of the tape "in various locations." Watling checked against fifteen different known prints in an attempt to make an identification. Whose prints those had been, Sowers did not ask. The two identified as belonging to McDonald "were near the end of the tape which was closest to the shank."

"Do you know how long the tape was? The entire tape?" Sowers asked.

"Right off hand, no, sir. I did not measure the entire thing," Watling answered.

Sowers asked no further questions. In total, he had asked only eighteen questions, taking less than five minutes for cross-examination. Later, Sowers constructed almost his entire closing argument around those few tidbits. Whether Sowers had any right to base his client's fate on so thin a thread could be debated by trial lawyers — and might have been the opening for a later attack upon McDonald's conviction for Sowers's failure to provide constitutionally competent and adequate representation. However, Sowers's strategy won vindication when the jury acquitted McDonald. Success needs no defense.

Prosecutor Wilkes, on recross, asked a question he should not have, establishing that Watling checked the prints against fifteen individuals before finding matches to McDonald, without making any further effort to identify the other two fingerprints.

The state rested. The prosecutors hadn't repeated their blunder from the first trial by introducing either Goff's or Farmer's exculpatory claims of self-defense given to investigator Stan Elkins.

Sowers began the defense case on the seventh day by defying every convention. He permitted his client, William James McDonald, to be called as the first witness. In criminal cases, the defendant does not have to testify.

The Fifth Amendment privilege against self-incrimination enshrines this right and affords so substantial a protection that the prosecutor cannot make any comment in closing argument to the jury drawing attention to a defendant's failure to testify during the trial. Any breach of this rule by the prosecutor automatically affords a convicted defendant a new trial. The defendant, however, has an equally absolute right to testify in his own behalf even if the defense lawyer thinks he should not. This decision often presents the most difficult strategic choice of the defense attorney and his client. Conventional wisdom suggests the defendant never be his own first witness, for it's tactically prudent to allow the defendant to hear all the testimony from his own witnesses before committing himself to his story.

McDonald told the jury of his convictions for armed robbery and escape, his job as maintenance electrician and mechanic in the print shop in November 1977, and his familiarity with the print shop from having built its rooms. This familiarity allowed McDonald to provide technical and convincing explanations for the sewer pipes frequently backing up, making the November 30 plumbing problem nothing more than a coincidence. According to McDonald, the print shop plumbing pipes were only "three-eighths copper tubing and sometimes those back up."

On the day of Small's murder, the inmates waited outside Tower 3 for their number to be called so that each inmate could be accounted for as they passed through the gate from the industrial yard to lunch. McDonald remembered seeing Small and Farmer talking. "I was standing up against the wall where I always stand at on the northeast corner of that building. Waymond Small called Terry Farmer over. Small was black and he called this white boy over there. And being that he was a fish, everybody got it in their mind, as soon as they seen that, that he was going to get hit on. Waymond Small was hitting Farmer up to be his kid. I thought that was pretty funny. Waymond told Farmer he wanted him to be his kid. Terry told him that he didn't want to be nobody's punk. He wanted to do his own time and be left alone. Waymond told him: 'Well, that ain't the way it's going to be. You don't do what you want to do here. You will be or I will kill you.' About this time, they started calling the number up and Waymond had to leave. He told Farmer: 'Come over to where I work at, and we will talk about it.'"

McDonald then told the jury technical details about grinders and wheels. The print shop grinder only had "finishing wheels" of "about

200 grit," suitable only for "knocking burrs off." It was suitable "to finish something, not to make it."

"Did you have any foreknowledge that this was going to happen?" Withers asked.

"No, I did not," McDonald answered.

"Did anyone ever tell you Waymond Small was going to be killed?"

"No."

"Did you ever participate in any conversation to plan this occurrence?"

"No, I did not."

This left McDonald to make specific denials during cross-examination, and he did well, throwing in gratuitous tidbits to help his cause.

"Was the grinder used frequently?" prosecutor Ford asked.

"No. Most of the time it was taken apart. I would take the spindle off it," McDonald answered.

"Did you have anything available to you in the print shop for grinding larger items?"

"Only a file."

If he had to grind anything heavy, McDonald said he had had to go to the tag plant or the sign shop.

McDonald adroitly manipulated the prosecutor's own questioning about the shank itself to steer blame for its construction in other directions. "Did you have any pieces of metal like that in the print shop?" Ford asked.

"I didn't, but when I saw that the other day, I knew what that was originally," McDonald answered.

"You didn't ever have any pieces of metal like that in the print shop?"

"No, I did not. But, when I saw that the other day—those holes in the handle—I knew what that was originally."

"Do you know what it was originally?"

"Yes, sir, I do."

"Was it a piece of metal used in the print shop?"

"No."

"Where was it used?"

"Mainly, in the tag plant area."

"Was the grinder that you had in the print shop, was it capable of putting on a fine edge, such as is on this shank?"

"Yes. Just a fine edge, but not to make it down the way it is."

McDonald, however, readily identified the tape taken from the shank as "a waterproof, moisture proof tape, primarily used in the silk screening part of the print shop or tag plant," which he used occasionally.

McDonald never appeared anxious to say much in answer to prosecutor Ford's questions, making his few zingers score that much more.

"Do you know an individual in the Arizona State Prison by the name of Jerry Joe Hillyer?" Ford asked.

"Yes, sir," answered McDonald.

"And does he have a nickname?"

"Yes, sir."

"What's his nickname?"

"Stretch."

"Do you know whether or not he is a member of the Aryan Brotherhood?"

"I have always been told that."

"That he is?"

"Yes."

"Do you know what position he holds in the Aryan Brotherhood?"

"Just what I heard."

"What is that?"

"General."

"You never heard of anything about the Aryan Brotherhood in prison?"

"Just jokes."

"Jokes?"

"Admirals, you know, stuff like that."

"Who was admiral?"

"Well, like I said, it was joking. I don't know if generals is the highest or admirals is the highest. I heard a lot of jokes about it."

"I see. You know an inmate by the name of John Watts?"

"Yes, sir, I do."

"Do you know if he had any relationship to Mr. Hillyer?"

"Not that I know of. I know Stretch had been locked up since he shot my cell partner a few years ago. Since that time, until we came down here to court, I never seen him."

Ford's cross-examination had proven inept. It generated empathy for McDonald while doing nothing for the state's case. It even allowed more leeway for further questions by the defense, so Withers asked McDonald to fully explain the origins of the metal of the type used to make the shank. The holes in the handle were "the exact size of the pop rivets" on metal strips used in the carpentry shop as pipe hangers, but, said McDonald, "I haven't seen any in the print shop." When in use, the grinder made a loud noise "like a drum head" and caused sparks to fly, making it all the more probable its use would have been noticed by guards and supervisors. To the end, McDonald knew how to score points that could make a difference during jury deliberations.

John Vargas, the tower duty officer, told the jury he saw a black man running very fast out of the north door of the tag plant just after receiving the excited call from the tag plant and issuing Code 3, meaning assistance was needed immediately.

Co-defendant Paul Bilke testified as effectively as a professional FBI witness. He denied ever having a key to unlock the gate, and he denied conspiring with anyone to murder Waymond Small, but he admitted he'd been a prospective member of the Aryan Brotherhood. Bilke confirmed Farmer's tale of being jacked up by Small to be his punk during the lunch hour of November 30, and Goff offering a ten-dollar bill to buy off Small. Bilke told the jury that Small was "extremely aggressive and violent, mostly to the white inmates. He was a racial activist." Judge Platt struck the "racial activist" comment, but the jury had heard it. Bilke told the jury that McDonald was not a member of the Aryan Brotherhood; that McDonald and Hall "never would talk to each other"; and that McDonald and Farrell never associated with each other.

It was on the fourth question of cross-examination that prosecutor Stan Patchell planted the seed that torpedoed the state's case, though the ticking time bomb wouldn't detonate until the next witness testified.

"Mr. Bilke, isn't it true that you have been charged with the conspiracy to kill and the murder of Waymond Small?" Patchell asked.

"That's correct," Bilke answered, not blinking an eye.

Patchell asked Bilke four more innocuous questions and then said, "No further questions."

Ernest William Goff, who had been acquitted in the first trial, looked as innocent as a choir boy, though his prison denim garb clashed with his cherubic appearance. He testified about Waymond hitting up Farmer over lunch hour on November 30 to be his punk or to be killed; Waymond telling Farmer to come over to the tag plant after lunch to "talk about it"; offering Farmer his ten-dollar bill to buy off Small; accompanying the unarmed Farmer on his trip to the tag plant to talk to Small; Small pulling a shank from his waistband; Goff yelling at Farmer to look out; Small yelling, "I'll kill you right now"; Farmer side-stepping Small's first knife thrust; Farmer, in defense, picking up a hammer lying on the roller coater; and then Goff running away for his life. Goff denied conspiring with anyone to kill Small; denied either he or Farmer changed clothes after the trip to the tag plant; denied joining the Aryan Brotherhood or being recruited by Hall or Farrell.

But now Patchell's one question of Bilke came back to haunt the prosecution. By taking advantage of this one tenuous and slender opening, Withers earned his entire fee of $13,344. He could have blundered at every turn and nonetheless been completely redeemed for exploiting in the heat of the moment Patchell's single, subtle miscue. And if Withers had not played his only trump exactly right, Patchell's question would not have been a miscue at all. Having the brilliance and insight to realize he'd been dealt one good card, Withers asked Goff the question that Patchell had made relevant by his miscalculation but that Withers otherwise could not have asked. Knowing he was on sensitive ground, Withers asked for a bench conference with Judge Platt and Patchell so that the jury would not hear the question unless the judge gave his approval ahead of time.

At the bench, Withers asked Judge Platt for permission to ask Goff the same question Patchell had asked Bilke: "Have you been charged with conspiracy and murder?" He also requested a follow-up question: "Were you convicted or acquitted of the charge?" Judge Platt told Withers he could ask Goff if he had been charged, but he could not ask Goff if he had gone to trial and been acquitted.

Since Patchell had opened the door by asking Bilke if he'd been charged for this conspiracy, the Arizona Supreme Court much later decided that Withers had been entitled to ask Goff if he had been acquitted. The court reasoned it was unfair to permit the state to ask if a coconspirator had been charged with Small's murder and in so doing suggest that this witness had a bias or interest that influenced his testimony, when in fact this inference was untrue. Once Goff had been acquitted, he no longer had an interest in shaping his testimony to avoid conviction. Therefore, prohibiting the jury from knowing Goff had been charged and acquitted had been unjust and unfair to Farmer. When the Arizona Supreme Court reversed Farmer's conviction, it wrote the following opinion:

When a witness has been attacked on grounds of his bias or interest, the party calling him is entitled to prove any fact tending to show the absence of such interest or bias. Here, when the state was allowed to ask a witness whether he had been indicted for purpose of showing the possible bias and motive of the witness in testifying, the defense should have been allowed to show that fear of pending prosecution was not the motive. Allowing the state to leave the inference with the jury that the witnesses were awaiting trial on the same charges as appellant and therefore had a motive to testify falsely, was error.

After the appellate review of Farmer's first trial, the jurors at the fifth trial knew about all the acquittals. No jury—knowing that other jurors had repeatedly rejected the State's case—would be likely to convict the other co-conspirators. This conundrum spelled doom to the attorney general's efforts to convict the last of the Florence Eleven in the fifth trial, the retrial of Compton and Harbin.

So ended the seventh day, the seeds of reversal sown by Withers's clever exploitation of Patchell's mistake. Upon this seat-of-the-pants ability to seize upon the smallest opening, a few criminal defense lawyers become famous and their guilty clients walk free—once in a great while.

The eighth day of the trial brought dazzling testimony from creative inmates willing to help out their fellow convict. Inmate Jose Mejis told the jury he worked in the tag plant where "quite a few" hammers were "just laying around." On November 30 he saw Small "running pretty fast, but I didn't see anything happen. It seemed he was carrying something [in his hand], but I couldn't tell what it was."

Inmate Edward Lawrence told the jury a freshly minted, brazen lie. He testified that Dominic Hall asked him to make a shank early in the morning on November 30 while Lawrence worked in the print shop in the letterpress area, and that he obliged. "I ground it down some on a wheel and then I took it back in the area where I was working and used the file on it there." He got tape for the handle from McDonald and gave the finished shank to Hall. Lawrence told the jury he told Warden Cardwell about making the shank for Hall "four or five days after Waymond Small was killed." Lawrence testified he'd made exhibit 17—the shank introduced by the state as the murder weapon.

Lawrence's testimony was nearly as dramatic and sensational as any from the Perry Mason show, in which the real killer screams out from the back of the courtroom, "I can't stand it anymore, I did it!" But, Lawrence hedged his gamble because he added an all-important caveat: He denied any knowledge of a conspiracy brewing inside the print shop to kill Waymond Small.

Inmate Randall "Sonny" Harbin, the brother of co-defendant Russell Harbin, told the jury he had worked in the print shop on November 30. He saw Lawrence filing a piece of metal, "saw that it was none of my business," and went back to his own work. Harbin also knew Small's reputation "as a bulldog. He'd tend to prey on younger, less experienced inmates." A bulldog is "someone who takes things from other inmates who aren't capable physically of defending themselves," Harbin explained. He then told the jury he saw the fictitious lunchtime argument between Small and Farmer. On cross-examination, Harbin admitted that he was McDonald's good friend and that he'd been a member of the High Wall Jammers but not the Aryan Brotherhood. His brother Rusty, however, was a member of the AB, he testified.

Inmate Ben Abney told the jury he worked as a maintenance man in the tag plant, where hammers were readily available. "Most of the people could just walk into the maintenance yard and pick up any tool they wanted," Abney said. He confirmed McDonald's testimony that the shank was made from materials used to make strap hangers for electrical conduit and water lines and was found "mostly in the tag plant."

Black inmate John Jackson told the jury about Small's fondling him outside the chow hall at lunchtime on November 30 and pointing at nineteen-year-old Terry Farmer, asking, "Does she belong to anybody?" Jackson responded, "I don't think so and I think she's a he anyway." Small responded: "Well, I'm going to find out. I'm going to make him mine." After lunch, he saw Goff handing a bill to Farmer. He told the jury Small "was definitely a very violent person." Jackson's use of prison vernacular made his account believable. Reinforcement of Farmer's self-defense fairy tale was coming from a black inmate who claimed he had been fondled by Small, a sexual predator always on the prowl.

Capt. Dale Davis, head of prison security, was forced to admit he had "received information a few days before the twenty-eighth day of November 1977, that there was a possibility that Waymond Small had been threatened with injury." Davis said that Small had told him "he'd gotten heat on the yard. Small said it was nothing he couldn't handle himself. I told him I thought we ought to put him in protective custody and he said, 'No, I don't want to go to PC.'" Davis admitted, however, that the prison administration could have placed Small into protective custody against his will. According to Davis, Small told him "he kept a hammer close by or with him, words to this effect, which would be immediately available to him to use to protect himself." He also told Davis he intended to testify before the Arizona legislature about prison violence and in court about the Koolaid Smith stabbing. In the prison culture, snitches get killed. "The penalty when you testify for the state against another inmate or give a statement or agree to testify, the penalty can be as severe as death. It would be administered by some inmate," explained Davis.

On the ninth day of the trial, Sowers began by calling his next witness, William Bates.

"Mr. Bates, do you remember the events of November 30, 1977?"

"Yeah. It was kind of a memorable day for everybody," the white prisoner deadpanned.

Bates testified he worked in the tool room at the tag plant. He explained that Small had come to the tool room about 10 a.m. and had tried to take Bates's hammer. "Nope," he told him, so Small took a claw hammer off the wall instead. Small placed this hammer beside the roller coater. He saw Goff and Farmer in the tag plant that afternoon, but neither came to the tool room.

"How was the situation at the prison in terms of racial tension?" Sowers asked.

Knowing his cue, Bates grabbed the ball and ran. "It had been pretty bad. They had a kind of a bulldog collection agency, what have you, and I'm sure Waymond Small—"

"Objection, Your Honor," prosecutor Wilkes screamed out, cutting off Bates's prepared slanderous speech.

"Sustained," Judge Platt vigorously agreed.

Turning back to the scene, Bates recalled hearing Small shout, "I'll just kill you, I'll just kill you." Small "took the hammer off of a metal encasing that was over a belt and chain thing, I think; and was chasing him. There was about forty blacks around, there was only the two white fellows; and Mr. Goff ran, I guess out the side entrance, you know, at the side around the office; and Small chased him with a hammer."

Knowing that Bates intended to talk about Small's bulldogging, prosecutor Wilkes cut him off, insisting that Bates only talk about Small's general reputation for violence but not any "specific incidents." Sowers and Withers, more ethically constrained than Stephen Bogard, Goff's attorney, had been during the first trial, didn't push it. But Bates proved too wily and got to say his piece anyway during the prosecutor's cross-examination, when Wilkes made the mistake of asking Bates, "Now, protection, isn't that where one inmate pays a group of inmates money, or sexual favors, or something like that?"

"That's right," Bates answered nonchalantly.

"Have you ever paid protection since you have been in the Arizona State Prison?" Wilkes asked.

"No, but I paid it for another guy in—well, anyway, the form of it, it cost me a twenty-one-jewel watch, which Waymond Small got. They wanted sexual favors and the kid checked himself in, that's what I know."

Why did Wilkes tempt fate? These seasoned old convicts were simply too good at twisting any question around so they could say whatever they wanted. The defense's purpose for calling William Bates had been accomplished because of injudicious questioning by the prosecutor: the jury learned about a "specific incident" in which Small bulldogged a young kid for sex and got Bates's fancy watch!

Richard Benjamin, the print shop supervisor, had told the jury at the first trial that he had worked continuously and closely with Michael Belt on November 30 to solve problems in the darkroom, making Hall's story of Belt's involvement in the conspiracy a virtual physical impossibility. His testimony in this trial now proved just as helpful to cast doubt on Hall's story of McDonald's involvement. The grinder in the print shop was kept under a workbench when not mounted for use. When mounted, it was visible from Benjamin's office desk.

"Was the grinder used much?" Sowers asked Benjamin.

"It was very rare. The only time we used it—make a part for a press, or something of this nature; otherwise, it was disassembled and kept under the table," Benjamin explained. It had a "medium grade of cutter on it." The grinder was so noisy it could easily be heard above the other noises inside the print shop. Before any inmate used the grinder, he "checked with me first; but if the grinder did start up I could identify it, and would check to find out why they were using it." Benjamin did not believe the grinder was used at any time between November 28 and 30.

"How good a repairman was McDonald?" Sowers asked.

"He was the best we ever had in there," Benjamin enthused. As a repairman, McDonald had access to duct tape from large rolls. Tape was used everywhere for temporary repairs, on printing presses, "any place that tape would be used we would be forced to use that type of tape." "Anyone in the print shop needing tape would go to McDonald and get it. For a while there was extreme shortage of that tape. Because of our silk-screen operation, we had tape, so if anyone from other areas, plumbers, electricians, needed the tape, they would borrow some from us."

"And McDonald was generally the one they would come and ask for it?" Sowers clarified.

"Yes."

With these simple explanations, McDonald's fingerprints on the tape around the shank became readily understandable as innocuous coincidence. Rather than casting doubt on Benjamin's account, Prosecutor Patchell's cross-examination of Benjamin bolstered his usefulness to the convicts.

"Would you say that prior to November 30, or on November 30, for that matter, that it would have been possible for an inmate to have worked about two hours during the day making a shank?" Patchell asked.

"I would say it would be impossible in that shop," Benjamin answered.

"Pardon?" Patchell blurted out in surprise.

"I would say that it was impossible in that shop," Benjamin repeated.

Digging his own hole deeper, Patchell blundered on. "If a witness had testified that he had made a shank in the print shop on the twenty-eighth of November back here in a corner somewhere, and spent over a period of the day — a couple of hours — making it, would you say that that was possible?"

"No, I would say it was not possible."

Patchell bulled ahead, digging deeper. Benjamin obliged by burying him again. Showing Benjamin the shank, Patchell asked, "Tell us whether or not the grinder that was back there and the wheel that was on it could have been used to make the edge on that piece of metal, or the edges?"

"I don't believe it would have."

"Tell us why not."

"There are very few scratches on the edge of the knife, the shank. The grinder back there I believe is quite a bit more coarse than what has been done here."

"If I told you McDonald said it was finer rather than coarser, would you say he was in error?"

"Yes, I believe he would be in error."

Next, coconspirator Willard Breshears, who was working in the shipping room at the tag plant on November 30, told the jury he had never been a member of the Aryan Brotherhood. Beginning his questioning about that day, Withers asked Breshears, "The person you saw in the tag plant that afternoon was Terry Farmer?"

"Yes," Breshears answered. He could have stopped, but he didn't. Going beyond the question, the crafty convict rambled on, "Well, I've been charged with him. I was charged in the case with him."

Prosecutors, asleep at the switch, didn't move to strike the answer. Instead, when their turn for cross-examination came, they stuck the self-inflicted dagger blow in even deeper. Following up Breshears's volunteered observation that he, too, had been charged with Small's murder, prosecutor Ford aimlessly asked, as his last cross-examination question, "I believe you testified that you were charged in this case last summer, of '78?"

"Yes."

Withers asked for another conference with Judge Platt, again wanting permission to ask a coconspirator what became of those charges. Had he been acquitted by a jury? Platt prohibited the question. Withers had done his job as defense attorney again. If Farmer was convicted, he would preserve the record for appeal and ask for a new trial. The state had "opened the door" when it asked Breshears if he had been charged, without allowing for the witness to state that he had also been acquitted. Like a sucker, Ford had taken Breshears's bait and tripped headlong into a unseen trap.

Defendant William McDonald took a second trip to the witness stand, this time to talk about his disputes with Dominic Hall. He claimed that two weeks before Small's death, Hall and he had had a conversation that "got drug out for quite some time. I didn't associate with him after that last falling out we had." He then elaborated on his role as tape dispenser: "For a while I think I was the only one that had it. Even silk-screen would get it from me sometimes." With his ready access to tools, McDonald had no need to bother with making shanks. "If I was going to make a shank for somebody, I'd give them a screwdriver before I would go to the trouble of making a shank." Even with the tape shortage, McDonald had been generous.

"With all the shortage of tape that was going around, you still never hesitated when anybody asked you for tape, the tape that they wanted?" asked prosecutor Wayne Ford.

"I wouldn't give them the whole roll; but I'm just a convict like anybody else. I'm not nobody to tell somebody they can't have something," McDonald quite rationally explained.

Next, Michael Belt, another acquitted co-defendant, denied cutting up clothes or conspiring to kill Small.

After Belt testified, Farmer took the stand in his own defense. How many times had one of the twelve jurors glanced at Farmer to see how he looked, how he reacted, as the damaging evidence unfolded? What impressions were formed? Did they think to themselves, "He looks like a killer," "He looks crazy," "He looks so young"? At different times, all twelve probably thought all of these things, for Farmer stood out, and not to his advantage. He was lanky, with long brown hair, wild eyes, and a nervous, high-strung disposition. Most of all, his eyes, the eyes of a madman, betrayed him.

Farmer denied that he had been a member of the Aryan Brotherhood or that he had ever been recruited. He told the jury that he was still new to the prison, a "fish," having arrived only six months before Small's death. He then testified that Small had approached him on November 30 at lunch, outside Gate 3, and announced that "I was going to be his kid." Farmer told the jury that he replied, "No way. I had a lot of time [to serve], that I wasn't going to be his kid or anyone else's kid," to which Small replied, "Either you're going to do what I want or I'll kill you." Farmer said he persisted in refusing and Small allowed, "Maybe there's something we can work out," so Farmer came to see him at the tag plant. During chow, Farmer discussed the problem with Goff.

"Did it occur to you to go to protective custody," Withers asked his client.

"In a sense, it did," Farmer admitted. "The reason I didn't want to check in was because I had a lot of time; and another reason, once you check in, you can't check out."

"Why can't you check back out?"

"They put a jacket on you."

"What happened after chow?"

"When I went back to the print shop, I had a conversation with Mr. Goff, and it was all over this Small thing. I was a fish to the joint. I never had anybody approach me and do something like this.

"Goff told me, 'I have some money. If you think you can buy Small off I'll give you this money,' and I thought I could, you know, I didn't know, so I said, 'Yeah, I'll take the money, I'll go try.'

Farmer told the jury, with complete plausibility, why he took up Goff's offer: "I figured if I went over there with somebody it would be a show of strength, just a strategy move to show this guy that I do have friends in the penitentiary. . . . When I stepped through the doors of the tag plant, I noticed that at least half the tag plant was black and that got me a little worried," Farmer told the jury. "I was just going to let this thing slide" when Small "motioned me over. I first started the conversation trying to beat around the bush, and I told him I'd worked the roller coater before," but Small forced the issue, Farmer said. He then recounted their alleged conversation: "Have you come up with a decision on what you want to do?" Small asked Farmer. "Yeah, I have a little bit of money here. I can give you this money but I can't give you anything else. I'm not going to be your kid," Farmer insisted. Small paused, and Farmer thought he was going to take the money until he yelled out, "I'll just have to kill you now, motherfucker," and he pulled a shank from his waistband.

Farmer said he grabbed Small by the shirt collar, pulling him off balance as he lunged forward. Farmer sidestepped and grabbed a hammer from a stool. Farmer struck Small with the hammer, who dropped the shank. Farmer picked up the shank and ran. "I just wanted to get away from the guy, that's all," he said.

Farmer ran for the bathrooms because he "knew there was a sliding door there that would let me out," but the door was locked. Small, hammer in hand, overtook Farmer at the door. "We just got into a big fight. And I swung with both hands and kicked. Apparently, I must have got in a good punch, or I must have kicked him, because he staggered back," and Farmer managed to open "the door just far enough for me to get through," then he "slammed it, hoping that it would lock, hoping that it would keep [Small] from coming on me again." Farmer then ran back to the print shop. Nervous and shook up, Farmer went to the bathroom to look himself over. "I was all right except I had a split lip and my nose was bleeding a little bit and I had a few red spots on me; but other than that I was okay. While I was in there washing my face off I got real dizzy, I got sick to my stomach, and I threw up. After that I just came back out and just stood around my press until they took us in."

Farmer's tale stretched credulity, for he claimed not to know even if he'd stabbed Small in the "big fight." Though bleeding from his nose, he had no blood on his clothing. He said he never told the prison administration or investigators what had happened because "you don't say nothing to the administration because you could get a snitch jacket put on you."

At this point, Patchell cross-examined Farmer. He established that Goff and Farmer had been cell mates for two months in 1977. He asked about the mechanics of the fight, obtaining Farmer's concession that the only way Small could have ended up with two shank wounds to his body "was during the fight we had" and that Farmer "could have stuck him," because he had the knife in his hands and had swung at Small.

On the next day, the defense ended with more stabs at the victim. Sam Withers called Small's lawyer, Bryce Beuhler, who had represented Small in 1972 on charges of aggravated battery and in 1977 on charges of the first-degree murder of Grace Ascher. Beuhler told the jury the obvious: Small "was known to be a violent man." Beuhler considered Small a "literary figure, an interesting character," and he wanted to write a book about Small's life and crimes. Withers next called Rufino Dominguez, who knew Small when he was a Maricopa County jailer. He agreed Small had a reputation for violence.

The state's rebuttal case consisted of plumbing and construction expert Jack Exline, a former prison employee, who testified that the toilets in the print shop had adequate suction to flush down torn-up denim jeans and T-shirts. Exline opined that the shank could have been made with the print shop's grinder and stone in ten minutes.

After Exline's testimony, the lawyers made their closing arguments to the jury. Patchell relished closing and fancied himself a skilled practitioner of the art form, his style straightforward and candid. He focused almost entirely on emotion and motive:

The administration, of course, runs the prison. But the inmates run the prisoners. That is a fact of life. An inmate who is able to get through the Arizona State Prison or probably any prison, for that matter, without running into any compulsion to act in any particular way according to the rule of another inmate, I submit, would be a rarity. The inmate's life is, of course, different from the lives of each of us. They are virtually captive within their own way of life. Because of the nature of prison, groups such as the Aryan Brotherhood exist.

It was the desire of the AB in November 1977 to silence a black inmate by the name of Waymond Small. That was to be done so that he could not testify in a couple of prison stabbings. Mr. Small knew this. Most of the prison knew of this.

Actually, when it is all boiled down, if you believe Hall and Farrell, Jones and Toney, the defendants are guilty. If you believe Mr. Farmer, the defendants are not guilty. That's about what it boils down to.

The people with the greatest stake in the outcome of this trial obviously are the defendants. That's something you should consider when you're deciding whether or not they're telling the truth. Is there a motive for them to color the story or to outright lie to you? That's a question you've got to ask.

Now, motive for testimony in a courtroom can be that if I go in the courtroom and testify against these defendants, the code of the prison is going to come down around my ears. The code is to hear no evil, see no evil, speak no evil. And if you do, you're going to be punished for it. Not by the authorities, but by the inmates. This code, of course, permits the prison inmate population to function in a way that allows the ABs, Mexican Mafias, Highwall Jammers, the motorcycle groups, people like that, to exist in the prison and to enforce their will upon other inmates. Extortion couldn't be carried out if an inmate would come forth and say when he is extorted. But the inmates don't come forth, as you've heard in this trial.

Most people like to know why a crime was committed. In this instance, you have the reason for the crime. The crime was committed because Waymond Small was going to testify concerning two stabbings in the prison.

Hall, Farrell, the rest of them. They're all there because they committed crimes against society. And the people who are in that prison are tough monkeys. Their code of conduct is: You will not testify, as someone said, for the man. You will not go and inform to the man against an inmate. See no evil, hear no evil, speak no evil. But if you go into court and testify in favor of a defendant, in favor of a convict, that's not against the code. Those people can come here all day and testify in favor of the defendants and suffer no ill consequences by going back to prison. They can go right back on the main yard and they haven't violated any of the code. In fact, and maybe just the opposite. It may be that they'll be patted on the back. The people who come in and testify for the state, those are the tough people to find, because they violate the code, and it's a tough, stringent code. Ask Mr. Farrell with nine stab wounds.

Defense Attorney Leonard Sowers then began his argument for Mac-Donald with a clever yet accurate feel-good nostrum: You can believe everyone and still find MacDonald not guilty.

One thing, as a juror I envy you in a way because unlike what the prosecutor has told you, that you have to believe one side or believe the other side, in my opinion you can believe everybody that testified and you still have to come back with a not guilty verdict on Mr. McDonald.

Let's look at Mr. Hall and Farrell's testimony, for instance. They're the only ones who have testified that Mr. McDonald made a shank. They also testified specifically that they did not tell Mr. McDonald anything about a conspiracy to kill Mr. Small.

They told this on direct by the prosecution—questioning by the prosecution, that they never at any time told MacDonald of any plan the AB had to kill Mr. Small. They also testified that nobody in their presence told Mr. McDonald that they had plans to kill Waymond Small.

To refute the idea that "everyone" in prison knew Small was going to die, Sowers turned to the prison's own chief of security, Captain Davis:

When Mr. Davis was on the stand and he was asked concerning an AB hit, he said, no, he didn't know anything about that.

This refutes right there that everybody knew . . . there's absolutely no evidence, none whatsoever, that Mr. McDonald knew the plan. He was not involved in it. . . . He didn't do any of the things that are required to arrive at a conspiracy. It isn't just enough that he has broad knowledge that prison life is rough, that people get hit. He had to know the specific knowledge. And they simply have not shown this. There is no evidence, even if you believe the state's case entirely and disregard everything else. You still have no knowledge proven.

Sowers accounted for McDonald's fingerprints on the tape by their location: the end of the strip.

[The fingerprints] don't prove that he had a hold of this tape for the purpose of putting it on the shank. His fingerprints were at the end because he had torn the tape off. You saw when we demonstrated how you tear the tape apart. Those fingerprints show that he tore the tape off.

Mr. McDonald gave pieces of this tape out not only to other people at the print shop, but to other people working in other areas. Mr. Benjamin testified, as a matter of fact, that he had seen Mr. McDonald go to the fence and hand pieces of this tape through the fence to other individuals.

There are also five other identifiable prints on that tape. We don't know what they are, we don't know whose they are. Fifteen people were all that were checked out. Mr. McDonald's fingerprints were the fifteenth, according to the testimony. And, therefore, we don't know who the other five fingerprints belong to.

The other five fingerprints, mind you, were found along the edges of the tape. Now it's possible that they could have been put there when it was wrapped.

Sowers then offered a plausible explanation that Hall and Ferrell threw McDonald into the conspiracy out of spite. By the time Hall and Ferrell had decided to testify against McDonald, they knew his fingerprints had been found on the tape. McDonald and Hall, he said, "had an argument some two weeks prior to the Small incident, and it's because of this argument that Mr. Hall and Mr. McDonald were on the outs at the time of the Small killing."

Terry Farmer's attorney, Samuel Withers, attempted a logically impossible straddle in his closing argument: while seeking to bolster the truthfulness of Farmer's self-defense testimony, he also suggested that someone else killed Small:

Mr. Farmer, at Mr. Small's direction, went to the tag plant with

Mr. Goff. He had a $10 bill from Mr. Goff, and he was prepared to try to buy his peace. He tried, and it didn't work.

I submit to you that Mr. Small may have had a number of enemies within that prison.

Waymond Small knew he was in danger because he was willing to go and testify before a legislative committee on prison violence.

He's a snitch. That isn't going to make him a darling of any group, not just AB, but any particular group. The Mau Maus, the possible black organization existing within the Arizona State Prison. The penalty [is] as severe as death for becoming a snitch. The AB is not the only organization that would sit over there in the prison and attempt to enforce a penalty for snitching. Any group can do that or individuals can do it.

Mr. Small was a violent individual. You don't make a lot of friends by being violent. He may have had any number of enemies.

You heard Mr. Vargis, the tower guard on Tower No. 3, saying that some—that a black inmate ran out of the north door and ran towards the west end and around the corner. Was this person involved? Those are all areas of reasonable doubt.

Now, I want you to put yourself in Mr. Farmer's place, if you would. Mr. Farmer took lunch on this particular fateful day of Nov. 30, 1977. And somebody comes up to him with a proposition that isn't particularly pleasant to consider. The man threatens his life. He thinks about it over the lunch hour and figures that he probably has a way out.

Can you imagine what his feeling must have been when he walked into the tag plant and saw all those black faces? He doesn't know them. They're presumably possibly friends, certainly coworkers of Waymond Small.

Waymond Small says, "Come on over." And he walks over. I ask you to put yourself in his position when he walks over.

They don't settle their arguments, Small draws a knife, lunges at him, and says, "I'm going to kill you."

Now, what do you do if you're in his position? What would you do if somebody lunged at you with a knife and says they're going to kill you? Would you stop and say, "I wonder if this guy is serious?"

Do you have time to do that? No, you don't have time to do that. I submit under the circumstances we have a classic case of self-defense.

If someone lunges at you with a deadly weapon, you do what you can to preserve your own life.

Sowers had done his job of understanding the mind of Pinal County citizens so well that all jurors agreed, even before selecting their foreman, that McDonald was not guilty. A five-minute verdict for McDonald! Jury deliberations for the next twenty-four hours became a contest of wills solely over the fate of Farmer. Juror Raul Alvilez tenaciously adhered to his belief in Farmer's self-defense fairy tale. Alvilez wanted to return a verdict of not guilty for both Farmer and McDonald or, for Farmer, of guilty of only second-degree murder. Slowly the other jurors wore down his stubborn resistance, and they finally agreed unanimously for acquittal. Alvilez, however, later gave an affidavit lamenting the verdict against Farmer.

Once again the jury's verdict produced utter consternation within the prosecution's team. The state's partial victory evaporated when Farmer's conviction did not stand up on appeal to the Arizona Supreme Court.

12 The Bailiff Did It

By any objective measure, the collective experience level and overall competence of the defense lawyers assigned to the Florence Eleven fell below the ideal for representation of any defendant facing first-degree murder charges and the death penalty. The eleven defendants, owing to substitutions of counsel that occurred for a wide variety of reasons, were represented by sixteen different lawyers in the course of the Waymond Small murder case. Of these lawyers, none was greener than me. Just three years out of law school, I had never defended anyone charged with a crime more serious than drunk driving. After nine months in Florence as a Pinal County prosecutor, I took the appointment to represent Richard Compton. This case was my ticket back to solvency and to Phoenix to practice law.

I met with Robert Bohm—who wanted off the case in order to take a new job in Phoenix—and Compton to discuss my substitution as Compton's attorney. All of us were locked together in a cell at the Pinal County jail, and it was the first time I had met Bohm's client. "Scary looking. I can see how he got the job as acting general," I thought as I shook my prospective client's huge hand. Compton was more than six feet tall, and his frame was big enough to carry 220 pounds, though he was emaciated to well below his natural weight. He had long, prematurely gray hair, which he wore slicked straight back, and he glowered as he held his mouth open, exactly like the young, tough hoodlums in gangster flicks. When he spoke, Compton never said more than four words without throwing in a "motherfucker" this or a "fuckin'" that. After each short sentence, he stared hard into my eyes, waiting for some expression of assent before continuing.

Compton asked few questions, apparently assured more by my intensity and earnestness than by my answers. On June 4, 1979, he signed a form for consent to substitution of counsel. Two weeks into private practice and I had signed up my first client—on a capital charge of first-degree murder. For the first time since graduation from law school, I began to think that being a lawyer might be satisfying.

Richard "Big Richard" Compton, Troy "Baby Peck" Killinger, William Steven "Red Dog" Howard, and Russell "Rusty" Harbin were tried in round three of the Florence Eleven trials and welcomed the trial perhaps more than anyone else gathered in Judge Platt's courtroom that day. It offered them respite for three weeks inside an air-conditioned building and the chance to ogle real women—the courtroom clerk, the court reporter, and female jurors.

Voir dire began the process of juror selection. Each juror in turn stood and answered aloud questions from a bulletin board: Name? Age? Occupation? Law Enforcement Background? Prior Jury Experience?

The beginning of a trial resembles a courtship. In voir dire (the name is from the French for "speak truth"), lawyers and judges ask probing questions, jurors must answer truthfully, and any obviously biased jurors are excused by the judge "for cause." From the remaining pool, the lawyers exercise their "peremptory challenges" to narrow the pool until the survivors of the process become a jury of twelve, just and true, empaneled to do justice.

The checking out during this voir dire went both ways.

"Check out juror six," defense attorney Michael Tidwell whispered into my ear. "She's looking over here at someone. Who is she looking at?"

Generally oblivious, and often blind, to flirtation, I had seen nothing.

"What are you talking about, Mike?"

"Juror six. She's looking at someone here at our table, and I think she's got the hots for someone, but I can't tell who it is. But I think it's me," Tidwell whispered.

The questioning of jurors completed, Judge Platt excused them, explaining that each side would now exercise challenges but that the panel would need to wait in the corridor for the bailiff's summons.

I looked at my handwritten notes furiously taken during voir dire inside the box assigned to the sixth juror's seat to decide whether I should exercise the defense's peremptory challenges.

"Amelia Jean Mays. Eloy, Arizona," Tidwell said. "Works for Arizona Public Service. No law enforcement background. No prior jury service. Attractive. Red Hair. About 40 years old."

"Okay Tidwell, so she's making eyes at you," I allowed. "What do we do about it?"

"Nothing," he answered.

Tidwell's hunch about this juror was reason enough to hope the State did not use its peremptory challenges to strike her name from the jury panel.

Noticing that the decided weakness and paucity of males on the panel, I suggested to the defense lawyers, "Let's use our strikes to get rid of all the males we can. The victim was a black rapist who killed a white woman. Women won't care what happened to him and might be more pro-defense than men." With cooperation from co-counsel, the defense used its peremptory challenges to rid males from the panel.

The final panel of twelve jurors included eleven women and one meek Hispanic male. No one on the defense team believed he'd ultimately be elected the foreman, or particularly sway the verdict.

The defense began the trial with its hopes riding on the decision of eleven women generally, and one woman specifically: a buxom, red-haired bombshell: juror number six.

This trial was actually two trials in one. According to snitch Dominic Hall, the four Aryan Brothers had ordered the hit on Waymond Small but had done so in two distinctly different ways. Howard and Killinger had sent kites to Hall ordering the hit; Compton and Harbin had given verbal orders directly to Hall. This difference gave Howard and Killinger the upper hand in their poker game with the state of Arizona. All their lawyers had to do was listen carefully to the evidence and object like hell if any undisclosed evidence implicating their clients was offered; declare "Objection, lack of foundation" before Hall testified about the kites signed by "Troy" or "Red Dog"; wait until the state rested its case; and then move Judge Platt for acquittal because the state had not introduced any admissible evidence to show they were guilty.

Sixteen days after trial began, the state rested its case against all four co-defendants. For the first time, Killinger's lawyer, Michael Tidwell, and Howard's lawyer, Michael Beers, were permitted by the rules of criminal procedure to ask Judge Platt to dismiss the charges against Killinger and Howard, for once a grand jury indicts the criminal defendant the trial judge has no power to dismiss criminal charges until the state has had its day in court by presenting its case for guilt to the judge and jury. Once the state rests, the judge enjoys the power to dismiss criminal charges if there is no credible evidence sufficient for the jury to reach a verdict of guilt beyond a reasonable doubt. Rarely, however, will the state's case be so weak that the judge will exercise this power to dispose of a criminal case by granting a "judgment of acquittal." The case against Killinger and Howard presented a textbook example of the judge's power to grant such a judgment.

The state's evidence had shown that James "Watermelon" Waltman picked up kites from Howard and Killinger while locked down in their disciplinary cells in CB-4's basement and delivered them to Hall. As the cell block porter, Waltman had hidden the kites while delivering laundry to prisoners. Hall testified that he received kites delivered by Waltman. Over defense objections to the admissibility of the evidence, Hall testified to the content of the kites and to the fact they were signed either "Red Dog" or "Troy." Hall had to admit, however, that he had never seen a document that he knew had been written by either of these two, so he could not recognize their handwriting.

At the close of the state's case, Tidwell and Beers renewed their objections to admission of all evidence about the kites. The state believed their evidence about the kites was authentic—that is, that they were in fact written by Killinger and Howard. The defense, of course, disagreed. Applying the rule of evidence on the authentication of documents involves a degree of subjectivity, as it offers only an analytical framework:

> Evidence Rule 901. The requirement of authentication or identification as a condition precedent to admissibility is satisfied by evidence sufficient to support a finding that the matter in question is what its proponent claims.
>
> The following are examples of authentication:
>
> i) Non-expert opinion as to the genuineness of handwriting, based upon familiarity not acquired for purposes of the litigation.
>
> ii) Comparison by the trier of fact or by expert witnesses with specimens which have been authenticated.

Hall had testified about the "content of a writing" when he told the jury what each kite said. Judge Platt found that the "original" kite did not have to be introduced into evidence, for the obvious reason that Hall had destroyed each kite to avoid its being found by prison guards. This meant the state was excused by Rule 1004 from Rule 1001's command that the proponent of a writing produce the original in order to prove what it says.

The more difficult question for Judge Platt to decide became whether the combination of Waltman's and Hall's testimony about the origin and content of the kites was sufficient to pass the rule's test. Had the state offered "evidence sufficient to support a finding that the matter in question is what its proponent claims?" Did the evidence from Hall and Waltman show that Howard had written the kite Hall said had been signed "Red Dog"? Did that evidence show that Killinger had written the kite Hall said had been signed "Troy"?

If Hall recognized the handwriting of either man, such as by having seen other letters known to him to have been written by Howard or Killinger, then the state would have been home free. But Hall had not. If the state possessed the kites, then a handwriting expert could have established their authenticity by comparing the handwriting on the kites with a known exemplar of Howard's and Killinger's writing. The state could have forced the men to sit down and provide a sample of their handwriting for that very purpose.

Because none of this was possible, Judge Platt found "insufficient evidence to authenticate the kites." Howard and Killinger had escaped the Small murder charge. Defense lawyers Beers and Tidwell went home victorious. Six of the Florence Eleven defendants had now beaten the state of Arizona and its attorney general's prosecutors.

When Judge Platt acquitted Killinger and Howard, he gave Bill Hackenbracht, Russell Harbin's lawyer, and me a choice. If we wanted a new trial, he would grant a mistrial since the jury had heard incriminating evidence involving Killinger and Howard that he had now ruled inadmissible. If we preferred, trial would continue with this jury. Judge Platt sweetened the pot. If we chose to continue; he would give the jury a cautionary instruction to disregard all the evidence it had heard concerning Killinger and Howard.

We faced a dicey decision. On the one hand, conventional wisdom suggests that the criminal defendant should take advantage of every mistrial and force the state to start over, especially when the state is picking up the bill for the defendant's attorney's fees — and Compton and Harbin had nothing but time on their hands anyway. On the other hand, there was juror 6. Throughout the trial, Amelia Mays proved to be the most attentive, pro-defense juror imaginable. Every day of the trial, Mays's behavior reinforced Tidwell's intuition that she had a romantic interest in someone at the defense table. Though married to his sixth wife, Michael let it be known to me that he hoped it was he. She took copious notes, and when snitches Dominic Hall, Danny Farrell, and James Waltman related key parts of their story, Mays had lifted her neck and leaned backward, physically drawing away. Every defense lawyer concurred that Mays's body language overtly expressed her skepticism.

Now relieved of their duties, Tidwell and Beers huddled to help Bill Hackenbracht and me reach our decision. "There is no way juror six will convict anyone. Go with this jury," Tidwell predicted.

"How much of a defense do you think we'll need to put on?" I asked.

"You could rest right now. You don't need to put on any defense. If you do, keep it short and don't take any chances," Tidwell advised me.

Michael Beers nodded assent. "You can't do much better than this jury. Juror six looks solidly with the defense. Write up the best instruction Judge Platt will give. If it looks good enough, stick with this jury."

Judge Platt had given the defense all the time it needed to reach its decision. I took up a yellow pad and a pen and began writing a nirvana instruction for Judge Platt, who most assuredly preferred that the trial continue. He then gave an instruction to the jury that sounded like he himself was repudiating Hall's testimony that he had received kites from Howard and Killinger.

Prison cases are hard for the prosecution to win. For entirely different reasons, they are no cakewalk for the defense lawyer either—especially a defense lawyer with a strict conscience.

Now that it was the defense's turn to present witnesses, I faced a difficult ethical dilemma. I had to act as the zealous advocate for my client's cause, yet I was required to temper my zeal and play fairly. I could not introduce evidence that I knew was false, nor call a witness that I knew was going to lie.

I knew that no prisoner's testimony was truly worthy of belief unless corroborated by physical evidence. Dominic Hall, Danny Farrell, and James Waltman testified that Waymond Small died because of an Aryan Brotherhood conspiracy to murder him in cold blood. Their story enjoyed corroboration: first and foremost, Waymond died from a stab wound to his heart inflicted in broad daylight in front of sixty eyewitnesses. Their story made sense: Waymond's brazen willingness to testify against gang members provided ample motive for the Aryan Brotherhood to carry out a murderous plot.

What corroborated the testimony of any prisoner who denied an essential element of the State's case? Usually, nothing.

Would prisoners lie when called for the defense? The convict's code of silence has one huge exception: a convict is expected to say anything he can to help another convict beat the system.

I interviewed many prisoners to prepare for Compton's trial. Some witnesses were suggested by my client; others had testified at the earlier trials; and still others appeared promising from witness statements conducted by the state's investigators, John DeSanti and Bart Goodwin. With eerie predictability, every interview played out as if drawn from the same script:

"Hi, my name is Terry Price. I am the defense lawyer representing 'Big Richard' Compton, the acting general of the Aryan Brotherhood in the Waymond Small murder."

The introduction was unnecessary, of course. The prisoner already knew exactly why and by whom he was being called out of his cell. Indeed, if he had not agreed to talk with me, no one inside the prison would have, or could have, forced him to do so.

"I think you know something about the case and wonder if you'd talk to me and tell me what you know," I would continue.

"Sure, Big Richard let me know you were coming," the prisoner invariably volunteered.

"Okay, what do you know?"

"What do you want me to say?"

"I don't work that way. I want to know what you know. You tell me what that is, and then I'll decide if I'm going to call you as a witness at Compton's trial."

"Then I don't know what to say."

After this scenario played out identically time and again, I decided against calling any prisoner as a witness unless Compton insisted. When Compton left every strategic decision to me, my preference carried the day.

William Hackenbracht, representing Rusty Harbin, readily agreed to the short-defense approach, and the defense's case began with his opening statement:

The defense has no burden to put on anything at all. The total
burden is upon the state. We're going to put on a few witnesses and
it's not going to take a terribly long time. Dominic Hall we're going
to prove is a liar. Danny Farrell we're going to prove is a liar. James
Waltman we're going to prove is a liar. Those three persons who carried the whole burden of the state's case have lied as to important facts
which are fatal to the state's case. Every person we'll call to prove
they are liars is an employee of the Arizona State Prison.

Mr. Blatt is going to say Mr. Waltman is a liar. He'll testify he
wasn't even working the day Mr. Waltman says Sergeant Blatt was
leading him around, getting all these kites, getting these kites from
Mr. Harbin.

Mr. Richard Benjamin will show you that Nick Hall and Dan Farrell are liars. He'll refute there ever were meetings in the print shop,
in the darkroom, like Hall and Farrell say. . . .

We're going to have Joe Sheridan from the Arizona State Prison
to come in with records to show that Mr. Hall did not go to church on
November 6 and November 27, 1977. It's pretty hard for Mr. Hall to
be talking to Mr. Compton when Mr. Hall wasn't even there.

We're going to prove to you Nick Hall is a liar, Dan Farrell is a
liar, James Waltman is a liar. Thank you.

Our defense case lasted only one day; no prisoners were called to
testify, not even Terry Lee Farmer. Four guards testified. Compton's high
school sweetheart, Rachelle Kilmer, told the eleven-woman jury of her
plans to marry Compton as soon as he was released from Arizona State
Prison, thereby vouching for Compton while offering nothing to refute
the criminal charges.

I introduced one exhibit, Exhibit 51. It was an Arizona State Prison
record that showed Dominic Hall had not attended church on November
6 or 27—the days Hall said Compton had given him orders to kill Waymond Small while the two attended church. Overly reliant on the force of
logic, I reasoned that this document—which the prosecutors agreed was
an authentic prison record of church attendance—provided irrefutable
evidence of Compton's innocence that the jury was bound to honor and
thereby acquit my client.

While Prosecutor Wayne Ford's closing argument for the state was
competent, pedestrian, workmanlike, unemotional, and uninspiring, mine

tried too hard to hit the ball out of the park. Portions of the argument required too great a leap to be accepted—such as my assertion that the real killer was a black inmate named Gilliam, prison number 36920, seen by tower guard John Vargas fleeing the tag plant after the hit. I told the jury that "to find either of these men guilty, you don't have to believe just one state's witness or even two state's witnesses. You've got to believe them all. And those witnesses contradicted each other and told you a story which is completely absurd. How could Goff and Farmer have left the print shop in clothes with no numbers on them and then Mr. Jones identified those individuals in the tag plant by the numbers that were on their clothes? That is physically impossible. They lied about that. They lied about that because that's the role that they're playing."

I recalled in chronological order each of Dominic Hall's statements about the conspiracy and how at first Richard Compton is never mentioned at all. Later, when Compton's name was added to the mix, Hall gave ever-changing dates for his meeting with Compton in church. From these arguments, I segued to my silver bullet: Exhibit 51, the records of church attendance.

How was this record made? Hall told you about how these records are made. You go to church. There's one door. You walk in the door. There's a guard and he takes down your prison number. It's a routine. You go in, your number's taken down. If he was there, his number would be on the sheet. His number is not on the sheet.

Mr. Farrell says he went to church, too. Look at these sheets and see if you ever find his number. He wasn't there. Why isn't Dominic Hall's number on there if, in fact, he was present? He lied to you again. There were no meetings with Richard Compton in church.

You've got to have a reasonable doubt that Dominic Hall was ever there. And if he wasn't there, he didn't meet with Richard Compton, and there were none of those conversations that have been testified about. And if they didn't happen, that man is not guilty.

Compton was due to be released from prison in March 1979 and was engaged to be married to Rachelle Kilmer. Ask yourself whether a person who was due to be released in a short period of time and had something to look forward to on the outside and was going to be married, is it more probable or less probable that he would be involved in what the state says he is?

I don't want to beat a dead horse, but look at those prison records. And if there's any way you can find Richard Compton guilty when Dominic Hall's numbers aren't even on this church attendance list, I'm shocked.

My complete faith in juror 6 permitted me to rationalize my decision to present a short, quick defense that was directly to the point of Richard Compton's complicity. I completely ignored the exculpatory tales from the mouths of other prisoners that had been offered by other co-defendants to win their acquittals at the first and second trials. Juror 6 fortified my faith when she maintained focused attention on every nuance of my closing argument, even boldly holding eye contact. When I stumbled, momentarily forgetting how many fingerprints had been found on the duct tape wrapped around the murder weapon, I glossed over this omission, telling the jury they undoubtedly remembered and could look it up in their own notes. Juror 6, however, interceded and supplied the missing number. Cupping her hands to her mouth, she whispered, "Seven." No one in the courtroom, especially other jurors, failed to see her sympathetic gesture.

When the jury retired to begin its deliberations at 6:25 p.m., I reasoned that surely there would be no convictions. How could it be otherwise when juror 6 had flashed sparks of yearning toward the defense table throughout the trial; when juror 6 had been so helpful as to coach me during my closing argument; when Exhibit 51 showed that Dominic Hall had not attended church on November 6 and 27; and when Tidwell confidentially predicted that all signs pointed to defense victory for Compton and Harbin?

Though the jury had been at the courthouse since 9:00 a.m., Judge Platt, following a Pinal County tradition of allowing late-night jury deliberations, permitted the jury to begin its deliberations at once, without giving any sign of how long or how late he expected the jury to work.

Lawyers Tidwell, Beers, Hackenbracht, and I kept vigil all evening, awaiting either the jury's verdict or a request from them to go home. We passed the hours in Pinal County's minuscule law library, a cubbyhole with one table and six chairs adjoining the Division I courtroom, where the trial had just ended and the jury now deliberated. Gallows humor and war stories dominated the long hours of the evening. Time passed slowly.

Tidwell, the humorous raconteur with a huge trove of stories as a lawyer, a six-times married paramour, a party animal, and a recovering alcoholic, fueled the nervous laughter spilling from the conversation, which ebbed and flowed and which was interspersed with slow walks down the corridors of the courthouse to the men's room or water cooler.

Guessing that a long deliberation would be to our advantage, Hackenbracht and I made no suggestion to Judge Platt that the jurors be instructed to recess their deliberations and return the next day.

The jury took six hours to reach a verdict, which they returned shortly after midnight. By 12:25 a.m., with the prisoners, lawyers, court reporter, judge, bailiff, and clerk all at their stations, the bailiff escorted the jurors back into the utterly quiet courtroom. Outside, the world slept, oblivious to the raw tension and exhausted anticipation of the prisoners and lawyers, who felt that their fate hinged on the jury's pronouncement of their verdict. Finally the clerk read from the verdict forms: "We, the jury, duly empanelled, do find the defendant Richard Compton, not guilty of first-degree murder." Compton and I were elated, liberated, set free, validated, given new life. But, just as quickly, the pendulum swung to the other side and punched my lights out as the clerk read the second half of the verdict: "We, the jury, duly empanelled, do find the defendant Richard Compton guilty of conspiracy to commit murder." A split verdict was a logical impossibility I had never considered. The jury's fallibility left me stunned, and the seriousness of the game—representing a man facing hard time for a verdict that made no sense—hit home. This was no fun, no game, no place for the timid, weak, or inept.

I crossed paths with juror 6 in the hallway and asked her, "Would you mind answering a question or two for me? I'd like to understand your decision."

"Okay," she said, in tired resignation.

"I was wondering how you decided Compton was guilty when the church records showed Hall wasn't in church."

"Those records could have been forged."

I asked nothing more about Exhibit 51, though I wished to scream back into her face, "You've got to be kidding! The state stipulated the records were authentic church records from the prison and the attorney general gave them to me; no one even hinted those records were forged!" Changing ground and maintaining decorum, I asked, "When did you begin to think the defendants might be guilty?"

"From day one," she answered. "One look at those guys and I knew they were all guilty as hell."

"How could you decide Compton was not guilty of murder but was guilty of conspiracy to commit the murder?" I asked, realizing this had to be my last question that night.

"It didn't seem serious enough to be a first-degree murder, but it obviously was a conspiracy."

As I drove home to Phoenix at 3 a.m., the illogic of the split verdict swirled inside my head. The more I thought about this defeat, the more my mind rebelled and I grew determined to salvage a rational ending to this chaotic episode. "Can a jury reach inconsistent verdicts of guilty and not guilty?" I asked myself. Logically, and in the eyes of the law, Compton was either guilty of both conspiracy and murder or neither. The state had alleged that Compton ordered Hall to "hit Small." That one act made him guilty of both murder and conspiracy. Could the state have it both ways? Could the state charge Compton with two crimes arising from one act and imprison him even if the jury found him not guilty of one crime committed by that act? Law school had never covered this.

The next day I went to the Maricopa County Law Library to hit the books, hoping the law required consistency in jury verdicts. The *Arizona Digest*, a volume that distills every appellate decision into bite-size legal morsels, showed that practical appellate judges have accounted for human folly. Appellate judges are adept at rationalizing away any inconsistency in order to uphold jury verdicts. The law does not require that jury verdicts be rational, logical, or consistent. The law ascribes any inconsistent outcome to a grant of undeserved leniency instead of an irrational proclivity to convict.

Arizona's criminal procedure allowed me only ten days within which to file any motion for a new trial. Eight days after the verdict was entered, I decided to call the jury forewoman, Dorothy Hartegin. We met for lunch, and she agonized about the verdict. "Is there anything you can do? We felt pressured that night. I'm not sure we made the right decision. The bailiff told us we had to decide the case that night. He said the Judge would not let us go home until we reached our verdict. Was that right?"

"I don't think so. When did this happen?" I asked.

"It was late that night, after our dinner break. We asked Tony, the bailiff, if we could go home because some of us were getting tired. That's when he said no, we had to decide that night. After that, Mrs. Montgomery and I changed our mind and we reached our verdict about midnight."

"Dorothy, I'll have to do legal research and find out if the bailiff should have done that. Would you be willing to tell the judge what you've told me?"

"Oh yes," Dorothy assured.

"What about Mrs. Montgomery?"

"I'm sure she'll remember it too."

To support Compton's request for a new trial, two jurors, Dorothy Hartegin and Marguerite Montgomery, gave me sworn affidavits, telling Judge Platt that, unbeknownst to him, his bailiff, Tony Larona, had improvised a few late-night jury instructions on his own to the effect that the jurors were his prisoners until they reached a verdict. According to Montgomery's affidavit: "The Bailiff made a statement that the jury had to come to a decision on the case that night. I began to experience heart problems arising from my arrhythmia condition. I needed to take a recess so that I might obtain my medication. When I requested that we take a recess for the evening, other trial jurors told me that based on what the bailiff had told us, we could not leave without arriving at a decision that night and therefore a recess was impossible."

Hartegin's affidavit agreed with Montgomery's and added a twist: "It was the understanding of myself and Ms. Montgomery and other trial jurors based on the comment of the bailiff that the jury had to decide the case that evening and the jury would not be allowed to recess its deliberations until the next morning in the event that a unanimous decision could not otherwise be reached. Because of this instruction from the bailiff, Ms. Montgomery finally agreed to change her vote on the murder charge, Ms. Montgomery and myself urged the trial jurors to reconsider their votes in favor of guilty on the conspiracy charges since we felt that the jury by voting differently on the two counts was failing to arrive at a verdict consistent with the instructions of the judge and the evidence."

Reasoning that the bailiff's admonition to the jury was an "instruction" from the court, I cited case law to argue that Compton's right to a fair trial had been short circuited by bailiff Tony Larona's interference. "Dynamite instructions"—defined by Arizona's Supreme Court since 1949 as any instruction that could "overemphasize the importance of agreement, suggest that any juror surrender his independent judgment, or say or do anything from which the jury could possibly infer that the court is indicating anxiety for or demanding some verdict, or subjecting the jury to the hardship of long deliberations"—can never be given to a jury, even by a judge.

Compton's motion read:

> The actions of the bailiff clearly had the same effect on the jury as if the court had given the jury a "dynamite" instruction, an impermissible and erroneous instruction under Arizona law. . . .
>
> The bailiff's comments left the jury with the completely erroneous impression that they had to decide the case that night and could not recess the deliberations. If the court had so instructed the jury, reversal would clearly be required. Instructions from the bailiff cannot be treated differently. The bailiff's instruction clearly consisted of the worst element of a 'Dynamite' instruction: the statement carried the clear message that the jury would remain until a verdict was reached and extreme hardship was imposed on the jurors since they heard testimony and instructions from 9:30 a.m. to 6:15 p.m. on October 3 and deliberated thereafter until 12:30 a.m. on October 4.

The state fought hard to keep intact their guilty verdicts of conspiracy against Compton and Harbin, which had raised the state's batting average at that time to three convicted (of at least conspiracy) and six acquitted (of all charges), with Bilke and Hillyer yet to be tried. The state claimed "no prejudice," a concept equivalent to "no harm, no foul" in refereeing basketball and football.

Faced with Compton's motion challenging the bailiff's conduct, Judge Platt subpoenaed every juror back to court twenty-five days after their midnight verdict. To their consternation, the lawyers were not allowed to ask the jurors any questions at the hearing. Judge Platt did all the questioning himself. Predictably, Hartegin and Montgomery stuck to their story as recited in their sworn affidavits. No one else, however, recalled any untoward action by the bailiff, except the twelfth and last juror, Dolly White. She, too, recalled the bailiff's intrusive demand that the jury reach their verdict that night.

"Did you hear the bailiff tell the other jurors that the judge said you could not go home until you reached your verdict that evening?" Judge Platt asked.

"Yes, I think he said that. I think he told all of us inside the jury room. We had to come with some kind of verdict before we left that night; and if we had calls to give them to him and he would make the calls to the families because we were going to go late that night," White answered.

"As you remember the bailiff, did he tell you that you had to make, or you had to reach, a verdict that night before you could go home?"

"Yes."

"You are certain that happened? He did tell that?"

"Yes."

"Do you remember any discussion by any of the other jurors concerning that at anytime during your deliberations that night?"

"Just that we have to come up with some kind of verdict before we left."

When the hearing recessed, Judge Platt took the matter under advisement and later mailed a minute entry with his decision to the lawyers. It read:

> Three jurors, Dorothy Hartegin, Margaret Montgomery, and Dolly White, claim to have heard the bailiff make a statement to another member of the jury to the effect that "the Judge said you must stay until you reach a verdict." One juror at approximately 10:30 to 11:00 p.m. on the evening of October 3, 1979, during the jury's deliberations asked for recess until the next morning because she was tired and she also thought the other jurors were tired. At the time of this request it appears that the jury had reached a unanimous verdict of guilty on the conspiracy charges and were deliberating the murder charge.
>
> The question to be determined is whether the fact that three trial jurors were under the impression that they would be required to remain in deliberation until they reached a verdict deprived the defendants of their constitutional right to a fair and impartial trial.
>
> . . . it is impossible to promote confidence in the administration of justice unless the jury is kept free from outside influences.
>
> Motion for new trial is granted.

On the same day, Judge Platt sentenced Harbin, Compton's co-defendant, "to ten to twelve years" for his conspiracy conviction. This sentence was to run consecutively to two prior convictions. Upon hearing the judge's sentence, Harbin sunk his head into his hands and moaned,

"I'm buried." His parole eligibility date stretched into the twenty-first century. In terms of punishment of the Florence Eleven, the state reached its high-water mark on this day.

Two months later, however, Judge Platt vacated Harbin's conviction and sentence because "said conviction was obtained in violation of both the U.S. Constitution and Arizona Constitution in that the jury which convicted the defendant had extra-legal communications with the court's bailiff during the course of their deliberations."

When the state appealed the grant of a new trial, Compton again asked Judge Platt to reduce his bail so he would not be in jail while the appeal ran its lengthy course. When Judge Platt reduced the bail to $10,000, Compton's sister and brother-in-law posted bond using their own residence in southern California as collateral.

Compton shafted everyone. Despite plans to marry his high school sweetheart, he staged a series of bank robberies in Los Angeles six weeks after his release. To pull his last job, he brandished a serious-looking pellet gun and handed the bank teller a note reading "This is a stik up," written on the back of his own laundry receipt. FBI agents quickly learned Compton's identity and showed up at his door. When they asked Compton how to spell "stick up" and he replied "s-t-i-k," the agents suggested they take a trip downtown. Compton caught a ten-year federal sentence to Lompoc. He was lucky he hadn't used a real gun.

On January 15, 1981, the appellate court affirmed Compton's motion for a new trial in the Florence Eleven case. The court reasoned that "the bailiff allegedly represented to the jurors that the judge said they could not leave without arriving at a decision that evening. In effect, it was as if the trial judge himself had made the same statement to the jury. The possibility of coercive tactics exists here. We find no abuse of discretion in granting a new trial." Now there would be a fifth trial of the Waymond Small murder case.

13 Stretch Hillyer Beats Two Murder Raps

The Waymond Small and Bobby Phillips hits, like so many others of the period, promiscuously interrelated identical players, motives, turncoat witnesses, prosecuting attorneys, and defense lawyers. The vendettas that started in prison and spilled over into stabbings, beatings, and killings were replayed in the professional battles pitting detectives and prosecutors against defense lawyers and their investigators.

The prosecution of Hillyer for the Phillips and Small murders epitomized their interrelatedness, for the prosecution's case was based on one confession in which Hillyer admitted ordering both hits as the general of the Aryan Brotherhood. Two murder prosecutions hinged on that one confession. The state tried the Phillips case first.

After reading the police reports on the Phillips case and learning that Hillyer had confessed, defense attorney Michael Tidwell faced an unusual task. While many criminal cases involve confessions, prison crimes rarely do. The hardened criminal knows he enjoys the right to remain silent. He has long shed the human need to purge his soul by confessing his sins and seeking forgiveness from a figure of authority. Hillyer's confession cried out for an explanation.

"One night the guards came for me," Stretch told Tidwell. "They took me from my cell without a word. I was taken out of the prison during the night, with a gun to my head, surrounded by six guards. They put me in a car and blindfolded me. We drove around in the desert, over rough back roads, for hours. I never knew where we were or where we were going. I was returned to the prison and put into a cell, but I don't know where it was in the prison. No one else was in the cell. I only had contact with one inmate in the cell next door for ninety-three days. This prisoner gave me drugs. I don't know what they were. After ninety-three days, I confessed that I ordered the killings of Phillips and Small. Then they took me back to CB-4 to the lockup unit where they had the other ABs locked down. I was out of my head when I confessed from the drugs and the isolation. Otherwise, I wouldn't have confessed."

For a while Tidwell ignored the tale. In Arizona criminal cases, the prosecutor must give to defense counsel copies of all statements of witnesses. In the Phillips case, instead of transcribing witness interviews, the attorney general gave Tidwell cassette recordings of interviews with no transcript. Tidwell put off listening to the twenty hours of taped interviews until a slow Sunday afternoon. Tidwell's attention drifted, until prison administrator Major Goldsmith's interview with the attorney general began to ring a bell. The major told a tale with eerie parallel to Hillyer's hallucination about having been taken out of the prison for a late night ride. The major's account omitted the blindfold and the gun but told of keeping Hillyer in solitary. It also omitted feeding Hillyer drugs through inmate Stanley "Kentucky" Shockley.

"Tell me some more about this confession," Tidwell asked Hillyer on the very next day that the prison's schedule would accommodate his attorney-visit request, his attention now fully riveted on a client enjoying newfound credibility. Using this information, Tidwell filed a formal motion to suppress Hillyer's statement and requested a "voluntariness hearing." Tidwell's motion to suppress was based on U.S. Supreme Court cases that inflamed the judicial indignation over "southern methods," including physical beatings and psychological stress, to coerce murder confessions from hapless blacks en route to death row. Since 1940, only confessions "freely and voluntarily" given by the accused have been admissible in evidence during criminal trials. What those phrases meant to Hillyer would be decided after a pretrial "evidentiary hearing" on the "voluntariness" issue—a sort of minitrial before only the judge, not the jury.

If Stretch lost the "voluntariness" hearing, the jury would hear his confession at trial, but it could disagree with the judge and disregard his confession if it believed his statement hadn't been given voluntarily—an exceedingly rare example within the criminal law in which a defendant gets two chances to win his case for the same reason. The hearing lasted three weeks, during which prison guards admitted that they had blindfolded Hillyer and taken him "for a little midnight ride" on the night of January 28, 1978, to disorient him once he was returned to prison. Warden Cardwell and a contingent of heavily armed guards had driven the blindfolded Hillyer to a deserted spot and commanded that he dig his own grave unless he confessed to every assault and murder he had ordered as general of the Aryan Brotherhood. The guards also confirmed that Hillyer was held in isolation for ninety-three days without knowledge of where he was and that the inmate in the adjoining cell, Stanley "Kentucky" Shockley, had been placed there by the administration for the specific purpose of getting Hillyer to talk to Shockley, who agreed in advance to testify against Hillyer. In addition, the prison administration had indeed given Shockley prescription drugs and powerful street drugs of unknown and unknowable concoction to feed Hillyer to win his confidence and loosen his tongue.

Judge McBryde found none of this shocking enough to the judicial conscience to warrant suppression of Hillyer's short and nonspecific confession, which amounted to nothing more than "Yeah, I ordered the Small and Phillips hits." As a result, Tidwell went to trial on the Bobby Phillips murder charge.

In addition to Hillyer's isolation and drug-induced confession, Tidwell added another unusual defense for the jury's consideration. Phillips had been attacked in the prison and hit repeatedly over the head, leaving him unconscious and comatose. He lingered twenty-eight days in a hospital bed until a blood clot broke loose from his leg, lodged in his lung, and killed him. Tidwell, however, read the twenty-eight days of nursing notes from the dead man's last days and discovered an alternative to the state medical examiner's finding that the blow to the head caused the blood clot in the vein. Apparently, the unconscious Phillips had masturbated with such force and fury that he knocked a bedpan onto his leg and the nurses had to tie his arms and legs to the bed. Immobilized for days on end, Phillips was poised to suffer blood clotting in his extremities, espe-cially his legs. The bruise from the bedpan compounded the likelihood of clotting.

The unsuspecting medical examiner knew not where Tidwell was going as he asked, "Doctor, were you aware that Mr. Phillips, in his comatose state, knocked a bedpan onto his leg?"

"Why, no," the medical examiner answered.

"Were you aware that Mr. Phillips was masturbating so frequently the nurses decided to tie his hands and legs to the bed to restrain him?

"No."

"Since he was restrained, did he get enough exercise to prevent thrombosis in his legs?"

"It appears not."

"So Mr. Phillips died from lack of exercise after he masturbated, knocked a bedpan on his leg, bruised it, and the nurses tied him to his bed?

"That may be so," the chagrined examiner was forced to admit. "Damnedest thing I ever heard," the exasperated examiner whispered to Tidwell as he left the witness stand. "Death by masturbation."

The jury had more fodder for acquittal, especially after the defense's forensic pathologist turned out to be Dr. Jack Copeland, who performed the first heart transplant in Arizona. Copeland opined that "the leg embolism could not be stated, to any degree of medical certainty, to have been caused by the blow to the head."

Tidwell began his closing argument measuring off the dimensions of the cell where Hillyer was kept for ninety-three days and constructing in front of the jury the imaginary walls of the cell by sticking a rectangle of duct tape onto the carpeted floor of the courtroom. Standing just beyond arm's length from the jury box, Tidwell gave his entire closing argument standing inside the narrow box. When the jury retired, Tidwell told the prison guards, "Don't bother to take Stretch back to prison. The jury won't deliberate even one hour." It took the jury forty-five minutes to return a verdict of not guilty.

The attorney general's office — by now well acquainted with Tidwell's zeal and charismatic charm over juries — decided to throw in the towel. The state voluntarily dismissed all charges against Jerry Joe "Stretch" Hillyer for Waymond Small's murder on January 11, 1980. With that dismissal, Tidwell beat the Small murder rap for his second client. When the case eventually closed, Tidwell had won acquittals for three of the Florence Eleven — Killinger, Hillyer, and Harbin. For a fourth, Terry Lee Farmer, he obtained a sweetheart deal, akin to the proverbial slap on the wrist — and exactly like the concurrent sentences meted out previously for prison assaults.

14 Farmer Quits the Gang

Kill Small, get a jacket for violence, and earn membership in the Aryan Brotherhood. It seemed like a surefire path to easy street for Farmer, who was facing life inside a prison run by rival gangs, each seeking a toehold for dominance. Given the environment of Arizona State Prison in 1977, his life term, and his immaturity, the choice possessed an irrefutable logic: Kill Small, then it will be easy street. Farmer thought that once he'd earned his bones, no one could ask more; he'd be left alone, respected and feared.

"Which side you on?" Baby Peck asked Farmer one day in March 1980. They were in the runs on CB-3, where the Florence Eleven and other gang members were still being held in investigative lockup. Farmer's conviction for the Small murder had been reversed, and he was awaiting a new trial.

The question confused Farmer. Though the Aryan Brotherhood insiders had been feuding and fighting since March 1977, Farmer was inconsequential to the bigwigs, and he had been kept in the dark.

"I stand where I am. I stand for who we are," Farmer answered. He wasn't trying to be cryptic or evasive.

"Oh," Baby Peck muttered and moved on, leaving Farmer perplexed and confused.

"What in hell's that?" he wondered to himself. Asking around, he learned about the split within the Aryan Brotherhood. The next time around, he again refused to take sides. "We're all white," he told Baby Peck. "We all stand on one side of the fence. We don't have two sides. If you got a problem with somebody, resolve it. I'm choosing no side." But the gang wouldn't let Farmer off so easily.

Though housed on different floors and far apart, inmates devise ingenious methods to communicate. String lines afford the means to exchange handwritten notes, or kites. The unwritten code grants special immunity to this form of communication. Exchanging kites between cells with fishing lines can only work if all the inmates cooperate, so they don't interfere with each other's efforts to use the line, or the phone as it's called. Of necessity, inmates work together to avoid detection by the guards. Using mirrors, they look down the run to see if the coast is clear. "Man!" the inmates yell if a guard appears while the lines are laying outside cells so that they can be quickly retrieved.

So when Little Ritchie yelled "Phone, Farmer!" Terry knew to look outside his cell. Once he spotted a string hanging down from the tier overhead, he threw his own line through the bars of his cell. A paper clip tied to the end of line served as a snare. With this physical connection in place, kites can be exchanged.

"Phone call, Farmer," yelled Little Ritchie from the run above. Their "phone" was actually a fishing line used to exchange kites. When he heard Little Ritchie yell, Farmer threw out his own line, which had a paperclip tied to the end to serve as a snare. When he pulled the wire to his cell, he couldn't believe what he read: "You got to hit Hendricks." The demand strained belief. The order came from Little Ritchie, the same dude who'd been at the epicenter of the Waymond Small beef. Little Ritchie had stabbed Koolaid Smith on the gun gang truck on November 3, 1977. In retaliation, Waymond Small and Gomes tried to strangle Little Ritchie with a wire. When Waymond Small went to Captain Davis and agreed to testify against Little Ritchie over the Koolaid shanking incident, Waymond declared his personal war on the Aryan Brotherhood, which ended when Farmer shanked Waymond to death.

Now Little Ritchie was ordering Farmer to kill again, this time a white inmate housed on Farmer's run, a few doors away. Hillyer's clique decreed that Hendricks be hit as tit for tat after the retaliatory rampage that left Dirty Dennis dead and Sneaky Pete, Wolf, and Buster wounded. Farmer's temper flared. He scribbled back his reply and yelled to Little Ritchie to pull in his wire. Little Ritchie read Hillyer's answer: "You must be nuts. Do it yourself."

"You don't understand what brotherhood means," Farmer screamed up at Little Ritchie. "You're destroying what we created. You're off the edge. To hell with it."

"You're down, you're finished, burned," Little Ritchie screamed back at the top of his lungs. "You with us?"

"I stand where I stand," Farmer yelled. "I won't do it, period."

"What, you scared? You weak?" Little Ritchie taunted. "You're getting stupid. You're a punk. Pussy, pussy, pussy. Got no backbone. No nuts."

"You're all a bunch of punks," Farmer screamed to the whole Aryan Brotherhood. "You want me to do something for you? You won't do it yourself. I made my bones. You all never do a damn thing 'cept run your mouth. I caught this stupid-ass murder beef for you, Little Ritchie. You little fat bastard. You're the reason. You're yelling at me? I got no nuts? You're out of your damn mind. You lost whatever sense your mom gave you? I protect my own. No rackets. Warriors stand for the weak. You want me to do my own? You're drunk."

Farmer's open defiance of Little Ritchie crossed the line. "We'll kill you. You're meat," Little Ritchie challenged back.

"Paint me gone," Farmer defiantly screamed, getting in the last word.

His mind made up and his words sealing his fate, Farmer took the only way out. He wrote Stan Elkins, Michael Belt's court-appointed investigator on the Small case, asking him to visit. Terry trusted Elkins. He had given his carefully choreographed, taped story of self-defense to Elkins—the pivotal statement in winning the acquittals of Goff, Breshears, Belt, and McDonald. Elkins came as fast as the mail delivered Farmer's vague letter. Once Elkins arrived, Farmer wasted no time. "I just gave myself the coup de grâce," he told Elkins. "I stuck my foot in my mouth. I quit."

"What?" Elkins stammered, unsure of the meaning of what he'd heard.

"I quit the gang. I need to get out of here. My butt isn't worth two cents," Farmer emphasized.

Elkins didn't need much convincing once he heard about Little Ritchie's demand and Farmer's refusal. He knew what to do. Elkins left to chat with Chief Davis and Captain Avenetti. Trusting Elkins's sense of urgency, they pulled Farmer straight from visitation to the main office. To check things out for themselves, they searched Farmer's and Hendricks's cells as Farmer waited for his fate to be decided. A thorough search of Farmer's cell found fragments of Little Ritchie's kites stuck in the commode. A search of Hendricks's cell discovered a zip gun inside his TV set.

After the search, a short interview confirmed for the prison administration that Farmer had given up the gang. "We got word that you were finished," Captain Davis began. "Are you serious?"

"I'm done," Farmer acknowledged. Farmer had punched his ticket out of the gang and into protective custody for life. He was moved to the basement of CB-4, where death row, administrative segregation, and protective custody inmates were housed. Since that day, Farmer has remained inside the most secure portions of Arizona's prison system, where the Aryan Brotherhood cannot reach him.

After Terry Lee Farmer's conviction was reversed by the Arizona Supreme Court on September 5, 1980, he asked Tidwell to represent him at his new trial. Perhaps unwilling to face further humiliation, the attorney general offered Tidwell a sweetheart deal. If Farmer would plead guilty, the state would agree to a concurrent life sentence without the possibility of parole prior to serving twenty-five years. The sentence would be backdated to the day of Small's murder. Already facing concurrent life sentences for his Arizona conviction for murdering the hitchhikers and his Texas conviction for killing Kelly Bryant, Farmer had nothing to lose. The Small plea agreement would extend Farmer's parole eligibility by only thirty days. On February 18, 1981, Farmer pled "no contest" to a charge of murdering Waymond Small. After five trials and millions in expense to the taxpayer, this was the only conviction and punishment ever obtained for Small's murder. In the end, the convicts' original assumptions had proven correct: Waymond Small's murder resulted in nothing more than a slap on the wrist.

PART IV AFTERMATH

15 Revenge and Rampage

Placed in administrative segregation and held in CB-6's maximum security lockup for the duration of the prosecution, each defendant expected to return to the main yard and the general population once they beat the Waymond Small beef in court. Little did they expect that incarceration under onerous special custody would become a nearly permanent fixture of their remaining prison existence.

So, the day Judge Platt dismissed all charges against them on September 28, 1979, Troy Killinger and William Steven "Red Dog" Howard expected to return to the yard where they could personally run their hustles, protect their kids, and flex their power within the feared Aryan Brotherhood hierarchy.

Their expectations never were realized, in part because civil war had broken out the year before within the Aryan Brotherhood, a battle for control of its business rackets, commissary, scams, and profits. After the November 1977 lockdown, the Aryan Brotherhood officers were forced to rely on their mules to collect the take and forward their share of the "zoo zoos," for the brotherly policy was to share all goodies among the brothers in lockup.

The Stretch/Troy/Red Dog faction, known as the "Old Timers," who received "store" every week; noticed that the biker group in the CB-3 lockup along with them, "got store" every day and shared nothing outside their own clique. The bikers called themselves the "High Wall Jammers." The Jammers were admitted into the Aryan Brotherhood by the Old Timers with the understanding they were "giving up" their "biker status" for the "better cause of racial supremacy."

Out of direct touch with the soldiers still on the yard, the two cliques of officers in the CB-3 lockup were sending conflicting orders about who should get what from store. Kites from the yard back to the Old Timers revealed that the Jammers were demanding of the Aryan Brotherhood soldiers that the profits, money, dope, and store be sent to them, because the Jammers were taking care of the Old Timers, not the other way around.

The Jammers claimed this was necessary because the Old Timers wouldn't share with them. Caught in the middle, the soldiers were in a quandary: who to believe, who to obey?

Among the select few of the Old Timers in CB-3, it was "voted and decided" to kill the selfish Jammers in CB-3 and "clean up the A.B."

Time was short. Construction of the new "maximum security" CB-6 lock-up was nearly complete. Its completion would greatly complicate plans. CB-6 would be "closed celled": no bars or openings in front of the cells; a modular design of pods and areas, each separately monitored by surveillance cameras. The four targeted for death—Sneaky Pete, Wolf, Buster, and Dirty Dennis—would be scattered around, making any hit that much more difficult.

The Christmas package program became the focus of a plan for retaliation against the Jammers. At this time of year inmates could receive gift packages from their families.

A gang member had a brother in California who was a brazier and welder. He would buy a large canned ham, remove the label, skillfully remove the top with a hacksaw, carve a cavity inside the ham, place a .25-caliber automatic pistol and seven-shot clip inside a plastic bag, insert the bag into the cavity, carefully braze the tin lid back in place, reglue the label on the tin, and mail the canned ham with a large package of Christmas goodies to his brother.

A fish and new recruit, like Terry Lee Farmer before him, volunteered for the hit to prove his loyalty and to become a member of the Aryan Brotherhood. Once briefed on the job, the fish was given the gun. He celled on the second-tier B-run in CB-3 along with several other AB members in other cells. The four targeted Jammers lived on A-run, first tier.

When the fish was let out to shower that fateful day in March 1978, the guard left for the other side of the building to let others out for their showers. The fish ran downstairs, dashing from one cell to another, firing the gun at the Jammers targeted for death.

He did his work well.

Sneaky Pete took two rounds in the back, suffering permanent partial paralysis; Wolf took one in the shoulder, maiming one arm permanently; Buster got off easiest when one shot grazed his left eye but did no permanent damage; Dirty Dennis died instantly from a bullet to his heart.

So far, the fish had followed orders to the T; suddenly he had to improvise to save his own skin when a convict yelled, "Six-five!" prison jargon that badges were swarming to the scene.

"I've got two shots left," he screamed out to the guards. "Shoot me and I'll bag someone else!"

In the tense standoff, the guards' weapons were trained on the fish, his terms laid down, loud and clear, for every badge and convict to hear and bear witness.

"If you won't fuck me up, I'll slide the gun across the floor to you. Swear to it that you won't and I'll give it up," the fish demanded, keeping his weapon poised to fire into nearby cells to shoot another inmate.

"Just slide it over careful like," the guards promised.

The fish surrendered only when assured repeatedly in the presence of many witnesses.

Even twenty years later, the rift from this feud permanently divides the Aryan Brotherhood into factions, one against the other, with contracts and hits yet to be fulfilled but not forgotten.

Dissension over the action was immediate.

Many Aryan Brotherhood members, both in the yard and in lockup, disagreed with the massive hit on four white dudes, who were supposedly their brothers.

Others were upset with the use made of the imported gun, reasoning, "When the brothers had a gun, why didn't they use it on the niggers in lockup instead of whites, since they're locked up over racial problems in the first place?"

A second round of vote taking—this time controlled by the Jammers—resolved to punish those AB members who had "conspired and voted" to have the four Jammers hit. Of the forty Aryan Brothers in lockup, the Jammers picked ten to be hit as soon as they were released back to the yard.

Knowing they were targeted, many chose to stay in protective custody or sought transfers to out-of-state prisons. Not so Red Dog, who decided to hang tough, wait his release to general population, and take his chances. He lasted three days on the yard before he was attacked in the chow hall and survived a shotgun-shell blast in the chest.

He still refused protective custody. The administration resolved to transfer the old Aryan Brotherhood members, including Red Dog, to out-of-state prisons.

16 The Demise of the Founder

May 1, 1978—after being held for ninety-three days in isolation and fed psychotropic drugs supplied by Warden Cardwell's minions—Stretch snapped and gave a rambling confession that he had ordered the Small and Phillips hits. As the convict code saw it, there is no excuse at all for snitching to the man.

Once released from isolation, Stretch expected to take up business where he had left off—in full command, the General of the Aryan Brotherhood, feared and obeyed.

It didn't go that way. No one talked to Stretch upon his release from isolation, and being ignored drove him bonkers. Even back in 1979 during the third trial, I'd hear the rumors that Stretch "went insane." In 1997, Red Dog confirmed the rumors: Stretch couldn't tolerate being ignored—for he got a complete snubbing and cold shoulder upon his release from isolation, the administration no doubt letting out of the bag his confession, knowing full well that this would prove his ruination. Stretch rubbed his body with his own feces, talked out of his head to no one in particular, and descended into a hideous void of madness. In later years, the rumor mill for nearly two decades repeated the story that a rival faction member had single-handedly murdered him after his transfer to an out-of-state prison, either the Federal "supermax" in Marion, Illinois, or Indiana State Prison. The rumors had it either way but agreed that Stretch got hit by his rivals.

Those rumors—started who knows when or by whom—proved untrue. Like Farmer and Red Dog, Stretch survived in prison, thanks to protective custody that kept him safe from gang rivals, into the twenty-first century.

17 Farmer Confronts Waymond's Brother

"There are no secrets in prison," so it's no wonder murderer Terry Lee Farmer knew long before their encounter in 1988 that Waymond Small's brother Curtis now was a protective custody inmate at Arizona State Prison. And no wonder Curtis knew his brother's assassin by reputation, name, and cell block location long before they came face to face.

Tension built for days once each knew of the other's presence. The grapevine—inmate and administration alike—buzzed with anticipation, since inevitably their paths would soon cross.

When the chance encounter materialized, Terry's and Curtis's eyes met as they entered the dangerous no-man's land of the cell block "run"—the alleyway between rows of inmate cells. Once out of his cell, every prisoner controls his own fate through his willingness to fight or to buy protection with his body, his goodies, or money. The alleyway's close confines, where one-on-one confrontation is unavoidable, presents more danger to inmates than the communal settings of the chow hall, the industrial yard, the main yard, or the exercise field, where the day is passed.

At a glance, each knew the other. Neither could escape.

"Are you the motherfucker who offed my brother?" Curtis asked, staring straight into the eyes that earned Farmer his nickname of Crazy—one blind, maimed, and terrifying, the other sighted, cold, and calculating.

"I am," Farmer answered, his voice deep, assured, and menacing. "If you need to make something of it, here's your chance." So saying, Farmer turned his back, arms at his side, completely defenseless, offering Curtis an opening.

In prison culture the turned back is a gesture pregnant with meaning at cross purposes, for in so doing Farmer offered Curtis his shot yet simultaneously showed his utter lack of fear and open acceptance of battle if Curtis struck first.

The pair stood motionless, in silence, time suspended. Farmer expected no mercy yet would have defended himself if attacked. Unarmed, he could offer no thrust to counter Curtis's first move.

After a moment passed long enough for his challenge to be clear and for Curtis to evaluate risks and spring into action, Farmer turned and faced Curtis again.

Forcing the issue, Farmer spoke first, "If you need a shank, I'll show you where they're stashed."

Curtis stood motionless and silent.

Farmer broke the tense quiet. "If you want, I'll explain why that black sonabitch had to die. You can tell your mother."

Close enough for noses to touch, the men stood silently, in a stare down.

Curtis moved off. Both headed outside to the exercise yard under the bright cloudless Arizona sky, a scene of blueness and light so pure that any feelings of hatred seemed impossible, unnatural.

Retiring to a corner, the two drew close.

"It was political," Farmer began. "It had nothing to do with race or personal vendetta. Waymond was a fucking snitch. He was going to testify against the Aryan Brotherhood, the Mexican Mafia, the Mau Maus, and the guards. He challenged the code. He knew the penalty and got what he deserved."

"Understood," Curtis answered, gazing beyond the yard to the sky as if his mind and vision were far away from this moment and place of confinement.

"Do you need to get even?" Farmer asked.

"Nah," the taciturn and distant brother softly added.

Farmer sized up Curtis as they spoke. The brothers were nothing alike physically. Curtis was light colored, effeminate looking, utterly unlike Waymond, his black, stocky, heavily muscled and bulldogging brother. The opposite of Waymond the predator, Curtis seemed the supine "prison girl."

The pair never spoke again.

Farmer sensed that Curtis had little love for his lost brother and accepted his brother's execution as the convict's judgment under their code. He accepted the convict's code as inviolate, immutable. Why defy it and attempt revenge for its judgment?

18 Waymond's Escape to Death

Arizona ostensibly prosecuted Waymond Small's murderers because he'd agreed to testify before the legislature about gang violence inside Arizona State Prison. He was murdered one day before his scheduled appearance at a hearing of the House Government Operations Committee.

Wanting to know what he might have said, I called William Smitherman in 1997. If anyone knew, surely he did, for he'd served as the counsel for the House legislative committee that had co-authored the committee's report on prison violence that had made such sensational news in December 1977.

Because of the specific instructions from the legislators, Smitherman told me that no one had ever interviewed Waymond. No one ever knew what he might have said.

In 1997 I asked John DeSanti and Bart Goodwin, the lead investigators for the prosecution, the same question. "Small knew nothing," DeSanti flatly conceded. "He was just scamming the system and looking for any chance to escape."

By its ground rules, the legislative committee made part one of Waymond's escape plan easy as milk toast. Just by volunteering, any prisoner could talk to the committee. He would be escorted out of prison without first being questioned ahead of time by investigators for the Department of Corrections or the Government Operations Committee. This special proviso was magnanimously extended in the legislators' wisdom to encourage inmates to talk. In addition, their identity would be protected by allowing them to wear masks over their heads while testifying. The legislators failed to grasp that the ruse fooled no one at the prison, and the blabbering inmate had no reason to fear John Q. Public.

19 Love in the Workplace

Defense lawyer Michael D. Tidwell's intuition proved correct during the third trial of the Waymond Small case; juror 6 was infatuated with his persona.

Three weeks after winning Harbin's acquittal, Tidwell received a call from juror 6. She made an appointment to inquire about a divorce from her husband of twenty-one years, a Baptist minister. To avoid the constraints of a stuffy office environment where Tidwell's sixth wife worked as his secretary, Tidwell suggested they talk about her divorce while taking a sixty-mile drive through the desert to the town of Globe in his goldenrod-colored Corvette. A torrid, scandalous affair ensued. Michael added a new quip to his repertoire of wit: "Waymond Small died for my sins." Defying the odds, Michael and Jean divorced their spouses, married, worked together in his law office for five years, hit it big on a few personal injury cases, retired to a life of complete leisure, and lived happily ever after, until November 2000, when Michael died in his mid-fifties suddenly but not unexpectedly, of a heart attack at their home in Missouri's Ozark backwoods.

Judge Platt married Elsie Coblentz, his courtroom clerk during the trials of the Waymond Small murders. Their marriage endures. They live in Coolidge, Arizona, where Judge Platt continues to practice law in semi-retirement and regularly goes on long fishing trips to Mexico.

20 The Tison Gang's Tribulations

The public had a nineteen-year wait before the death penalty claimed its forfeit for the six murders committed in 1978 during the Tison gang's prison escape and thirteen-day rampage. On January 23, 1997, Randy Greenawalt became the seventh man Arizona executed when it resumed carrying out the death penalty after a twenty-nine-year hiatus.

Arizona's justice system spent eleven years trying to execute Ricky and Raymond Tison for the Lyons murders, but the pursuit proved elusive.

A single fact proved too great an obstacle to execution of the Tison boys. The State could not prove that the boys had an "intent to kill." This nuance stimulated a protracted judicial battle, reaching the United States Supreme Court in 1987, ten years after the Tison rampage.

Ultimately, the State's bid to execute the Tisons could not clear the hurdle that remained in its way after Supreme Court Justice Sandra Day O'Connor delivered her opinion: the State could not show that the boys knew in advance that their father and Greenawalt planned the murders, or that the boys' actions exhibited "reckless indifference" for the Lyons' lives.

Nonetheless, the public need not worry ever again about Ricky and Raymond Tison. They are serving multiple consecutive life sentences for murder, kidnapping, aggravated assault, and escape, and their parole eligibility date extends many decades beyond their life expectancy.

21 Terry Farmer Twenty Years Later

Twenty years later what had become of Terry Lee "Crazy" Farmer, the neophyte to prison crazy enough to volunteer to kill Waymond Small?

I'd never talked to Farmer, and only seen him briefly when he testified as a defense witness at Compton's two trials. Michael Tidwell wrote Farmer in my behalf and gave me his prison address.

On September 24, 1997, we met in the large visiting area attached to the tower and entryway to the Kaibab Unit of Winslow's branch of Arizona State Prison, a medium-security facility.

We'd written over four months, my first letter to him a bolt from the blue asking if he'd talk to me about this book with no promises made how I might use what he might tell me. When nearly two months passed in silence, I feared Farmer, uninterested, had torn my letter to shreds.

The first response—and the four that followed until our meeting—offered full, unconditional cooperation from Farmer, expressed in humble, articulate terms.

As I walked across a cavernous room to the cafeteria-style chair where he sat, we greeted each other as if long-lost friends, shaking hands firmly, looking squarely with smiling eyes into relaxed faces.

Being seated, neither spoke for a long moment.

"What's happened to you since I saw you last?" I asked, breaking the silence.

"Well, I've had to file this federal lawsuit over my protective custody status. I don't know how related that is to your book," he began.

"Tell me and we'll see."

"I've been housed at my request in protective custody since 1980, when I quit the gang. The Aryan Brotherhood put a hit on my life because I refused to do a hit on a white inmate. That's why I quit. I wasn't going to kill a white man just because some AB didn't like him and told me to do it. That's why I'm here in Winslow now on Kaibab unit. CB-4 here has two hundred inmates in protective lockup. There's about

800 inmates statewide in protective custody at their own request. About three years ago, the Department of Corrections decided there were too many inmates in protective custody and so told us we had to go back to general population. That's when I filed a class action lawsuit. DOC can't make a hit go away and say I'm safe all of a sudden one day after I've been locked up for seventeen years for my own safety. I tried going out to general population twice. One time I went to Rincon down in Tucson. The inmates sent a kite to the administration saying I'd be killed because of the AB contract on my life. They pulled me out.

"A second time I was in protective custody at Perryville. When they told me they were going to release me to general population, I told them they weren't, and if they tried, I'd escape. They said I was, so that was when I stole some bolt cutters, walked straight across the yard with them in my hands and went back to lockup at night in my cell. That night, I cut out the bars of my cell and was cutting through the last fence when they caught me. The inmates had snitched me off."

"So you're saying that you had to file the federal lawsuit because the AB has a 20-year-old hit on you because you wanted out of the gang and refused to kill someone?" I asked, wondering if my ears had deceived me.

"That's about it, but my problems with the AB went back even further than that. They ordered me to hit someone who was in my cell block even before the Small trials were over, and I wouldn't do it, and the threats to hit me started then."

The first of many ironies I learned that day sunk in: Small's killer, at the orders of the AB, became the AB's intended victim — the predator's predator had became the predator's prey, forced to seek protection from his own assassination by the same prison system and society that condemned him to life imprisonment for murder.

"Another thing I can tell you, Hall made up those things he said about Compton. Compton never ordered Hall to hit Small."

I was perplexed. Was Farmer telling me this just because Compton had been my client?

"Why'd he do that?"

"I don't know. Probably to get back at him for not sharing the protection rackets and dope with him," Farmer offered.

"How about the rest of the case? Did it happen the way the State said it did?" I asked. Knowing that the conspirators couldn't be retried for the Small hit, I ventured to ask crucial questions I'd wondered about for years: Did the conspirators get off even though they were guilty? Would Farmer still maintain that he acted in self-defense when he killed Small and that no one helped him?

"Yeah, it was a conspiracy. I went over there to kill him."

"Had Small accosted you at lunch, tried to bulldog you into paying protection?" I continued.

"No, that never happened," Farmer offered before proceeding to tell me about his premeditated attack on Small, as described for the first time in this book.

For months before this interview, I'd read again the sixteen thousand pages of microfilmed transcripts from the trials of Waymond Small's murder. The study had been deeper than anything I'd had time to undertake twenty years before when preparing for *State v. Compton I* and *II.*

From that reading, a hypothesis formed in my mind about how the eleven defendants had concocted the clever defense that had won so many acquittals. The linchpin of the acquittals had been the interlocking statements of Goff and Farmer—rigorously adhered to through five trials—in which the attack was turned into an act of self-defense by two new inmates after Waymond Small bulldogged Farmer to be his kid or pay protection at lunch hour, an hour before his death.

Probing gently I suggested, "How did you pull it off? The slickest part of the conspiracy was the story. You came up with a believable one. How'd you do it? You were all locked down. You couldn't talk to each other."

As I reread the transcripts, the subtlety and perfection of this story to beat the rap became manifest to me. So how had eleven desperate men, locked down twenty-four hours a day, gotten their signals together and come to an agreement on this plan, which exposed Farmer and Goff to great risk of conviction and the death penalty by their mere admission of being present at the scene of the crime and which required all the defendants to remain confident that Farmer and Goff would stick to their story and never turn against their co-conspirators?

"Lots of ways. We'd slip notes to each other during the preliminary hearing. We'd send kites in prison. We'd have visitors slip notes to inmates. The cops and the guards made it easy. Some were sympathetic to the AB. They'd help too. We always knew where Hall and Farrell were being kept. Within twenty-four hours of them being moved to Avondale, we knew. The cops would tell us. The cops at Avondale would tell the cops at the sheriff's office, who would tell the cops at DPS, who would tell the prison guards, who would tell us. People that work as prison cops are stupid, very unprofessional, and really don't care about who they hurt, so they just blab away. You'd be amazed how fast news travels in prison, and its mostly from the cops talking too much."

"What's become of the other defendants?"

"Red Dog turned himself in last week on an unsolved murder he committed twenty-nine years ago."

"What?" I gasped.

"Yeah. He got out several years ago and ended up in a mission in Utah. He couldn't live with it anymore, so he confessed to a murder the cops had no idea he did."

"So you're telling me a man turned himself in on a murder he got away scot-free with for 29 years?"

"That's right."

"What about anyone else?"

"Rusty Harbin got killed by the AB on the outside three years ago. Got on the wrong side of a drug deal."

"When did he get out?" I asked.

"Three years ago."

"So after being in prison all those years, he went straight out, messed with drugs, and got himself killed in no time?"

"That's right."

"Willard Breshears died of an overdose."

"How about Hall? What happened to the snitch?" I asked.

"I ran into him right here in Winslow about three years ago. One day I was working at my job as an administrative porter when he walked into the same room and saw me. He turned his head, lowered his face, and tried to back out of the room right away. I told him he didn't have anything to worry about from me. We were in the same boat now."

"You mean that the AB wanted to kill both you and Hall?" I clarified.

"That's right."

"I ran into Waymond Small's brother too," Farmer continued, and he proceeded to tell me about that encounter.

The conversation drifted away from the case to Farmer's current state of mind.

"I've learned a lot. Used to be no one could tell me anything. I thought I knew it all. Now I've figured out there's a whole lot I don't know. But I'm happy with who I am now. I've got direction. I know where I'm going."

22 Red Dog Finds Jesus

After hearing Terry Farmer's highly improbable story that William Steven "Red Dog" Howard had just turned himself in on a twenty-nine-year-old, unsolved murder, a phone call verified Red Dog's presence in central Phoenix's main jail, where I paid him a visit.

Indeed, on September 4, 1997, Red Dog had walked into the Salt Lake City Police Department and confessed to the murder. When he provided unique details knowable only to the murderer, and his palm print matched one found inside Catherine Davis Newton's apartment in downtown Phoenix after her savage rape and murder on December 15, 1968, Phoenix police detective Ed Morland realized that Red Dog's confession was genuine.

Why would this man—a five-time felon who had served twenty-three years in Arizona State Prison, who had mocked the justice system when he beat the Waymond Small murder beef in 1979, who had never shown the least concern for his fellow human beings, voluntarily confess to an unsolved murder and ask the State to give him the death penalty?

As Red Dog related his story, some answers emerged.

Red Dog had maxed out on all his sentences in 1988. He had spent the next nine years on the streets in an utterly dreary life. Upon awaking each day, his ambition was fulfilled once he had hustled up enough money to buy a fifth of vodka, a quart of orange juice, some smokes, and landed a place to stay. For years he'd sponged off relatives and acquaintances, living with them, until his welcome wore out, and Red Dog found himself homeless. His aimless life appeared to be coming to an end in 1997, for Red Dog believed he was dying of stomach cancer. Homeless and destitute, Red Dog frequented the skid row missions of Salt Lake City. His mother having recently died and facing death himself, he felt moved to get right with God. Professing a profound belief in Jesus Christ and adhering to a literal, Apocalyptic interpretation of the Bible, Red Dog decided that confession and punishment for the unsolved murder were necessary preconditions for eternal life; for salvation, he must pay with his own life for his murder of Catherine Newton. Unspeakable crimes against help-less women carry a stigma and create unresolvable guilt in the minds of warriors like Red Dog and Farmer, who feel little or no remorse for their murders of men, especially black bulldogging convicts like Waymond Small who could defend themselves.

Though Red Dog asked for the death penalty, Judge Anna M. Baca couldn't oblige his request. The United States Supreme Court's 1972 deci-sion in *Furman v. Georgia* had required every state wishing to impose the death penalty to rewrite its laws and adopt specific criteria distinguishing which first-degree murders would receive the death penalty as opposed to life imprisonment. No murderer sentenced to death at the time of the Furman decision was ever executed, because of constitutional infirmities in the death penalty statutes on the books at the times of their crimes. Charles Manson, like countless other notorious killers of the era, avoided the death penalty through this peculiar escape hatch. Red Dog joined the club. Judge Baca's refusal to impose the death penalty made no sense to Red Dog, who reasoned, "There is no statute of limitations on the crime of murder and the punishment then and now is death."

Prosecutor William Clayton, addressing Judge Baca at the time of Red Dog's sentencing to life imprisonment, told the court he wanted to believe that Red Dog's confession and conversion were genuine, though he acknowledged that Red Dog might simply have been using the 1969 murder as a "Get back into jail free card."

Red Dog's new life in prison played out better than he'd imagined. On my first visit he complained of stomach pains. His pale, thin, weakened frame made him seem older than his fifty-one years. After my second visit, I lost any fear for his immediate demise. No longer plagued by guilt, removed from ready access to booze and cigarettes, receiving three meals a day, unstressed by worry about where to spend the night, Howard's color, mood, and frame testified unmistakably to quickly revived health.

Once inside Arizona State Prison, Red Dog spent his mandatory six months of solitary confinement inside Florence's Special Management Unit I for "validated" gang members. Renouncing the gang and submitting to the Department of Corrections debriefing about his knowledge of gang activities without the least resistance, Red Dog graduated from SMU-I to Buckeye's Morey Unit for laid down ex-gang members, where he now lives alongside Terry Farmer. Unlike Farmer, Red Dog does not face a twenty-five-year minimum term before he becomes parole eligible. Arizona did not adopt that get tough policy until five years after Catherine Newton's murder. Red Dog has already lived to his parole eligibility. In 1968 a first-degree murderer sentenced to life gained immediate parole eligibility at the sole discretion of Arizona's parole board. Red Dog's term of imprisonment is controlled by that law.

23 Parole, the Lifespring of Hope Eternal

Repeating its past mistakes, Arizona's legislature, in its political wisdom, chose to construct the "crown jewel" of its prison system—a $160 million, 4,100-bed colossus of incarceration appropriately located amidst virgin desert just west of Maricopa County's massive landfill for Phoenix's non-human refuse. This site for Arizona State Prison—Lewis, seven miles south of Buckeye, was ideal since it was far from any voters that could be unpleasantly reminded of our country's swelling prisons by the insult of public display in the city, and far from every NIMBY constituency that could have arisen to squelch building the prison in their neighborhood.

In 2000, two years after its completion, Arizona still could not open half its colossus for want of staff willing to commute two or three hours a day from their homes in the city for the privilege of working as Lewis prison guards at a starting salary of twelve dollars per hour.

Not knowing how long my own commute might take, I awoke in Scottsdale at 5 a.m. on December 19, 2000, confronting the same commute that dissuaded most prospective prison guards from accepting employment at the crown jewel. That morning I planned to visit Terry Lee "Crazy" Farmer and William Steven "Red Dog" Howard, conveniently for me now housed together at Lewis Prison, Morey Unit, by virtue of their designation by the Arizona Department of Corrections as "certified," "debriefed," and "inactive" members of the Aryan Brotherhood.

As I learned during this visit with Terry Lee Farmer, few prisoners inside Lewis's walls ever lose the last vestige of hope that someday they will walk out free men.

Terry qualified as one who could easily have lost all hope.

Sent to prison in 1976 at age 19, he was sentenced by Arizona to two concurrent terms of life imprisonment without the possibility of parole for twenty-five years. Texas gave him life as well, concurrent with his two Arizona sentences. Given his life terms, Terry never thought he'd live to see the day of his parole eligibility. As the years passed, the impossibly far-off year of his first parole eligibility in 2002 became less so. Then one day, the impossibility became real. A letter arrived announcing the exact date of his parole hearing: March 14, 2002, just fifteen months away.

The passage of the years is written on Terry's body. White and gray hair crowds out the brown around his temples; it softens his look. No longer thin, he carries thirty or forty extra pounds from the fighting days of his youth. His mind has adopted the more mellow and mature complacency that his body now dictates. He feels like an older, wiser man than the 118,965 inmates that have entered Arizona's penal system since his arrival. Every new inmate is assigned a lifetime number upon graduation to the custody of the Department of Corrections. Terry had been the 36,922nd customer. The year 2000 ended with Arizona's 155,887th.

"I'm really nervous about my parole hearing," Terry blurted out to me once our greeting had ended and serious talk had begun.

"What are you nervous about?" I asked. The single question opened the floodgates of the intriguing nonstop, forty-five minute monologue of a man who'd had nothing more worthwhile to hope for the last twenty-four years than the day of his release from Arizona State Prison.

"The hope that I'm going to get out has kept me alive all these years. Just the primal hope we all hang onto. The Department of Corrections takes everything from you. You have nothing except your word and your hope. I try not to get my hope up, because I truly believe I'm going to be denied because I'm in for multiple murder and I killed somebody in here."

"I truly want out. I do see a light at the end of a tunnel now, but it's still so distant."

"Once in a while it's flashed in my mind, '2002.' That seemed like eternity. All of a sudden here it was 2000. I'm two years from the parole board. When I found out my exact date I said 'Oh my God, I've done that much time in the hole.' I've done fifteen months locked up with nothing, in solitary confinement.

"What will the victim's family say? Will they still have hate in their hearts? I would have. Or will they say, 'He's done the time recommended by law'?

"I've been here 25 years. I've lost my dad, I've lost my grandmother, I've lost my uncle. I've felt the pain of losing someone. Now I understand that.

"I get completely depressed during Christmas, Thanksgiving, all these holidays, because of what I've done. I've taken people away. I feel sorry for my family because I took myself away from all these times when you're supposed to be a family.

"Time in here is not different than time out there. I wake up at two in the morning and go to work, I make fifty cents an hour to cook eggs and feed four to five hundred people. I come home, I take my shower, I watch some TV, I may go to school if I have the chance. Or I go out and play on the recreation field. But what don't I do in here? I don't pay taxes. I don't pay medical expenses. I don't have the pressures that they have out there. So, in actuality, I have it better in here than many people have it out there. I honestly don't have a hard life in here.

"When I start thinking about going back to the outside world, it scares the hell out of me. I'm not going to have somebody telling me when to go here or when to go there or what to do. I'm going to have to get up every single morning, go to a job, pay my taxes. Everyday pressure is going to drive me nuts because I've been locked up since I was nineteen years old.

"If everything went perfectly, I'd be paroled to serve my six-month escape sentence, then I'd walk through that gate a free man with a humongous tail behind me. I'd have a snap leash from this prison to wherever I go in the world for the rest of my life, and all they got to do is whoosh and I'm back in like a rubber band. It's going to be strong, real tight.

"I want people on the outside to understand that people in prison do change. Just being in here doesn't change a man. The man has to change. If you don't want to change, nothing society does to you, nothing the judge does to you, is ever going to change you. Never. It's not something that's offered. You have to make the change."

So if he'd changed, what had brought it about? I asked him to explain.

"The Waymond Small case didn't change me. As a matter of fact it made me harder. My changing point came when my dad died. When I started losing people in my family, that changed me."

For the first time in his life, he'd felt genuine pain, realized he had the capacity to love, and comprehended the pain and suffering he'd inflicted on others.

From the realization came a pledge. "I won't harm others. I just will not do it ever again. It's not me anymore. I will not bring harm. This won't ever occur ever again in my life. That's something I'm very proud of. Something I overcame on my own. I didn't get no help overcoming that. I overcame that on my own, and I feel that was just the first big step I actually took."

If society refuses to believe that the Terry Farmers of the world can change, if society refuses to believe that young warriors can grow into wiser men who can live by a simple creed of "Do no harm to others," then it must keep building and filling more and more Lewis prisons, more crown jewels.

In the twenty years since Waymond Small's murder, Arizona has invested millions of dollars in the premise that it can build prisons faster than criminals can commit crimes. In 1977 Arizona had the capacity to incarcerate 1,800 prisoners at Florence; in 2000, Arizona has ten facilities located throughout the state, from Winslow to Perryville, Safford, Buckeye, Yuma, and a greatly expanded Florence. While Arizona's population doubled between 1977 and 2000, its prison capacity increased by fifteen times. Arizona's prisons can hold 27,000+ inmates, more people than lived in Tempe in 1961 when my family moved to Arizona.

I give the last word to Terry Farmer, whose infancy as an abandoned and abused foundling made his fate tragically predictable.

"Here's what I want to say through this book. Everyone in prison doesn't belong there. For the first ten to fifteen years of my term, I fit into this place perfectly.

"I'm hoping people realize that people change. I want younger people to not go down this road. No matter how bad you're neglected, no matter how bad you're rejected, please don't go down this road. This is nowhere. This is not a life to live unless you want to just let somebody take care of you for the rest of your life and be a bum. That's basically what you are in prison, a bum. Everything taken care of, and you're just laying around on your butt all day long. I've been a bum for twenty-four years. I'm tired of being a bum. I've taken so much away. I want to give back."

Illustration Credits

Index

About the Author

Thornton W. "Terry" Price III practiced law in Florence, Arizona, as a deputy Pinal County attorney in 1978 and 1979 and in Phoenix as a sole practitioner from 1979 to 1988, emphasizing criminal defense, insurance bad-faith litigation, and general commercial litigation. He now lives in Durango, Colorado, where he maintains a solo law practice and operates Price Llama Ranch, an irrigated eighty-acre llama breeding, boarding, training, and sales operation. Terry enjoys llama packing, rock climbing, golfing, and alpine skiing.